To Jill

With Best wishes

Beryl E Scott

To Jill
with a day to remember
Best wishes

Saunders
as Cériside

MISSION
IMPROBABLE

Patrick Stephens Limited, a member of the Haynes Publishing Group, has published authoritative, quality books for enthusiasts for more than twenty years. During that time the company has established a reputation as one of the world's leading publishers of books on aviation, maritime, military, model-making, motor cycling, motoring, motor racing, railway and railway modelling subjects. Readers or authors with suggestions for books they would like to see published are invited to write to: The Editorial Director, Patrick Stephens Limited, Sparkford, Nr Yeovil, Somerset, BA22 7JJ.

MISSION IMPROBABLE

A salute to the RAF women of
SOE in wartime France

Sqn Ldr Beryl E. Escott

Foreword by Air Commodore Henry
Probert MBE MA RAF (Ret'd) former
head of the Air Historical Branch (RAF)

Patrick Stephens Limited

First published in 1991

British Library Cataloguing in Publication Data

Escott, Beryl E.
Mission improbable: a salute to the air women of SOE in wartime France.
1. World War 2. Army operations by Great Britain. Army.
Special Operations Executive
I. Title
940.548641

ISBN 1-85260-289-9

Patrick Stephens Limited is a member of the
Haynes Publishing Group P.L.C.,
Sparkford, Nr Yeovil, Somerset,
BA22 7JJ.

Typeset by Burns & Smith Ltd, Derby

Printed in Great Britain

2 4 6 8 10 9 7 5 3 1

Contents

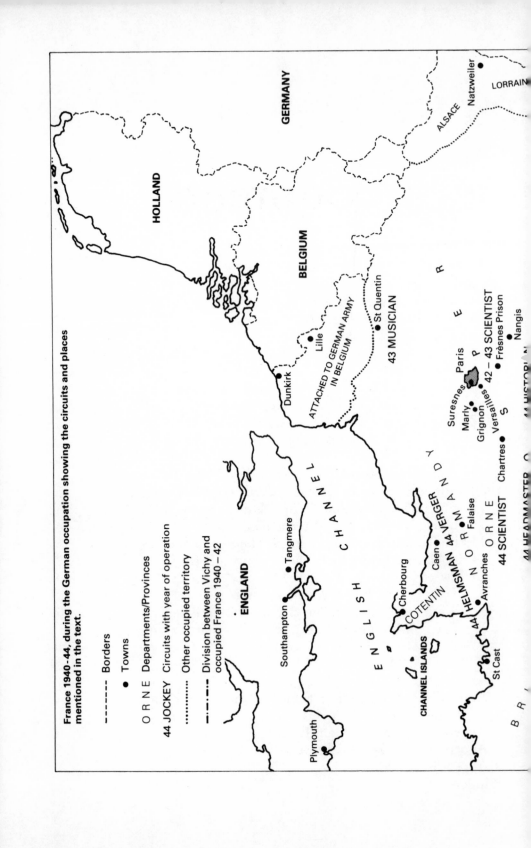

France 1940-44, during the German occupation showing the circuits and places mentioned in the text.

Legend:
- - - - - - Borders
- ● Towns
- O R N E Departments/Provinces
- 44 JOCKEY Circuits with year of operation
- ············ Other occupied territory
- -··-··- Division between Vichy and occupied France 1940 – 42

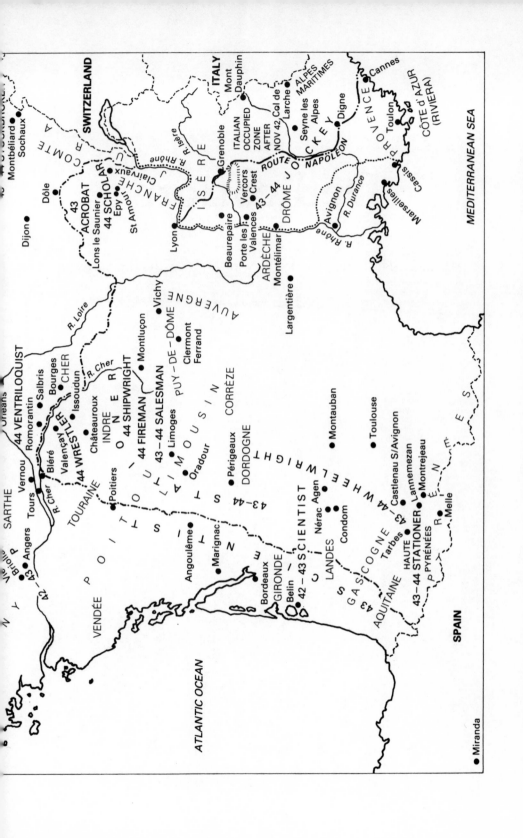

Dedication

To those who served, selflessly, without breaking their trust;
and
To those who died with their secrets unspoken.

Foreword

by Air Commodore Henry Probert MBE MA RAF (Ret'd), former Head of the Air Historical Branch (RAF)

I count it a great privilege to have been invited to write the foreword to this book, and thus join in the tribute to the courage of those featured herein. During the war I was a teenage schoolboy living on the outskirts of Manchester, and for over three years, starting in early 1941, my family played host to some 60 men and women who were training to become wireless operators with the Special Operations Executive. Each spent a week or occasionally a fortnight with us, the purpose being to simulate as far as possible the work they would later be doing in France or elsewhere. They came with their radios and set up shop in our spare bedroom, from where they established regular contact with their training school at Thame Park; they would also disappear from time to time to rendezvous with other 'agents', normally school instructors. All this activity had, of course, to be hidden from our neighbours, and while my parents and I knew virtually from the start what it was all in aid of, I do not think anybody else ever guessed; most of our visitors wore uniform, and ostensibly we were looking after them while they enjoyed a spot of well-earned leave. A few visited us again while they were undergoing their parachute training at nearby Ringway, but that was the last we ever saw of them.

I wish now we had kept a record of their names, but at the time we felt it wrong to do so; in any case we thought they were probably using pseudonyms. We were wrong, and on reading some of the SOE books over recent years I have spotted many who stayed with us, including a number who ended up in German hands and did not survive. They came from many countries besides our own, including France, Belgium, the Netherlands, Denmark, Norway, Poland, Czechoslovakia, Yugoslavia and the USA, and while most were men, at least a dozen were women. I am reasonably certain that two appear on Beryl Escott's list: Muriel Byck and Lilian Rolfe.

Altogether, as this book now reminds us, 15 members of the Women's Auxiliary Air Force were involved in SOE. Chosen by virtue of their special qualifications, all were sent to work 'on the ground' in the occupied countries, and their stories are recounted here. As Beryl Escott tells us, theirs was a very special kind of courage; they were indeed fighting in the front line in a way that few other British women did during the war, and some paid the ultimate price. Now, almost 50 years later, members of the Women's Royal Air Force have at last been allowed to pilot operational aircraft, and it is proper to be reminded that certain of their predecessors did in fact have to do their job in the face of the enemy.

Generally, when we recall the work of the Special Operations Executive and the role of the Royal Air Force in supporting it, we think of the operations of the Special Duties squadrons. We remember the Lysanders, the Hudsons, the Whitleys, the Halifaxes, the Stirlings, the Liberators that flew, usually by night, across much of Europe and the Far East, delivering supplies and ferrying agents in support of the local resistance movements. Theirs was an unspectacular but very demanding role, calling for much courage and great skill, and one which must always be remembered alongside the RAF's many more publicized activities in the Second World War. But the men of those squadrons would be the first to agree that the women of SOE who had worn Air Force uniform must also never be forgotten. This book is a worthy record of their contribution.

Author's Introduction

I first became interested in the women of the Special Operations Executive (SOE) while I was writing *Women In Air Force Blue*, the history of my own service. For *this* book I am seeking to capture their stories before the record is lost.

In this world which we inhabit, we take so much for granted. It is therefore both salutary and necessary for us to look back to see the terrible sacrifice that these girls were willing to make so that we could enjoy freedom today. Freedom is hard to define. It is a delicate plant, but peculiar in that it often flourishes strongest in a hostile environment. Only those deprived of it understand and value it. Likewise to comprehend the anatomy of courage can be likened to pulling the wings from a butterfly to see how it flies. It comes in so many forms, and here it can be seen in its diversity.

I have wandered through many byways while tracking down the accounts in this book, but in all my life I have never descended to such depths as I discovered in reading about what these girls of SOE were prepared to face. Nightmares or Bruegel's visions of hell fall short of the horrors, the calculated sadism, cruelty and murder inflicted by the Nazi regime on its race rejects and conquered countries during the Second World War. Just to encounter in cold print the eyewitness accounts of the War Crimes Trials is to be physically sickened, and even the horrific spectre of Belsen blanches at the terrible toll of these atrocities. Yet the astonishing fact is that these awful things happened on our doorstep, in our civilized world, scarcely 50 years ago.

It was against this inhuman system, that the 15 women whose stories are told here left the relative security and comfort of the United Kingdom to venture into the hostile and dangerous territory of an enemy-occupied country. They went on what seemed a most improbable SOE mission, namely to assist the French in driving out the Germans. They were not the first nor the last. Many men and women did similar work, there and in other countries, depending for their effectiveness and their very lives on the courage of the people who sheltered them and with whom they worked. The miracle was that such a number of these missions were successful, but the cost in lives was high.

I apologize for subjecting you, the reader, to yet another war book, but it has this difference. It takes a homogeneous, identifiable group in its entirety — partly representative of the many brave individuals in SOE — and it shows something of its work and experiences in one theatre of undergound war. It is a perfect illustration of the typically British trait of supporting the underdog, David against Goliath, bravery against the odds. It is also a proud tale for the annals of the Women's Royal Air Force today and the Women's Auxiliary Air Force from whose ranks they came. Essentially it covers the stories of 15 very human, sensitive and skilled women, who were called to display a true courage far and above the call of duty, for the love of Britain, France and Freedom.

In attempting to piece together a simple narrative of the exploits of these very brave girls, as unclouded by emotion and factually accurate as possible, I am indebted for information from some who still survive, other members of SOE, and those connected with them, who recalled those days and events, as well as generously helping me in my search for the truth. They all have my sincere thanks, and I have listed my principal sources under my Acknowledgements. However, five people must be specially named here. Air Commodore Probert of the Air Historical Branch has continued his wise and careful counsel, and Barbara Barrie, an ex-WAAF, has carried on her Trojan efforts in typing my manuscript and checking it with her husband. Without Vera Atkins, who worked with F Section, and after the war spent an investigative year in Europe, we would not have known the fate of those who disappeared, and for her advice and reading of the draft manuscript. I am most grateful, as I am to all my checkers. The world-wide trails I followed and the oceans of ink I spent in tracking down photographs of the women in this book, form a detective story of their own — the last one appearing at, literally, the last minute of the eleventh hour, when I had given up hope! Unfortunately, and for various reasons, some cannot be reproduced, which is why they are drawn, thus extending equal treatment to all. Their portraits have all been copied by Pat Sturgeon, another ex-WAAF, with whom I have enjoyed a lively correspondence and whose search for character in her drawings has helped me greatly in understanding my subjects. Lastly, but certainly not least, I must thank my long-suffering mother for her continued patience with the restricted, disciplined life of a writer.

Now it remains for you to travel down the years and meet these girls on their improbable mission for SOE. We should remember them not only to wonder and admire, but also to pay a grateful tribute to those who lived and died, alone and steadfast. They gave their future for ours. France was liberated and for 50 years we have not been forced to face another global war. Their struggle against a mass conqueror must alert the generations of today, then unborn, that they should ensure that the evils of what once happened in our world, will never be allowed to happen again.

Beryl E. Escott

I vow to thee, my country, all earthly things above,
Entire and whole and perfect, the service of my love:
The love that asks no question, the love that stands the test,
That lays upon the altar the dearest and the best;
The love that never falters, the love that pays the price,
The love that makes undaunted the final sacrifice.

Cecil Spring-Rice

'Look for me by moonlight,
Watch for me by moonlight,
I'll come to thee by moonlight, though hell should bar the way.'

Alfred Noyes

Animula, vagula, blandula,
Hospes comesque corporis.
Quae nunc abibis in loca,
Pallidula, rigida, nudula,
Nec, ut soles, dabis iocos?
Emperor Hadrian (c.120AD)

(O winsome spirit, loth to rest,
The body's guardian and guest.
At last you launch for lands untold,
Poor spirit, pallid, stiff and cold.
You loved a jest, but on the shore
Of silence, you will jest no more.)
(*Translated by J. M. Todd*)

1
The Exigencies Of War

'About half-past seven on the morning of the 15 [May 1940], I was woken up by the news that M. Reynaud [the French Prime Minister] was on the telephone at my bedside. He spoke in English and evidently under stress. "We have been defeated." As I did not respond he said again: "We are beaten; we have lost the battle." '

Winston Churchill

'The Battle of France is over. I expect that the Battle of Britain is about to begin. Upon this battle depends the survival of Christian civilization. The whole fury and might of the enemy must very soon be turned on us. Hitler knows that he will have to break us in this island or lose the war. If we can stand up to him, all Europe may be free ...'

Winston Churchill, 18 June 1940

'From Reichsmarschall Goering to all units of Luftflotte 2, 3 and 5. Operation Adler. Within a short period you will wipe the British Air Force from the sky. Heil Hitler!'

Order of the Day, 8 August 1940

The Special Operations Executive was born in the heat of that blazing summer of 1940, when, in the blue skies and golden sun, the mighty German Luftwaffe locked in daily battle over Britain with the small embattled Royal Air Force. Watchers on the ground shaded their eyes as they gazed upwards at the deadly dogfights, the black swastika against the tricoloured roundel, knowing that they all lived under the battlefield and that their freedom was at stake.

At that moment, patriotism — love of country — inspired everyone to quiet heroism, from the pilot in his Spitfire or Hurricane, to the radar operator gazing tired-eyed at the squiggles of light on his green screen, or the harassed housewife facing endless queues with screaming tots and unwilling, unwanted evacuees. Each felt involved, and 'doing your bit' became a byword. People accepted carrying identity cards, coping with ration books yielding small amounts of everyday foods like tea, sugar, meat and fats. Women drew recipes for fatless cakes from the dwindling pages of newspapers, making do and mending with black-out curtaining and shortages of all imported goods.

It was a time of air raid shelters, barbed wire, seaside minefields and walking in blacked-out streets. Men and women, kitted in khaki and blue, filled the crowded, steam-hissing railway stations, kissing partners and crying children goodbye. Wives took their place in the services or at work in the buses or the factories. It was the days of ARP, WVS, 'Dad's Army' and 'Boffins', the 'V' sign, National Savings and 'Careless Talk Costs Lives'. Everything stopped for the nine o'clock news on the BBC, the speeches of Winston Churchill, or the relief of *ITMA*. Uplifting war films alternated with Hollywood extravaganzas, pride for the King and Queen balanced an equal detestation of Hitler and the Nazis. Casualties knew no class or boundaries, and produced the comradeship of companions in misfortune. Throughout the nation a feeling of togetherness spread and with it a welling up of sympathy for others.

For at this time of trial, Britain was still thinking of her European neighbours, and the disasters that had come upon them thick and fast. Long before war was declared, Russia, Japan, Italy and Germany, the great powers of east and west, were already flexing their muscles and embarking on conquests. Britain had shared with Europe a desire to preserve peace, and therefore contemplated uneasily the advancing power of Mussolini in Italy, and then the rise of Hitler, who in 1933 became Chancellor of a Germany still yearning to avenge its First World War defeat. Secretly he also nursed the dream of a rich German European Empire with agricultural colonies to the east. Internal squabbles and fear of war reduced Europe to appeasement while Hitler put his plans into action. Starting in 1936, and using the most plausible of reasons, Hitler began his absorption of territories, first the Rhineland, then Austria, the Sudetenland and Czechoslovakia. Safeguarding himself on the way by forming pacts with Italy and Russia, in September 1939 Hitler was already invading Poland, before Britain and France, realizing that concessions had only increased the danger they most feared, declared war. It made little difference to Germany's relentless advance and Poland fell, being followed in quick succession in 1940 — neutrality being no protection — by Denmark, Norway, Holland and Belgium, whose governments sought shelter as exiles in Britain. France, too, was on her knees, and by the beginning of June 1940 Britain had withdrawn her forces, and as many French as possible, from the beaches of Dunkirk. Soon Britain was left on her own to face the full weight of the combined powers of Germany and Italy, in the first check to their ambitions that was to become known as the Battle of Britain.

Little did Britain then know, though she certainly guessed, that

The two sides of a lottery ticket, one of the last sold before the Germans took over France — note the date. (Mrs D. Scandrett)

matters would become a great deal worse before they became better. The war moved to North Africa, while in 1941 Yugoslavia, Greece and Crete joined the ranks of the conquered. Then Germany turned on Russia and shortly Hitler, with his allies Italy and Japan, found the United States and China joining Britain and her far away Commonwealth and Empire, against him. So a European conflict had become the Second World War.

Thus, in the summer of 1940 it must have seemed almost the height of stupidity in a nation about to face its own defeat that Britain should at such a time turn aside and try to help keep the spirit of resistance alive within those already conquered. Some might have called it a triumph of hopeful optimism over reality. Yet this was when Churchill's War Cabinet approved the setting up of a new and different secret service, answerable only to the Prime Minister and the Minister of Economic Warfare, Sir Hugh Dalton. It was a strange stroke of fate that the man who drew up the details and remit of the new service was none other than Neville Chamberlain, the former premier and man of peace, whose policies of appeasement may themselves have been instrumental in bringing about the war. Not only that, but he also named it, and so the Special Operations Executive, SOE, came into being, absorbing three earlier bodies created before the exigencies of war.

Its work was not to be confused with that of MI5 which dealt with security at home, or MI6 which gathered intelligence from sources abroad and was sometimes known as the SIS. Occasionally SOE was referred to as AI10 and by some as the Inter-Services Research Bureau, but it had other names at home and abroad. It was designed, as Churchill instructed Dalton, to 'set Europe ablaze', and its role was to nourish resistance to enemy occupation. In simplistic terms it was to aid occupied countries in showing their conqueror that they did not want him, that they did not like him, and thereafter to help them to get rid of him. It was to be, in Churchill's phrase, 'the Ministry of Ungentlemanly Warfare'.

In pursuit of these aims SOE used many methods, but at the start it mainly consisted of trying to hamper the enemy in the occupied country by damaging factories, railways, roads, submarine pens, supply depots, troop encampments, airports or radio stations and any other installations that strengthened his occupation and war effort. Aerial bombing was difficult and still far from accurate, as well as likely to cause many civilian casualties, whereas more effect could often be gained by men on the ground with local knowledge. This meant sabotage, and on so large a scale that it required huge supplies of explosives and arms. These had to come from outside — hence the parachute drops. It also meant gathering intelligence on suitable targets, and men expert in the skills of using the materials and information.

In the early days SOE concentrated on small scale sabotage then later, when the possibility of re-entering Europe to drive out the Germans became more of a reality, the European part of SOE (for it dealt with many parts of the world) was given the two-fold task of building up arsenals of weapons and resisters, and then keeping them from dissipating their strength until the invasion, or its forward advance, would be most usefully served. Grave misunderstandings also arose from the postponement of the date of D Day in the north of France from 1943 to 1944, and even some confusion, when this took place, as to whether the northern or southern coast invasions were to trigger internal uprisings.

All occupied countries nurtured resistance against the invader. This was to be found even in the heart of Germany itself, as several attempts on Hitler's life proved, where so eminent a General as Rommel was one implicated. But perhaps the fiercest opposition came from the Czechs and Poles, some of the earliest peoples overrun. One outstandingly brave Pole had himself arrested to report on what was really happening, and to organize resistance, inside the terrible concentration camp of Auschwitz. The Jews of Poland and Austria were all but exterminated by Hitler's policy of genocide. Poland's capital Warsaw saw two bitter uprisings, the last of which was intended to assist the advancing Russians, who watched the city razed to the ground before in their turn absorbing the country still restless under any outside control. The uprising in Czechoslovakia's capital, Prague, was more successful. Yugoslavia, Albania and Greece also had active resistance movements. Greece had held her own alone, like Britain, and defeated her Italian invader until overwhelmed by a subsequent German assault. The armies of the resistance in all three countries, however, were afflicted by left-wing and right-wing quarrels, the left usually communist-supported. These sometimes led to more bloodshed among the resisters than among the Germans. There were also resistance movements in the Far East against the Japanese and in Africa against the Italians and Germans, but those in Europe — in Denmark, Norway, Holland, Belgium and France — were possibly more bitter and less easy for the Germans to extinguish because those countries were within sight and support of Britain, who remained fighting against and free from the German armies.

Inadvertently, this tangible evidence of outside support in the form of men, materials and broadcasts, had incalculable effects on the resisters' morale and national pride, even in their darkest hours, qualities impossible to measure but essential to their survival and then recovery after the war.

Of all the European countries under the Germans, France had some rather peculiar features. At the beginning of the occupation she enjoyed a more privileged position in her treatment by the conqueror, who ordered his soldiers to show politeness and take less hostages than in any other country. Only three-fifths of France was occupied by German troops, but she also changed shape. Two *départements* of the north-west were attached to the German army administration in Belgium, Alsace-Lorraine was annexed to the Reich, and, after Vichy was occupied in November 1942, a large area in the south, east of the River Rhone, with Toulon and Nice on its sea borders was controlled by the Italians, who made somewhat indulgent guards. The local government of France and its police were allowed to function with less interference, and with their French staffs. True, strikes were forbidden and no movement in prices or wages allowed, but in the early days things continued almost as before and relations between the French and Germans were encouraged to be cordial, not to say friendly.

Moreover the French President Lebrun, after the resignation of Reynaud, called on Marshal Pétain, an 84-year-old French hero of the First World War, to head the government. After he had signed the Armistice with the Germans on 22 June 1940 he was allowed to keep the south of France, with its government now transferred to the town of Vichy at its centre, free at least nominally of German occupying troops. France, however, had to pay for the privilege of keeping German troops on its soil to the tune of 400 million francs a day, an impost certain to bring eventual economic impoverishment.

In geography too, France had unusual features, with two of its borders alongside the neutral countries of Switzerland and Spain. In addition, its Mediterranean coast was within reach of boats or submarines from British-held Gibraltar, and later North Africa, while the north was at some points within 20 miles of the British coast. Nevertheless despite such distractions, to many good Frenchmen Marshal Pétain unquestionably represented the continued legal government of the Republic, and whatever orders were issued under his seal were to be obeyed.

Shortly after Marshal Pétain took office, a rival Free French Government, set up by an unknown General de Gaulle in London — 'France had lost a battle but not the war' — swung away a few loyalties, but de Gaulle's government was of his own making and therefore not deemed by most Frenchmen to be lawful. The Roman Catholic Church, the largest religious denomination in the country, was torn in its allegiance. Officially it advised its congregations to submit to the rightful authorities, quoting Christ's words to the Saducees, but many of its bishops admitted in private to being conscious of the German hand behind the Pétain Government, and demurred. A few braver than the rest openly criticized its anti-humanitarian actions, such as those against the Jews. Also, no priests in the confessional gave away secrets of resistance or resisters, and later many gave active assistance to them.

Then there were the communists, more independent of Russian policies than most European communists of that era, whose sympathies might have been expected to lie with the anti-fascist resisters. They were kept virtually immobile because of the Russo-German Pact, but when this pact was finally broken by the German invasion of Russia they were released to violent and effective action against the Germans, although they also posed a danger of taking over the country after liberation.

As winter followed winter of occupation, the French faced increasing hunger and cold. Shortages started almost immediately; food queues grew longer, rations became tighter, with little bread, no butter, only ersatz coffee, few vegetables, foul-smelling, useless soap and coupons for clothes and shoes, when they could be found. RAF, and later USAAF, air raids disrupted the factories and power supplies, so that electricity was often cut off with no warning. Bombs disrupted the roads and railways but the Paris Métro still ran. The black-out and frequent house and body searches frayed the nerves. Controls and checks appeared everywhere. People needed a wallet of identity cards, permits and passes to move, and pity help those who were so careless as to lose or forget them!

Life was hard in towns but there were also difficulties on many farms, short of labour, tractor fuel, animals and seed for planting. Most women remained at home or worked on their farms, for without them life would soon disintegrate, and the Germans fully approved of this preoccupation.

Before March 1943, families in the north of France could not send mail to those who lived in the south, and everywhere there was censorship. Petrol was almost impossible to get, so the few who had vehicles for their work usually relied on steam-powered engines fuelled by coke or wood. Even in Paris taxis disappeared and people relied on *vélo-taxis*, chairs on wheels pedalled by bicycles. The black market was vicious, dealing with everything — food, clothes, shoes, fuel and forged papers of every kind at unbelievable prices — while the shops were filled with scent, hats and luxuries useless to the population. Most things had a price and bribery was widespread. While potatoes and bread rations were so diminutive that people almost starved on the streets, restaurants for the Germans and the rich had no limits. Erratic curfews kept all indoors at night, with fearsome punishments for those not obeying. The German police and soldiery later became subject to bouts of arrogance, injustice and atrocities. Pogroms for extermination of Jews, communists, freemasons, 'gipsies', dodgers of labour drafts to Germany and resisters resulted in the prisons filling with potential hostages who were mercilessly shot at the rate of 10 to 50 for any German death or act of sabotage, and the hated and feared red and black execution notices became more frequent over the years.

French minds, confused over the legality of their government and the advice of the Roman Catholic Church, were divided on whom to blame and whom to follow, but few were so blind as not to recognize that their country was being milked for the German war machine. Collaborationists and resisters appeared. An outlawed secret army and Maquis took to the woods and hills looking for its chief support and aid from its old friend and enemy Britain, which a Lorraine prophecy had promised would be the ally of a young French leader who would drive out the Germans. On hidden wirelesses they listened to the BBC for news from Britain, of how the war was going or for coded messages.

SOE agents sent to France from England were the key to effective support of the resistance, for though resistance could function in isolation it was made much more effective when working in co-ordination with London. The work of agents was four-fold: to bring radios by which communications could be set up with the headquarters from which they came; to arrange supplies of arms, if safe dropping places could be found and parties could spirit them to safety before they were discovered by the Germans; to find safe houses (often also used for assisting the escape lines) and people who could be trusted to help agents; and to organize as much sabotage as was sensibly practicable.

FRANÇAIS!

SAVEZ-VOUS CE QUI S'EST

PASSÉ À *ORAN?*

Voici les faits !

Jugez-en vous mêmes . . .

VOTRE GOUVERNEMENT VOUS A DIT que l'amiral anglais avait remis à l'amiral Gensoul un ultimatum le sommant ou bien de se rallier à la flotte anglaise ou bien de detruire ses bâtiments dans un délai de 6 heures :

LA VERITE, LA VOICI :

Le 3 juillet l'amiral français a reçu des mains d'un officier britannique un document déclarant que, la Grande-Bretagne se trouvant dans l'impossibilité de laisser les navires français tomber aux mains des Allemands ou des Italiens, le gouvernement britannique demandait aux unités françaises à Mers el Kebir et à Oran de choisir une des solutions suivantes :

SOIT de continuer la lutte contre les Allemands et les Italiens aux côtés des Alliés jusqu'à la victoire.

SOIT de se rendre à la Martinique ou dans un port britannique, pour y être demilitarisées, les équipages devant être repatriés dans le plus bref délai.

Le document précisait en outre que *quelle que soit la decision adoptée*, les bâtiments seraient rendus à la France à la fin de la guerre.

C'était seulement dans le cas ou le commandement français opposerait un refus à toutes ces propositions honorables que le gouvernement britannique lui donnerait à grand regret l'ordre de détruire ses bâtiments.

L'amiral français a fait connaitre au commandement anglais son intention de se battre. Voulait-il donc remettre ses bâtiments au pouvoir des Allemands ?

VOTRE GOUVERNEMENT VOUS A DIT que l'Allemagne n'exigeait pas la livraison de la flotte française mais seulement sa démobilisation et son rassemblement dans des ports français.

OR, RETENEZ BIEN CECI :

L'Allemagne a déjà renié sa parole. Dès le 1er juillet la Radio allemande déclarait que, s'il en voyait la necessité, Hitler n'hésiterait pas un instant à utiliser la flotte française *contre les Anglais*. L'affaire d'Oran vous en apporte une preuve.

Sous la pression allemande le gouvernement de Vichy a donné au commandement français l'ordre de résister aux alliés de la France, à ceux qui combattent pour la France et qui sont animés de la volonté inébranlable de la libérer du joug étranger.

FRANÇAIS!

Le maréchal Pétain a declaré qu'il avait abandonné la lutte parce qu'il ne voulait plus sacrifier inutilement des vies françaises. Son gouvernement qui refusait hier de faire couler le sang français pour la France vient sciemment de le faire couler pour l'Allemagne.

The two sides of a pamphlet dropped by the RAF on France. It explains why Britain had served an ultimatum on the French fleet gathered at Oran and Mers-el-Kebir, asking it either to join her or be demobilized, at a British port. It indicates that for the fleet to obey Vichy instruction and oppose the British would be to hand the fleet over to the Germans to use against their ally. (Mrs D. Scandrett)

Such work was essentially team-work, so agents usually functioned in groups of three; one was the mastermind or organizer, one worked the wireless transmitter — the most vulnerable part of the whole enterprise — and one was the courier, a kind of postman for money, and messages, often more secure when oral, passing back and forth between local individuals and the organizer.

The area in which an organizer aimed to build up his resistance network was called his *réseau* or circuit, usually named after a profession or type of employment. It is estimated that F Section had around seven circuits in France during its early days in 1941, about double that in 1942, while in August 1944 it numbered something like 52. It may have had 70 to 80 circuits in total, not all operating at the same time and many with numerous sub-circuits, all of which were supposed to be independent and with no contact with each other. If possible an individual was not to know who else was in the circuit except those closest him, and the agent's whereabouts and person were not to be known to any except through the courier. The organizer had a large degree of independence, being the person who knew the locality intimately, and was only subordinate to F Section instructions from London, which in any case relied heavily on his suggestions. Occasionally the basic team of agents was joined by an expert instructor on arms or explosives, but any member of the team, from force of circumstances or with additional skills, could carry out more than his own task.

In the background, however, were the fearful penalties for resistance — prison camps, torture, concentration camps, death by slow and humiliating starvation or other, worse cruelty. Always the steps of the agent were dogged with dangers. His situation was rather like that of being among icebergs, whose jagged tip above water indicates an even more immense and lethal base in the midnight depths, far out of sight. Not only did he have to keep out of the clutches of the Germans he could see, but also there were often more widespread hazards among the people with whom he lived, many quite innocent but just as deadly . It might be the prattle of a child, the slip of speech of an adult caught off guard, boastfully drinking or talking about something that puzzled him, a confidence or a message mislaid, accidental words overheard, a suspicious object, or having the wrong papers at checkpoints or in police raids. Then there were informers, sometimes pitiable souls forced by unbearable torture or threats to their families to give unwilling information to their captors, or other more Judas-like creatures parting with lives for money, spurred on by a host of promptings ranging from love, jealously and hate to pure greed. There were also others, loyal to the Nazi creed, planted as quislings or infiltrators to spy out the secrets of the resistance. Little wonder that many of the populace, before the scent of victory changed their thinking, wanted nothing to do with resisters but just to carry on their lives in peace. They ranged in shades from outright hostility to apathy or intentional deafness and blindness.

On top of all this, there was rivalry between different secret services and sometimes the agents themselves who had to work so closely together, even if they disagreed with or distrusted their supporters. Knowing all the secrets of the circuit, they could do irreparable damage if they were captured and threats or torture weakened their resolve to stay silent, or, far worse, turned them round to work with their enemies. In addition, controversies emerged after the war pointing the finger of suspicion at the High Command, questioning whether agents and their helpers were not at times being deliberately misinformed or actually sacrificed in order to mislead the enemy for the greater good of the cause. This accusation is bitterly denied and lacks any satisfactory evidence. These difficulties in themselves were enough to discourage any faint-hearted agent, but they were no less than the skirmishes going on in the Cabinet in Britain over aircraft and supplies. The web into which an agent stepped when he took to the field was certainly a very tangled one.

Because of the difficulties both in France and London, SOE had to tailor itself and bow to prevailing circumstances. In 1940, a Cabinet injunction ordered it not to offend Vichy by sabotage, and to recruit only those who were at least nominally British citizens. In 1943 it was told that the activities of the Foreign Office-controlled and long-established Secret Intelligence Service (SIS) were to have priority over those of SOE, particularly in the field of supplies and aircraft, a policy not reversed until 1944. Not unnaturally these two bodies did not see eye to eye, although sometimes forced into some sort of collaboration, better in the field than the office. Intelligence gathering is a quiet, secret occupation, eschewing noise and notice, while SOE with its predilection for sabotage and loud bangs was the direct opposite and very often produced conditions leading to nullifying the work of the SIS man, if not his actual discovery.

These were not the only secret services involved in France. General de Gaulle in London set up his own, calling it the *Bureau Central de Renseignements et d'Action* (BCRA). As the General, never a patient man, felt that Churchill wanted to direct his actions, and there were often very strained relations between them, he needed to prove that he was no British puppet. Unfortunately de Gaulle also fell out with the Americans, whose Office of Strategic Services (OSS) was created later in the war for similar work. Because of de Gaulle's attitude, SOE formed two main French Sections, RF (*République Française*) which worked along with his supporters in France, and F, which was independent of him and annoyed him by its very existence. F Section worked with those Frenchmen who did not favour de Gaulle but still wanted to resist the Germans. In 1941, Maurice Buckmaster was in charge of this part. By 1942, the French division of SOE also had several other smaller sections sending agents to work in France from Britain. One was labelled DF and dealt with escaped Prisoners of War, there were also two separate Polish organizations and one Czech, as well as Belgians and Dutch running French escape routes. Eventually these were joined by Jedburghs, commando-type teams and an Algiers-based force.

As time went on and SOE grew, there were inevitable changes as internal and external politics, as well as inter-service wrangles and wartime emergencies, all had their effect. Early in 1942, the MP Dalton was replaced as head of the Ministry of Economic Warfare by the man who became Lord Selborne. Those who directed SOE from within also went through changes, first with Nelson and then Hambro, settling finally with Sir Colin Gubbins, who remained Director, or CD as he was sometimes known, until SOE was somewhat hastily disbanded.

It is interesting to notice that its headquarters used many buildings during its short life. One of the earliest, and the one where most of the

French F Section continued to be located was, very appropriately, in Baker Street, London, but as time went on and the various areas where its agents worked proliferated, or it acquired other interests, SOE as a whole extended to buildings in different London streets, then towns and countries. Offices were described as having 'desks', which indicated their country. There were also headquarters in Egypt, Algeria, India, Ceylon and elsewhere. All these closed down when SOE ceased to exist on 15 January 1946, after the ending of the war it had been created to help win.

2
Forewarned Is Forearmed

'As SOE was secret, no one could recruit for it directly by advertising.'
'SOE 1940-46', M. R. D. Foot (BBC)

'There are plenty of women with marked talents for organization and operational command, for whom a distinguished future on the staff could be predicted if only the staff could be found broadminded enough to let them join it. SOE was such a broadminded staff.'
'SOE in France', M. R. D. Foot (HMSO)

When young men or women walked through the doors of the dingy London building to which they had been sent, the chances were that they had no idea why they were there. If they did, they had probably found out about the Organization, fondly referred to as the Org, the Company or the Firm, by pure accident, after which they usually had spent a great deal of time finding out how to be recommended to it and then where it was. Information was purposely vague. Otherwise there were few barriers for entry to SOE, except for the expected weeding out processes.

Race, class or sex, very definite obstacles in previous days, made little difference to the final selection if the person was right for the job. In fact, where speaking a foreign language as well as the natives was the overriding necessity, SOE could afford tacitly to sidestep the British Nationality Only rule that the government sought to impose. As it turned out there was little need to do so; the Commonwealth and Empire providing volunteers from India, China, Africa, Canada, as well as North and South America. It was hardly surprising, therefore, that its recruits ranged from peers to those picked up almost literally, in the old-fashioned phrase, from the gutter. Some of their previous occupations give a notion of how widely they ranged: journalist, débutante, burglar, Oxbridge don, shop assistant, singer, con man, fashion designer, chef, barrister, lawyer, film director, engineer, wine merchant, artist, accountant, receptionist, teacher, and salesman. Again, there were famous names among them: Julian Amery, Richard

Crossman, Peter Fleming, Anthony Quayle, Hardy Amies, Pat Hornsby-Smith, Eric Maschwitz, Francis Noel-Baker, and F. Spencer-Chapman.

Only a select few members of SOE were sent into their chosen country — 'in the field' as it was expressed. But for every 'sharp end' of an organization there had to be many more at home who worked to support them, from the tea or office boy to the housekeepers, secretaries, planners and drivers, or those wearing headphones who listened to messages or coded and decoded them. There were also those who were attached to the organization for special duties or worked with them for a time, like the RAF pilots who took them on mission or those training them. A total staff of 13,200 of which about 3,200 were women, is not unduly high for a body which put about 5,000 agents into the field. Of course figures can only be estimated, as this was a secret organization, but Air Ministry did record around 300 men and women on its books. To fuel this organization, therefore, there must have been a 'home' staff of about 8,000.

All this cost money but fortunately money was one headache SOE did not have. It was of course needed for the funding of agents and their training, for payment for expensive weapons and materials and for all the vast paraphernalia of wirelesses, devices, bases and staffs, that such an enterprise entailed. Large unaccountable sums disappeared into secret funds, manipulated by the Treasury, handled by SOE's own treasurer, Wing Commander Venner, and free from Parliamentary investigation. No agent suffered from lack of money to bribe or free a fellow resister, and yet very little was misused or wasted.

One beguiling beneficiary of this secret vote was the number of establishments, workshops and laboratories set up to provide for the peculiar needs of agents. Exploding animal droppings, coal lumps, nuts and bolts, fountain pens, milk bottles and improved plastic explosives stemmed from laboratories at the V & A and Kensington Natural History museums and the Thatched Barn Roadhouse at Barnet. Much energy went into making articles small enough to be secreted on an agent's body — James Bond was behind the times in comparison with some of the ideas! Microfilm dots on spectacles, button compasses, tiny escape saws, silk scarf maps these and many others — like forged papers, invisible ink, death pills, and abrasive lubrication grease guaranteed to seize up and destroy any ball-bearings or moving parts treated by a 'helpful' mechanic — emanated from the fertile brains and workshops of Newitt, Wills, Russell and Hutton. John I. Brown was the designer and world expert of a team which, in the age before transistors, managed to produce a succession of clandestine radios for SOE, each an improvement on, and smaller than, the last. Professors of science, Jewish tailors, burglars, and film studio staffs (the natural purveyors of a make-believe world, where anything goes) took to the work like ducks to water, forming an inventive, happy and productive alliance, where many colourful and unusual characters found an unexpectedly useful niche.

In accordance with the non-discrimination policy SOE followed, and where only ability counted, from its early days women were to be found in many important positions at home. This was not so unlikely as it seemed at the time. It was not new to have women who were clever and who worked for their living. Among the poor, girls had often worked outside the home, at least until marriage and sometimes afterwards, to supplement family incomes in such tasks as maids, cooks, washer-women and seamstresses. It was girls from the better-off families who had been most limited by Victorian conventions and education to the sheltered, rule-bound, narrow upbringing in the home, from which only the strongest had been able to break away and make a career for themselves in such fields as typing, nursing, teaching and occasionally in business. But in the First World War of the twentieth century, the shortages of men called to the fighting front had forced women to take over many apparently male jobs, from delivering coal or running trams to joining one of the armed services. Though the post-war years had seen most women return to their former roles, attitudes had imperceptibly shifted so that girls were already with such bodies as munitions factories, the Forces and the Air Transport Auxiliary, early in the Second World War. The 1942 National Service conscription carried this movement forward. Though it was only an extension of the notion that women were useful and capable, to many families it came as an unwelcome shock. Strangely, it was often those higher up the social scale, used to boarding schools and homes abroad, who took to it most readily.

Those women who found themselves working with SOE, like the men, were drawn from varied sources such as the armed services of Britain and other countries, the Women's Transport Service FANY's (First Aid Nursing Yeomanry), the civil service, or they were just plain civilians with special attributes. They acted as controllers and planners working in the air sections and arranging the dropping of agents and armaments into occupied countries. Some were intelligence or escorting officers and others liaison officers between various bodies. These all held positions of great influence and responsibility which they carried out faithfully and secretly. One started as the personal assistant to the head of F section and ended as the *éminence grise* of it. Nor did they stay in the same place, but might be moved to Cairo, Algiers, Bari, Calcutta, Meerut or elsewhere, as the course of the war altered.

Women appeared 'in the field' in the teeth of much considered opposition, for two overwhelming reasons. First, the numbers of trained male agents, particularly those who were wireless operators — the most vital and vulnerable of all functions in occupied countries — were at a critical low level in 1942. In answer to urgent requests from SOE, the Cabinet swallowed its objections and sanctioned the sending of women as agents into the field. Secondly, it was recognized that women would probably be able to move around in an occupied country far more freely than men. Men were very much more restricted in their movements. If a man moved out of the direct area where he worked, he would immediately come under suspicion that he was working for the resistance. If he were young he would be suspected of dodging forced labour or belonging to the maquis. On the other hand, young girls and older women were to be seen cycling along the roads in abundance. They often substituted for a missing husband or brother, as the wage earner of the family. They travelled to faraway places to look after sick or aged parents. They searched for missing relatives or children. They covered incredible distances hunting for scarce items of fuel or clothing and particularly on a regular search for food to feed their families, with the fierce and protective care that distinguishes a mother for her children. They were to be found on all the roads — in their locality and out of it — most going about their lawful and innocent duties equipped with the legal and correct passes and papers required of every French citizen. A girl on a bike with a carrier was therefore a common sight everywhere and the Germans had such a stereotyped idea of the role of women that it could take a long time before they would suspect one of being an agent. She was therefore more unobtrusive and less liable to be caught. She might also be able to use more charm and devious wiles that might hoodwink a questioner. Many trainers objected, but they soon discovered that women could be just as skilful and brave as men and this was soon proved in the field, where they also had to overcome the extra obstacle of the ingrained prejudice to women of the peoples in the countries where they worked, no small task in itself. Thus the most unlikely of agents became assets.

A girl's first encounter with SOE might be when she believed she was being sent to London to be considered for an interpreter post. The interview was usually in a spartan, dingy, requisitioned building near the War Office, like the Northumberland Hotel, full of scurrying people, in and out of uniform, carrying official-looking files.

In the large echoing marble entrance hall her letter of introduction is checked by a sceptical custodian, from whom shortly she is rescued by a young man who leads her upstairs and then leaves her to wait in the dim light on a hard chair outside an office door. As she is nearly always early, the minutes will seem like hours and she will be growing still more nervous before she is summoned into the presence in the room beyond, exactly on time. A tall man of indeterminate age comes to meet her: 'Good morning, will you take a seat?' He indicates one of the two

uncomfortable wooden folding chairs in the room. No names. The room
is dark and grimy, with only a black-out screen, a table at which her
interviewer sits and a solitary light bulb hanging from the ceiling without
a shade. She wonders what she has come to and why she is here. She
does her best to answer a few questions, and suddenly finds that she is
speaking in French or the language in which she is most fluent. She
blinks and they stop. 'How do you know the language so well?' he asks.
She explains. Perhaps she was brought up there before the war, or spent
long lazy holidays up and down the Mediterranean, where one of her
parents worked or was born. 'Where was this?' She does her best to
explain the ramifications of her family, the areas she knows, her friends.
He seems interested, that is if the questions he asks urging her on to
further disclosures are any guide, and he seems to know much more
about her than she had first believed, but his face gives nothing away.
It remains masklike and polite. 'Why did you leave?' 'What do you think
of what has happened to this country since?' 'What do you think of the
Germans?' 'What more do you want to do to help this country?' And
so the questions continue, searching, probing into her private life,
sometimes releasing thoughts that she had never realized were there deep
within her. Occasionally her answers are a revelation to her as well as
her interrogator. But still the insistent quiet voice drives her on. Then
suddenly it is over. He stands and holds out his hand. She scrambles to
her feet, puzzled and faintly disappointed. She is still not sure why she
is here. It seems a funny kind of interview for an interpreter post, but
it must have been reasonably satisfactory as he has arranged another
meeting in a few days' time. Outside she consults her watch. Surely there
is some mistake. It is only 50 minutes since she entered the room.

A few days later she is ushered into the same room to be greeted by
the same man. From various indications she has an idea that she has
been the subject of security vetting in the interval. They get down to
questions almost immediately, and she accepts it when she finds that no
English will be spoken from now on. 'Why do you want to be an
interpreter?' 'What do you think could be the most useful or damaging
work against the enemy? Would it be at home or abroad?' 'What sort of
contribution do you want to make?' 'What if you could get closer than
a mere interpreter?' 'How would you feel if you could actually work
against the enemy in that country?' 'Do you realize what dangers you
will run, your treatment if you are caught?' Finally he ends: 'Don't
commit yourself in hot blood or you will live to regret it. Sleep on it.
'It's a life or death decision! No, I won't let you say any more — oh, and
one thing further. This interview is secret. I repeat, you must confide in
no one about what we have spoken or my head, and yours too, will roll.
Your decision must be your own, alone. I shan't think less of your
wisdom if you decide not to take it on, but I shall rely on your secrecy.'

She leaves the room considerably shaken and at the same time exhilarated, sure that she will not change her mind.

At a third and last encounter, she makes her final decision. Despite the terrible risks pointed out to her on a cold statistical basis, she still wishes to carry on if she is acceptable. So well have the candidates been screened before being sent for interview that at this stage few refuse.

Girls who were sent for selection a year later, in June 1943, faced a different kind of procedure. Now, instead of talking to one person for a few carefully spaced interviews, they found themselves staying for a few days with a group of people, who were in fact mainly psychologists, who probed their characters and motives in different, more scientific ways, but the results were usually very similar. Those who did not pass scrutiny were returned to their previous work.

Afterwards came the training, averaging from four to ten months, according to their previous knowledge and the work the agent was to undertake. It was necessarily short because trained agents were few and needed urgently. Many went into enemy-occupied territory more than once. In comparison with the 10 years usually spent in training Russian spies this was woefully inadequate; but then SOE agents were not professional spies, just men and women volunteering to organize and supply resistance in an enemy-occupied country for the duration of the war. Their pay was absurdly low and their abiding motive was to help in liberating the country that they loved.

All the volunteers, men and women together, spent between two to four weeks at an Initial Special Training School for final selection. For those going to France in F Section this was at Wanborough Manor near Guildford, an earl's fine Tudor house with large rooms and a wide private park. Here, while FANY's looked after the well-being of its inhabitants, they underwent a stiff preliminary course of basic military and physical training, where they learned the rudiments of living in a wartime occupied country, the Morse code, elementary map-reading and how to handle pistols and sub-machine-guns. Outside it was believed that they were being given commando training, though locals were mystified to see girls among them, but inside it sometimes more resembled a country house party, an atmosphere which could catch out unwary students who unwisely drank too much at the bar, became too garrulous and confiding, or talked English in their sleep. Indeed, if they were going to France they had to speak French continuously. All the time they were being watched and assessed by the staff, including Commanding Officer Roger de Wesslow from whom regular reports reached Baker Street. At the end, the least promising were quietly encouraged to drop out.

At this point, or even before Wanborough, those intended to become wireless operators had their specialized training. Later it was realized that basic knowledge of radio work would have been useful to all agents, except that insufficient time precluded it.

To understand the kind of wireless course that faced SOE recruits, a glance at that given to an ordinary WAAF is helpful. When airwoman Diana Scruton told an acquaintance that she was going on a wireless operators' course, she was annoyed by the response that she had better give up the idea as 'you had to be pretty intelligent for it'! Consequently she worked for the next six months with such determination to get her treasured sparks, 'that the old experienced sergeant who was my examiner for Morse sending said he'd seldom heard such perfectly spaced morse'. In early 1943, another airwoman, Irene Gozzard, arrived at Blackpool for her first three months of learning the Morse Code. 'Olympia had been taken over and as you succeeded in reading Morse at different speeds you moved on to the next table. Each table represented a certain speed, so that by the time you reached the last one you could read morse at 18 words per minute. We also had to learn all about the radio set, Ohms Law, triodes, pentodes and so forth. They had acid batteries in those days and we used to sing a little song to the tune of an Hawaiian seranade, to which we used to march:

"Sal-ammoniac ammoniac, ammoniac,
Sal-ammoniac, ammoniac, ammoniac,
A two volt 20 acc
An unspillable venti-acc
Sal ammoniac, ammoniac."

The next six months were spent at Compton Bassett, where it was very cold and bleak. Apparently it was a two-year course condensed into nine months for us.'

If this was the training for ordinary WAAF, how much more difficult was it for the SOE volunteer, who had to cover it in much greater detail in a much shorter time. Even for those fortunate enough to know their trade already, like Noor Inayat Khan and Yolande Beekman, there were still long hours to be spent in the laboratories learning the vagaries and composition of their set, fault diagnosis and how to repair it with makeshift materials. In Special Schools like Thame Park in Oxfordshire, most of the agents had to learn from the beginning, starting with Morse and climbing to speeds in excess of 22 words per minute. They also developed a 'fist' or style by which it was said that someone receiving could tell who was transmitting — a kind of fingerprinting in Morse. But there was much more. Learning the skills of transposition into cipher must have been quite a headache as no message was ever sent or received except in cipher. According to the period of their training several methods of enciphering were used. There were also the refinements of atmospherics, wavelengths, oscillation, static, skip, dead spots, jamming and the mysteries of aerials, with the thousand and one other details they had to acquire, as well as ways of hiding sets and security.

They additionally learned to incorporate into their messages certain features peculiar to each operator, known as safety checks. Receivers in Britain would then be able to judge if the message was genuine or sent by the Germans. It was not the agent's fault therefore when occasionally, if they were captured, their purposely-omitted safety checks went unrecognized by London.

Agents knew that once in the field their messages would, with the aid of the specially tuned crystals supplied with their set, go to a particular station in Britain where there were banks of receivers and relays of men and girls, the latter often FANY, who listened out perpetually to send and receive their messages. Sir Colin Gubbins called the work of the SOE wireless operator 'the most valuable link in the whole of our chain of operations. Without these links, we should have been groping in the dark'.

Male and female recruits next passed to the Group A Special Training Schools, F Section to Number 26 STS at Arisaig, one of a clutch of big houses found in the wildest and most inaccessible parts of the highlands of Inverness-shire, where the weather could be as hostile as the environment beautiful. They were far enough from habitation to practise blowing up bridges with dummy explosives and to carry out various nefarious activities without causing remark, though the canny Highlanders seemed to have some wind of what was going on. Occasionally it was only at this point that the purpose of such training really sunk in. 'I only answered an advertisement for a bilingual secretary', bemoaned one girl. Dressed in blue denims, with no concession to sex, agents were trained in the use and handling of British and German arms, loading slippery weapons by touch in the dark. They learned fieldcraft, how to cross rough country and creep silently through the undergrowth, how to avoid the skyline and wade rock strewn streams, how to live off the land and kill silently. There was more Morse, map and paperwork, advanced raiding tactics, forced marches, all-night schemes, unarmed combat, knife work, rope work, boat work and, despite the rough conditions, they were brought to a peak of physical fitness, unless they were some of the unlucky one-third who were usually weeded out as unsuitable before they could harm themselves or someone else more lethally. They were taught by commandos, poachers and jailbirds, and a sense of humour became a piece of necessary equipment in their armoury. Conducting officers often went through the training alongside their candidates, so as to get to know them all the better.

Somewhere in their last few months, if it was felt necessary, agents were sent to Special Schools for their own particular mission. Some did

courses on industrial sabotage, some learned the skills of choosing and
describing dropping zones and creating special reception committees for
parachuted supplies, others learned how to teach men to use new forms
of armaments, or safe and lock breaking. One of the final specialized
courses was for parachuting. Agents lived at Tatton Park, near
Manchester, and learned at nearby Ringway Airfield, where all troops
were trained in parachuting. They usually did four or five practice
jumps, the last one at night and in later years with a leg bag for carrying
equipment. Of course the station had its usual complement of airwomen.
Having spent about two years at Ringway working on parachutes,
'where most of the time 1,000 troops were dropped day and night',
Winifred Smith has clear memories of '... cycling across the tarmac to our
section, seeing girls preparing to parachute, complete with lipstick and
make-up — otherwise it was hard to tell that they really were girls, what
with their parachute suits, crash helmets and so on. We often watched
them waiting to board their plane. It was like follow-my-leader. The girls
were towards the back but they were always laughing and we would
wave and call good luck. I don't ever remember more than about three
or four together boarding the same plane, in fact often I could only see
one.' Trainers sometimes said that they put the girls to jump first out of
the aircraft into the grounds of Tatton Park, since they reckoned that
the men would not hold back if a woman led the way. As part of her
work on modifications to 'chutes and packs, Winifred also went into the
training hangar: '... and saw them training on what we called the Fan.
They were completely fearless. They were also quick off the mark in
getting away afterwards. One had the feeling they didn't expect to come
back, so they were living for the moment. When VE Day was over and
we could talk more freely, it was agreed by all who had contact with
these WAAF, that they had an inner strength and sheer determination
which allowed them to do what was asked of them. They were inspired
by something greater than the ordinary person.'

  Girls like Winifred were clearly very conscious of their responsibilities,
illustrated very well in this poem called the *Parachute Packer's Prayer* by
G.D. Martineau:

'When they posted me here to the section,
I was free as the pitiless air,
Unashamed of confessed imperfection,
Having no sort of burden to bear.
I was not an incurable slacker,
Neat, not fussy — I fancied of old,
But today I'm a Parachute Packer
And my heart takes a turn at each fold.

When I think how I snugly resided
In the lap of this land we could lose,

I believe if I left one cord twisted,
I would place my own neck in a noose.
So I lay the fine silk on the table
And I lift each pale panel in turn.
They have said that my folding is able,
But it took me a long time to learn.

For the cords must come free for smooth flowing,
And the webbing attachment be stout,
For the brute of a breeze will be blowing
If the aircrew will have to bale out.
'Cos the flyer must float unencumbered,
Come to earth to complete the design.
See the 'chute has been carefully numbered
And the name in the log book is mine.

So is conscience awakened and care born
In the heart of a negligent maid.
Fickle Aeolus, fight for the airborne,
Whom I strive with frail fingers to aid.
Give my heroes kind wind and fair weather,
Let no parachute sidle or slump,
For today we go warring together
And my soul will be there at the jump.'

Out of the approximately 60 Special Training Schools in many parts
of the world as well as the UK, those in Group B acted as Finishing
Schools. Of these, Beaulieu in the New Forest, now famous for its
vintage cars, housed the different country sections in its grounds in
cottages and lodges rejoicing in such romantic names as the 'House by
the Shore' or the 'House in the Woods'. The family in one wing kept
aloof but often watched with curiosity verging on hilarity the antics of
their unusual guests. The staff of the School lived in and used the main
hall. This was the School for Security, whose laws were constantly
driven into the students. They learned more about codes, map reading,
microphotography, how to use and arrange messages on the BBC, and
the ways of recognizing and making forgeries. The finer points of
espionage too were stressed, constant vigilance, the routine of organizing
safe letter boxes and safe houses, and, if it became necessary, the cut-out,
using intermediaries in contacting leaders, so as to keep their identities
secret.

The students also learned in greater detail of the counter-intelligence
forces of the enemy, and how to recognize and deal with them. Such
knowledge was vital. Thus they discovered that there were, of course,
the ordinary German Soldiers of occupation and the normal French
police, later assisted by the French Milice — pro-German, suspicious and
local, and thus much feared. There were, in addition, two services,

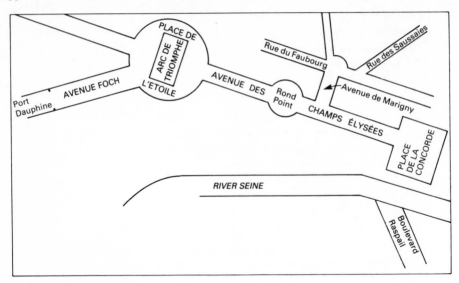

Paris, a diagram showing the streets where German Intelligence Sections were located.

military and civil, which dealt with any secret opposition to the Germans, and used the methods of counter-intelligence against them, such as the collection of information, capture of agents and supply dumps, interrogation, breaking up of circuits, playing back captured wireless sets in order to misinform Britain, (the so-called Wireless Game) and infiltrating opposition groups to destroy them. Because of the distrust by the Nazi state of its own people, several different counter-intelligence bodies had grown up, confusing in their roles and overlaps. When the system moved to France it became no less confusing, though to the SOE agent the results seemed the same. But an agent's treatment might vary if he encountered the methods of the Abwehr of the military arm, with its Paris headquarters at the Hotel Lutetia on the Boulevard Raspail, headed by Admiral Canaris in Germany, or the SD (Sicherheitsdienst) in its headquarters at 82-86 Avenue Foch — sometimes known as Avenue Boche — the intelligence wing of the SS. This SS was the much hated and feared Political State Police, headed by Himmler in Germany, a vastly powerful organization which also controlled the Gestapo, whose Paris headquarters was 11 Rue des Saussaies. These bodies often clashed over their victims, agents, and methods, and eventually in the spring of 1944 the Abwehr was absorbed by the SS.

It was at about this stage in the agents' final preparation, that their new identity was created and then put together, piece by meticulous piece, their new name and occupation, the places and people they knew, where they were born, and so forth. Always truth was mixed with fact, so that if detected the French or Germans would find it hard to disprove them. Then last of all came the culminating test, a task that might take them to the ends of the country with a special mission to perform by guile, skill or bravado. At the end they were taken for interrogation by mock Gestapo, who gave them the hardest grilling of their lives, albeit without the torture of the real thing, but which at least one agent was to say saved him. From this experience, faults could be corrected while there was still time, or the agent could be dropped and sent for a short time to the 'cooler', a place well isolated in the remote Scottish Highlands. This was done if SOE felt that this particular individual could not withstand interrogation by the Germans for the minimum period of 48 hours, calculated as sufficient to enable a network to take cover, should he be captured.

A plaque was later unveiled to commemorate the work done at Beaulieu.

'Remember before God, those men and women of the European Resistance Movement who were secretly trained in Beaulieu to fight their lonely battle against Hitler's Germany, and who before entering Nazi-occupied territory, here found some measure of the peace for which they fought.'

The agent was thus prepared, as far as it was humanly possible for the mission. Now there was nothing else to do but go over and over the cover story and wait for the call on operations. Sometimes, if the wait was long, it would be at a holding station. This was often a large house like Fawley Court, where smiling FANY hostesses helped an agent while away the days, maybe months, dictated by the weather, numbers of planes available, politics, accidents of people or war. At other times it might just be a short stay at a London flat, spending the last day at Orchard Court, famous for its sybaritic black marble bathroom and its obsequious, skilful butler Parkes. This was comfort indeed, unfortunately not enjoyed by British counterparts on the outskirts of Algiers, who suffered the weeks of waiting in extreme discomfort, only alleviated by the call on mission.

3
Flight Into Danger

'I am off to RAF Tempsford, near Bedford, tomorrow to take up a new job which will give me a lot of fun and a real chance to make some personal contribution to the war as a whole. As the war swings from the defensive to the offensive, so do I go from Fighter to Bomber Command. My particular job will be an outstandingly important one that I'm afraid I cannot describe to you. It will involve a little operational flying... Personal fears and hopes must shrink before the importance to millions of people of shortening the war.'

Letter home from 'We Landed By Moonlight' by Hugh Verity (Ian Allan), Pilot and Officer Commanding the Lysander Flight (A Flt) of 161 Special Duties (SD) Squadron

The waiting time was over. The long expected phone summons had at last arrived. Now the first women agents to go by plane to France reported to Baker Street for a few words from their chief, Colonel Buckmaster, who gave each a small gift, like a silver cigarette case or compact, which could be sold if necessity arose. Then, with their luggage packed in nondescript suitcases, they trooped to the car ready to take them and their conducting officer to their unknown destination.

They had no idea of the battles that were being fought over their heads, but this time it was not due to the fact that they were women going to do an agent's job. That battle had been fought earlier and won! This battle was on the essential means of getting them, men and women alike, to the country where they were to risk their lives. With the Battle of Britain over, Bomber Command, under its redoubtable Commander Sir Arthur Harris (as well as Sir Charles Portal at Air Ministry) was certain that the way to weaken and destroy Germany was by an increasingly heavy bomber offensive against its factories, power plants, railways, and any other targets which would damage its war effort. It was Harris's belief that this was the way to shorten the war. He therefore guarded his aircraft like a hen with its chicks, firmly setting his face against losing any, particularly large ones (other than by enemy action), which might detract from his heavy bombing raids, which in his eyes were far more effective than mere sabotage pinpricks. For this reason he opposed diverting aircraft for SOE activities.

The Moon Squadrons, so called because they could only work during the bright moon period between the quarter wax to quarter wane, ferried agents in and out of occupied countries, and also transported their vital armaments and supplies. They were therefore limited in their number of sorties, but additionally they could only fly according to the number and state of their aircraft. There were other uncertainties too which might abort flights, such as weather in England or over France, aircraft shot down by enemy fighters or anti-aircraft guns, finding or losing the way to a tiny pinpoint in a huge country, the suitability or obstacles of the site with marshes, high trees, mountains, telegraph wires, or meeting a reception committee not of members of the resistance but of Germans. Their task was to support SOE in the second, secret type of warfare that was being waged against the all-conquering enemy in his very home and backyard — the clandestine war of resistance.

Thus 138 Special Duties Squadron was formed in August 1941 at Newmarket, equipped with Whitleys, Lysanders, and a few Halifaxes used by Polish crews for long distances. Eventually in March 1942 it found a home at Tempsford, near Sandy in low-lying Bedfordshire, after being joined by the Hudson, Whitleys, Lysanders, and Wellingtons of 161 Squadron. Later more aircraft were released and Stirlings made their appearance. Planes were modified for their special roles using Tangmere in Sussex by the sea as an advance base for short distances and Tempsford for long hauls. Their crews came from many nationalities, starting with British, soon joined by Poles, and later other European nationalities, followed, after Pearl Harbor, by the Americans who, using many airfields, eventually deployed Dakotas and two squadrons of Liberators. After spring 1945 personnel and planes were transferred, their task accomplished. The Whitleys were relegated to training by the end of 1942 and the Lysanders had already been taken off operational flying in March 1944. As the *Aeroplane* wryly notes: 'They have been honourably retired to several non-combatant duties like Air-Sea Rescue!' Most of the SOE women who climbed down on to French soil landed from a Lysander or Hudson, while those who were parachuted in came by Halifax.

Some of the most skilful, secretive and courageous pilots flew these aircraft, calculating drops and landings to a hair's breadth in the few moonlit nights of a month, taking their precious cargoes through the teeth of the enemy artillery and paying a terrible toll for their actions. Nevertheless they could joke about their work. 'It's expecting too much of anyone to be able to talk French *and* fly by night,' wrote Wing Commander Hodges in Group Captain Verity's *Cottage Line Book*. Others, like Robin Hooper broke into rhyme:

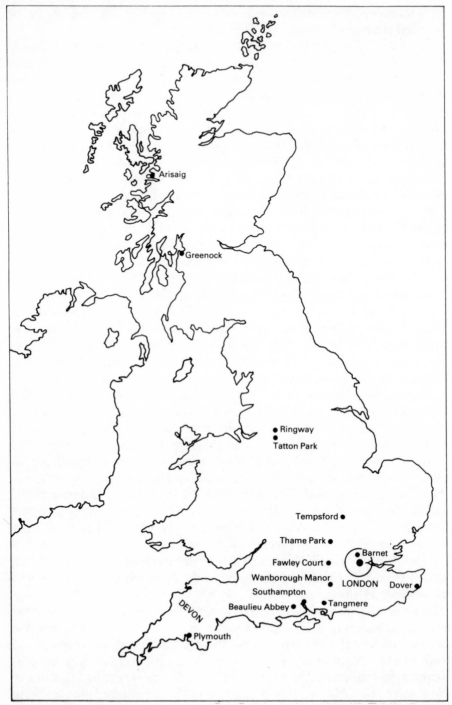

The main UK centres, training bases and airfields connected with SOE agents sent to France.

'The moon is sinking in the sky,
We know we've damn well got to fly
Or get into a fearful mess
With SOE or SIS.
The messages come thick and fast,
"We've got a field for you at last,
So come tonight and try your luck..." '

Despite all the precautions for secrecy these special missions could not be hidden from the all-seeing eye of radar. In common with many others, Pearl Panton, a WAAF working on Ground Control Interception, GCI, knew immediately one of these special flights set out. They were noticeable in being only single aircraft going out across the Channel and then later returning homewards. 'They were given quite a different code, plus a special time for the moon to light their way, and they flew very low.' She might have speculated but she really had no idea what the mission was. Nevertheless, like all controllers, she never spoke about it.

In her diary she recalled what happened to one of these flights. 'It was a full moon last night, an essential factor for the special mission pilots taking off and returning. At 21.30 hours, I was driven from the Officers' Mess to the "Happydrome" [the building from which the aircraft were controlled]. The officer of the watch gave me my orders. I was to work on the Skyatron radar. A special mission was going out before midnight, due to return just before dawn.

'P for Peter 141 took off at 22.00 hours. One of the girls working the watch was startled as she recognized her husband's voice calling to confirm that he was airborne. She wouldn't have known of this mission, of course. I didn't know her well, but I had met her recently in a nearby café. There she had introduced me to her husband and I remember her delight at a pair of fur-trimmed gloves he had bought her that day. During the night watch she told me she was expecting her first baby.

'It was a busy night as usual. P 141 was due to return at 03.00 hours. There was no R/T contact at the scheduled time. I was told to call him and keep calling at regular intervals. He should at least have crossed the French coast. The girl sat next to me, watching the Skyatron, listening intently for her husband's voice. His call would have included a coded message to be passed to Air Ministry. It never came through.'

However these aircraft were not always involved with SOE, and indeed sometimes, though not often, aircraft joined them from other squadrons, or their special skills of location were needed in the main bomber stream if Air Ministry so decided.

The work of another WAAF at Air Ministry, Yvonne George, was to liaise with SIS and SOE headquarters. 'Each morning SIS and SOE would inform me which operations they could put on that night. This information I would phone to the Intelligence Officer at Tempsford

Station and according to the availability of aircraft, weather, and so on, the final programme would be decided upon. Code names such as Lettuce 1 and Cabbage 2 would be used. No names of agents were ever disclosed. Drops were made in France, Belgium, Holland, Denmark, Poland and Czechoslovakia. Additionally we flew Lysanders from Tangmere from where the pilots would fly out and back agents, mostly from France. On one occasion I was at Tangmere to see the take off of an aircraft with three agents aboard and waited till about 3 am, early morning, for its return. As one of them alighted I caught a strong smell of Guerlain perfume — something we in England had not known for some years!'

Faith Spencer-Chapman has similar memories. 'I was in "Air Ops" and mostly we did work on dropping agents into Europe, and then the "Pick up Ops" which meant taking agents down to RAF Tangmere and waiting for the Lysander to return with agents who had to be got out of France urgently. Then we had to drive back to London in the early hours and hand them over to be debriefed.'

At Tangmere crew and passengers usually shared the same ivy-clad, overgrown house called 'the cottage'. Here was where they slept if their flight was delayed and it was usually in the fairly spartan dining room that they toasted their future flight and had their last meal on British soil. No names would be exchanged but everyone would be extremely cheerful.

Then in the last of the daylight they would straggle out to the field where usually the Lysander stood ready to transport them to France. Once aboard, the passengers were totally reliant on the pilot who had to do his own navigation in the small unarmed, one-engined plane. It looked an ungainly aircraft with its high wings and fixed undercarriage, but its high rate of climb and descent, together with its ability to come down on tiny pocket-handkerchiefs of ground, no matter how rough, endeared it to its pilots and made it perfect for undercover night landings. Properly speaking it carried its pilot and one other person in a rear cockpit, but when the Lizzie worked for SOE it usually carried two, or at a pinch three, passengers in great discomfort from which they climbed down a fixed metal ladder to the ground. Its disadvantage was its short range of 600–700 miles, which was why it was chiefly confined to France.

Tempsford, on the other hand, took the larger aircraft and therefore larger numbers of passengers on a flight. They usually arrived with their conducting officer in a FANY driven car, via the Great North Road, at teatime. The food was magnificent (no rationing observed), and so was Tempsford House, the large country mansion where agents awaited their flight call. Again various reasons might delay their expected flight, but a blackboard in the drawing room, using their code names, informed

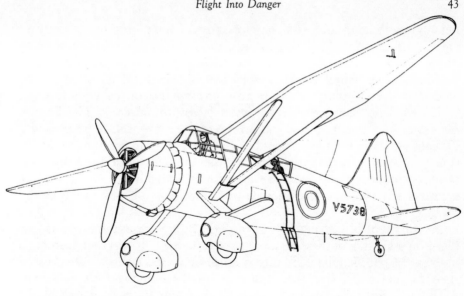

Drawing of a Lysander. (Lt Col P. Lorain)

them when it was time to go. Bedrooms were allotted one to several women if the wait was prolonged.

On the destined evening another car would take them down a winding lane, through a railway crossing, towards some farm buildings in flat country. This was the famous Gibraltar Farm, the well-camouflaged base in RAF Tempsford. The Nissen hut that looked like a cowshed from the outside was a veritable Aladdin's cave inside, with a proper fire, an RAF uniformed officer, and racks and tables for the final equipping and briefing of agents. Clothes and suitcase contents were checked for betraying British labels or laundry marks. Pockets and bags were turned out for the forgotten bus or theatre ticket. Money, in large quantities, was handed over, a loaded Colt revolver was added and then came the four tablets — for doping an adversary, keeping awake, counterfeiting a dangerous illness, or for death if all else failed. Wireless operators also received the little crystals for their transmitters. When everything was ready came the jumping suit, the helmet and the parachute harness, after which, all Parisian elegance lost, passengers waddled out to be greeted, still nameless, by their captain and his crew, whose confidence transmitted itself to them, cheering them on their long cold journey to France.

They might be taking off in the sturdy twin-engined Hudson with its range of 1,000 miles and capacity for eight to 10 passengers or a heavier load of parcels and containers. But the greater likelihood was that they would be taken up by the four-engined Halifax, with its chattering guns and extremely long range. It also had a special ability to take off when heavily overloaded and was therefore perfect for taking big loads, and parachuting men and supplies in large numbers to the waiting reception parties below. Later in the war the Halifax was also equipped with a homing device called Rebecca, which could read off distances or be guided to a particular spot by a tiny ground beacon called a Eureka, which used no power unless triggered off by the aircraft. The French resistance had fixed two Eurekas on top of the cathedrals of Rheims and Orléans, known by aircrew as 'boot and shoe', and aircraft could get timely navigational aid from their 60 mile signal if wandering from their target. The same applied to the Eurekas positioned in the heart of three great French forests, at goodness knows what risk to life and limb by the French.

On the night of 12 May 1943, Frank Griffiths was co-pilot for his first flight on a Halifax of the Special Duties Squadron. 'It was such a smooth uneventful trip, it lulled me into a false sense of security... We crossed the Channel at 200 feet, then "jumped" the French coast at Cabourg at 4,000 feet. Nothing came up at us. Then down to tree level in bright moonlight. We called at two receptions east of Paris and dropped our loads, then off to Belgium to drop a Joe [agent] and his pianist [wireless operator] to a reception, then back round Paris to, of all places, a sewage farm just south-west of Versailles. A curious place to have a reception but no doubt few people hang around sewage farms at 3 o'clock in the morning [13 May]! So back to Cabourg to jump the coast, then to Tempsford and bed.

'As Jack and I walked back to the mess from debriefing, I remarked on the utter smoothness of the trip, the lack of excitement, the way the moonlit countryside rolled by underneath, the way all the water checkpoints came up dead on time. "Why," I remarked, "to hear the chaps talk in the Mess, you'd think it was hellfire all the way."

' "That's Al Roach [the navigator]," he replied. "If you don't get lost you shouldn't get shot at. The more trips you do the bettter you do the job, but if you once get lost it can get quite exciting."

'How right he was for I then started operations with my own crew and for the first four trips we didn't do well. We delivered our loads and passengers all right but we kept being shot at.'

And eventually what everyone feared happened — he was shot down. His aircraft and crew went up in flames but, badly wounded, he was passed along a French escape network to freedom — an adventurous journey, which he describes in his book *Winged Hours*.

In November 1942, after the invasion of North Africa, the Inter Services Signals Unit 6, code-named Massingham, was set up outside Algiers. As well as taking and sending messages, it packed and sent supplies to the resistance. It also began training and, in time, sending agents and finally commando groups. Such tasks required special

The Form.

1) Go to Intelligence. Take ¼ million map of your target area, and mark the field accurately.
Note letters (Ground to Air, and Air to Ground)
Note times of reception.
Note previous reports of operations on that field.

2) Make out ½ million maps, measure distances, and work out approximate times :—
   a) Take-off.
   b) Crossing English Coast (OUT)
   c) Crossing Enemy Coast (OUT)
   d) Time over Target.
   e) Crossing Enemy Coast (IN)
   f) Crossing English Coast (IN)
   g) Land Base
   h) Latest Time of Take-off.

3) Hand these in and then go to lunch.

4) Measure your tracks, mark flak areas, and tidy up your maps.

5) N.F.T. Have parachute, dinghy, Mae West, and helmet in the kite.

6) Met. briefing.   Find out movements of our bombers.

7) Collect :—
   a) Colours of the Day, and Very Cartridges.
   b) Letters of the Day.
   c) List of Pundits.
   d) Rations.
   e) Escape Kits.
   f) French Money.
   g) Parcel for Agent.
   h) Coffee.
   i) Operational Call Sign.
   j) C.H.L. Station to call (OUT and IN)

8) When you get the Met. winds, work out your courses and ground speeds, and mark off time or distance intervals on your map.

9) Relax until take-off time.   EVERYTHING UNDER

PERFECT CONTROL

Advice to pilots of 161 Special Duties Squadron (written by W. Taylor and copied by Flt Lt R. Large).

aircraft, so it was eventually decided to send a Special Duties wing out to North Africa to obviate aircraft having to fly over enemy-occupied territory to the less heavily occupied area in southern France. Yvonne George opted to join them. 'I was finally posted to MAAF HQ Algiers where Eisenhower was Supreme Commander. I remember arriving by boat in Algiers, which, in the sunlight with the smell of orange trees, seemed like heaven after the blackout, bombing and austerity of England.'

In 1944 she was moved to the Balkan Air Force HQ in Bari, southern Italy. 'Here aircraft dropped hundreds of thousands of tons of equipment, guns, and ammunition to the beleaguered Yugoslavian partisans who were working in close collaboration with the British Special Forces, hindering the movements of the occupying German troops in the mountains.'

Indeed from its early days, SOE had spread its activities into as many different areas as theatres of war — Europe, Near, Middle and Far East; but its main energies were centred on Europe and the largest numbers of its agents, about 480, were sent to France. In such dangerous work around 130 were captured. Of these the survival rate was tiny, only 26 emerging from their captivity.

The men were usually given a commission in one of the three armed services, but for the women it was slightly different. About 90 women were trained, from whom — allowing that in such work there will always be a few who fit into no category — in the region of 50 were actually sent to France as agents. Among these, 11 were either American non-service girls or belonged to the *Corps Auxiliaire Féminin* (the French equivalent of the British Auxiliary Territorial Service). The remainder were Women's Transport Service FANY, but not entirely so. Mrs Davidson of the FANY explains. 'As the women's services were not allowed to carry arms, the Women's Auxiliary Air Force, WAAF, who volunteered for SOE would automatically be seconded to the FANY where there was no such inhibition.' They were therefore all serving members of SOE, only nominally in another service for administrative convenience or for cover. Of course none could wear any type of uniform in their secret work in France, unless they were with a uniformed Maquis or after liberation, but it caused less comment while the girls were training in this country, doing service-type activities in the FANY khaki uniform. It made them look official at any rate.

The position of WAAF was therefore strange at the very least and untangling service alignments can pose difficulties. The SOE Adviser at the Foreign and Commonwealth Office illustrates the position by quoting the case of Noor Inayat Khan, an undoubted WAAF. She was an Aircraftwoman I when she joined SOE on 8 February 1943. On 12 February 1943 she was enrolled as a FANY. On 15 June 1943 a standard type formal letter was sent to Air Ministry (the same for all WAAF). 'I shall be glad if you will arrange for the above-named airwoman to be discharged from the WAAF and given an honorary commission under the special arrangements made between us.' In the early hours of 17 June 1943 she landed in France. On 22 July 1943 her appointment as a WAAF Assistant Section Officer was agreed and it was gazetted on 1 January 1944. However, the recommendation for her George Medal is made out in the name of 'Ensign N. Inayat Khan, a Volunteer FANY', but it was granted by the Central Chancery of the Orders of Knighthood on 5 April 1949 to Assistant Section Officer Nora Inayat Khan. With such a mixture it is a wonder if Noor herself knew what service she represented, but on balance I think it is fair to say that she was, as she had begun and ended, a WAAF!

As in Noor's case, before going into the field most of those who had previously been in the WAAF had the same letter sent to Air Ministry and were granted honorary commissions, if they did not already hold one, in the expectation that as officers should they be captured by the enemy they would be treated better and given more suitable accommodation and conditions of imprisonment. They would also be prisoners of war and could not be sentenced to death without trial. This proved to be a forlorn hope, but it was the reason that of the 15 WAAF sent to France (14 for F Section, one for DF), three were originally WAAF officers and 12 were made honorary officers. Seven went as couriers, eight as wireless operators, and out of these, six were imprisoned, one died of natural causes and five were executed. Their casualty rate was about par for the course and they represent a good cross section of the characters and actions of the many other women sent into the field by SOE.

To know what they did and what happened to them can therefore act as a memorial to those who died, and a reminder of the great courage shown by all these remarkable individuals who, in abnormal times, when their world was turned upside down, displayed extraordinary qualities to match their unusual and perilous role.

'These are deeds which should not pass away and names that must not wither.'

Byron

And these are their stories!

4
The Girl Who Came In From The Sea

Mary Katherine Herbert

'Mary was naturally courteous and considerate of other people, generous and trusting and in some ways naïve. She was attractive with an engaging smile, made and kept friends easily and her knowledge of art, literature and languages made her an interesting companion.'

Claudine Pappe

Mary Herbert, known by her friends as Maureen, was one of the first girls to be chosen by SOE to go into France, and the first woman taken from the WAAF. In April 1942, the authorities had only just agreed to allow women into the field and their training took a long time.

At the beginning of the war, Mary worked first in the Embassy in Warsaw and then as a civilian translator at the Air Ministry in London. On 19 September 1941 she joined the WAAF at Innsworth, Gloucester, as an airwoman in the General Duties trade group, where she remained until March 1942 when she was released at her own request so that she might join SOE in May of that year. Here she became one of the second group of women to be trained for work in France. She was, however, granted a retrospective WAAF commission to 15 January 1941 as a Section Officer. But the problem in that year was how to get agents into France, especially German-occupied France. Mary was an experiment, and unlike the WAAF who came after her who went in by air, she was to arrive another way. She was to go in by sea.

Thus it was in October 1942 that she found herself sitting in the comfort of a large flying boat, floating on the choppy waters of Plymouth harbour, waiting to take off for Gibraltar. Together with her were others — some were follow trainees — and Roger Landes, all destined for French circuits, although she and Roger were to belong to the same one.

The engines of the plane were already warming up when the outside door clanged open and a head appeared in the opening, talking fast. It and the steward, with whom it spoke, looked in their direction. 'Not again,' groaned Roger, who had already been on three abortive flights. But he was right. A minute later the steward appeared beside their four seats and whispered apologetically, 'Sorry, ladies and gentlemen, your journey is cancelled.' As they followed one another out of the seaplane, Mary must have felt bitterly disappointed. Having wound herself up ready to face the dangers of a difficult mission, it was not easy to come back to earth and a standstill. While they went back to the quay, their escort told his glum passengers that the felucca, expected to meet them in Gibraltar and transport them on to France, was overdue. 'What could have happened?' they asked. But the question needed no answer. Any of a dozen fates could have befallen it — treachery, capture, submarines, storms, accident, the list was endless. Their guide turned up his collar and shrugged: 'It might turn up yet.'

Carrying their nondescript suitcases, in their shabby French clothes, they formed a dejected huddle on the quay before being taken to a quiet hotel where they might wait. Each day when they came down to breakfast they asked the same question: 'Any news?' But each day there was the same answer: 'Nothing.' They took brisk walks looking at the sea, and explored the town in ones and twos, afraid to go too far away for recall. But nothing happened. At the end of the third day, their guide brought them together. 'It's gone I'm afraid. I'll settle your bills and take you back to London.'

Once more waiting to be called forward, Mary did not feel like painting the town red in her brief days of freedom. She knew the call would come sooner or later, so instead she kept very much to herself, and spent her time reading in any one of the five languages she spoke, taking long ruminative walks in the grey, gathering, winter weather, and mentally rehearsing in meticulous details her cover story. Even the very air around her seemed to be suspended into a throb of expectancy. And then suddenly, there it was, a telephone call. Just the briefest of messages. She was quickly packed and ready when the car came to pick her up.

This time the sea transport waiting in the gathering dusk was not quite what she had expected. It was a submarine, and though her quarters would have been considered palatial by the crew, it still felt very cramped and stuffy. Her companions were the same, except that George

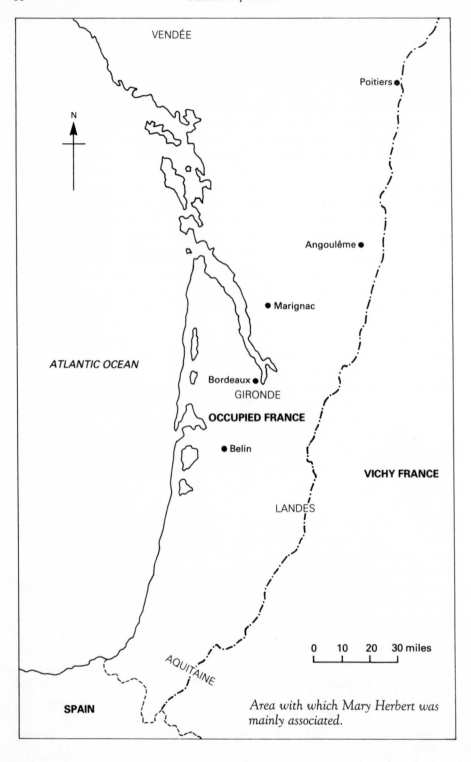

VENDÉE

N

Poitiers ●

Angoulême ●

● Marignac

ATLANTIC OCEAN

Bordeaux ●
GIRONDE

OCCUPIED FRANCE

● Belin

VICHY FRANCE

LANDES

0   10   20   30 miles

AQUITAINE

SPAIN

Area with which Mary Herbert was mainly associated.

Starr escorted them, himself bound for a further circuit, since Roger Landes was to be parachuted in elsewhere. At Gibraltar they boarded their felucca. It wasn't the same one for which they had first waited, but no one asked about that for fear of bad luck. This was a net-strewn little fishing boat of 20 tons, a sturdy craft with a strong smell of sardines and a head of steam peculiar in any vessel of such a trade. Finally on a moonless night, with only a phosphorescent spray breaking on the rocks of the cove to show the place, and where high cliffs blotted out the stars the fishing boat hove to with silent engines. Eager hands lifted them into a cockleshell boat propelled by muffled oars, whose ripples glimmered oily and silent on the waters. Then the boat slid ashore and she jumped out and fell, to find the wet sand of France in her hands. She had landed near Cassis, on the coast between Marseilles and Toulon. Around her she heard the accents of southern France from the shadowed figures, who were urging them away before they were discovered. It was dreamlike, exhilarating and magical, all in one. It hardly seemed real! At last Mary was in France, and it was 30 October 1942.

But this was only a beginning. After a meal — more fish — and a short nap at a fisherman's home, with the others she boarded the early train to the still popular holiday town of Cannes, where they all assembled in a room behind a beauty salon. Here they rested before finally saying their goodbyes, ready to make their own way to their various circuits. By daylight they had quickly dispersed, knowing that they might never see one another again. Passed from friendly house to house, they travelled by train, bus or bike to their several destinations.

For Mary, the first big obstacle after her journey from Cannes west to Tarbes and then north, was to cross the demarcation line which separated the unoccupied Vichy zone from occupied France. Up until then, she had been on the safer side of the border, notable mainly in its absence of Germans. Few willingly wanted to exchange their freedom for the opposite side, yet Mary had to. However, the papers and documents she carried, though carefully prepared by SOE in London, were not considered by those around her as sufficiently good forgeries to pass the border controls and rigorous examinations of papers and passports. She therefore had to trust to the services of a local guide, who would take her across at a quieter place and under the cover of darkness. This she accomplished quite smoothly with little more than a slight loss of sleep and a few breathless minutes of running and hiding. What she did not realize at the time was that she was almost the last person to leave the zone when it was unoccupied; the next day the German army marched across the border and their tanks rolled in. The Germans explained, very apologetically of course, that they had only done it to safeguard the French, but few believed that. No one in the north showed much surprise. Each felt that the surprise was only in the length of time that Vichy's special immunity had lasted. Mary, having crossed the border, was no longer concerned and continued her careful way westwards towards Bordeaux, reaching it in early December, sooner than expected. However, a room was found for her with a courier who shuttled between Bordeaux and another group in Tours, which at that time provided her organizer with his only wireless communication with London. Here her contact took her to Claude de Baissac, code named David, who was the organizer of the Scientist circuit. He was an attractive, forceful man, the son of one of the richest and noblest families in Mauritius. Mary must have been delighted to find that she was to be his courier. She then moved out of her cramped room and found herself a comfortable flat to use as her base. But she was not the only new arrival. Roger had preceded her and was safely ensconced as Claude's wireless operator, code named Aristide, and she was introduced to Charles Hayes, known by the code name Victor, who was to train the resistance in explosives and demolition. As courier Mary was to be known as Claudine, thus completing a fully manned and operative SOE circuit.

Mary was probably not what Claude had been expecting. She was well educated with training in art and a degree, had travelled widely and like Claude was of a very good family. She was tall, slim and fair-haired, but at 39, four years older than he. Apart from being highly intelligent and sincerely religious, she had one useful characteristic born from experience, in that she could merge into a crowd without attracting attention, an enormous asset for an agent who wanted always to be inconspicuous. However, her peculiar status in a small mostly male circle, combined with her special closeness to her chief, and being the willing recipient of the compliments and courtesies paid by all true Frenchmen to any female, brought her more vividly to life in the coming year.

As a courier her task was rather as maid of all work. First and foremost she carried messages both verbally and, less often, on paper. She took these between the officers in her circuit and the leaders of the various groups. As well as messages, she carried money and sometimes wireless sets, usually using the tramway. On one occasion when she was struggling with a particularly heavy set, a German naval officer politely carried it for her to the tram, obviously totally oblivious to its incriminating contents. Another task was to act as a post-box for the circuit. Anyone who came to Bordeaux to see Claude had to see her first and she arranged future meetings. She also looked for 'safe' houses and useful people who might be good recruits. Additionally she helped to arrange for parachute drops and was frequently there when they took place. Other facets of her work might involve her in helping escapees from the prisons or aircraft crashes, and she remained on the lookout for

SOE's early tasks, apart from the infiltration of agents, were spreading propaganda and
building up supplies for sabotage. It occasionally also found itself drawn into other
clandestine spheres such as assisting the escape networks, which were set up in most
countries, to hide and take to safety fleeing refugees, prisoners of war and shot-down
airmen — usually the care of such bodies as MI9. This drawing depicts an actual event
— the arrival in April 1943, at the Ferme du Mont de Vauxrot, near Soissons, of the
pilot of a shot-down Wellington bomber. He was welcomed and hidden by the owners
of the farm, Monsieur and Madame Dupuis, before being passed along an escape line
back to England. Their nephew drew the picture used as the 1989 Christmas card of
the RAF Escaping Society. (M. Tabarant)

possible dangers, road blocks, good routes away from suspicion. In fact she might be called upon to do anything.

Indeed the Scientist circuit was a wide one. It started of course at Claude's headquarters in Bordeaux, a large thriving port, particularly important to the Germans for two activities. One was as a centre for the ships which ran through the British blockade between Europe and the Far East. The other was as a home for the German submarines which prowled the oceans, preying on merchant ships. However, even the Germans dared not walk unescorted or unarmed into the dockland areas, where warrens of French labourers who worked with the resistance were only too glad to pass on information or cause minor acts of sabotage that were almost impossible to trace. One amusing foray they managed was to sprinkle itching powder on to the clean shirts of the submariners before they were delivered, another was to 'doctor' a consignment of ships' accumulators which fell into their hands. Nevertheless the most damage to the U-boats in their pens was done by the limpet mines set by a small British commando raid in December 1942. In an unfortunate after effect, the Germans guarded the dock areas even more rigidly than before, and despite the unusually detailed information Claude managed to collect and pass to London, little could be acted upon.

In the hinterland beyond Bordeaux, Mary found herself travelling through the German controls far and wide over the surrounding country of the Gironde with its outliers of the circuit in rural Landes, near Angoulême and even in Poitou and the Vendée. Nor was this enough. Claude occasionally took her even further afield on some of his frequent visits to see Francis Suttill at Paris, where parts of his own circuit functioned. Soon Mary was visiting Paris herself, having found a small hotel not too concerned with registration. Claude also took her to see his sister Lise de Baissac, at Poitiers. Lise was organizer and also a courier of a loosely interconnecting circuit called Artist, who maintained contact with further circuits from the Gironde to Paris. Consequently Mary became very friendly with Lise. All this was, of course, strictly against all security rules, but Claude felt that his circuit was so secure that he could afford to ignore such regulations.

This could sometimes prove useful. On one occasion Roger needed Mary's help because one of the transmitters in his wireless set had burned out and he learned that a spare could be obtained in Paris from the Prosper network. Therefore, despite the risk, and using Mary, who now knew how to find Francis Suttill, they both travelled to Paris by train, the best way to avoid the majority of German identity checks. There Mary led him to Francis, the new transmitter was handed over and Mary assisted him in carrying it back to Bordeaux. Such chances had to be taken by all individuals in all organizations, however much they tried to remain hidden and inconspicuous.

In 1943, after Mary's arrival, London became more generous to this circuit, increasing the quantities of explosives and armaments parachuted to its members. Knowing its potential for sabotage SOE hoped to build it up. Nor was London to be disappointed. Satisfactory types of explosions began to mushroom in numbers of key areas, greatly damaging the German war effort, such as the huge blast shattering the radio station at Quatre Pavillions, which provided the necessary communications between Admiral Doenitz and his German U-boats in the Atlantic. Another well-placed detonation crippled the power station supplying the *Luftwaffe* airfields near Marignac, and in the same way the power station at Belin was damaged. This supplied power to German anti-aircraft batteries as well as the radar establishment at Deux Potteaux. These were large scale blows but lesser ones continued, such as the cutting of railway lines, roads and telephones — an annoying war of attrition in which it was difficult to catch the perpetrators or forecast where they would strike next.

A walled town on the way to Poitiers.

Mary must have been proud of such an active organization and even more pleased with the feeling that she was so much involved with what it did. Nevertheless, by Claude's wish she saw only a few of his chief lieutenants and this was to prove fortunate for her. One of these was André Grandclément, a former colonel in the French army, who headed a regional branch of the *Organisation Civile et Militaire* (OCM), a right-wing body of dissatisfied ex-servicemen and civil servants, one of the many conflicting organizations, unfortunately endemic in France. His members swelled Claude's numbers and Claude came to rely heavily on his support. Roger felt uneasy about the man and in any case he thought that Claude was expanding the circuit too widely and quickly, exposing himself to infiltrators and double agents. But Claude would not be warned. Their characters and outlooks were dissimilar, Roger very careful and Claude more expansive. They disagreed, but Roger continued transmitting almost daily from about four different houses in Bordeaux.

Matters were at this pass when in May 1943, Claude and Francis Suttill flew back to Britain to discuss the circuits and for new briefings. In the eyes of many in France such a visit indicated that the invasion of France was not far distant. Less than a fortnight later they returned, and with him Claude brought a new wireless operator to help Roger. But all was far from well. Within a few weeks, in June, the Gestapo pounced in Paris and began rounding up the members of the Prosper network, Francis Suttill among them. It was therefore inevitable that from torture the Germans would discover the links with Claude and Bordeaux.

As the Paris arrests proceeded, news of the disaster filtered through to Bordeaux, in time for the SOE officers there to take cover. Mary was badly shaken and moved to another flat. She changed her disguise and adopted a new name and identity. Everyone knew that now the Gestapo would be after them. After a while Claude became busy trying to extricate some of the Paris members of his group from the débâcle and checking with his sister, on whose judgement he relied very heavily. Mary quietly shuttled to and fro, trying to hold together the fraying edges of the huge circuit.

It was at this point that London recalled Claude for consultations on the mid-August Lysander. Many thought that since Mary had been in the field working hard and conscientiously for nearly a year, it was perhaps time for her to have a break and a short rest, but because Lise was then in imminent danger of being arrested, at the last moment Claude took his sister with him instead. Nevertheless, before he left, Claude gave instructions that André Grandclément was to stand in his place.

Shortly afterwards Roger was informed that Claude was being sent elsewhere and that he, Roger, was to replace Claude as the head of the circuit. When Mary heard that Claude was not returning, she was inconsolable. Charles Hayes saw her, and finally she broke down and told him what he had for some time suspected. She was going to have a child and the father was Claude de Baissac. Claude had promised her — and she had it in writing — that he would marry her, so she had hoped that this would be soon. They dared not marry yet in case their forged documents betrayed them. But now Claude was not returning, what could she do? She was quite certain that she did not want to be sent home, and soon because of her condition she would not be much help as a courier. She had cleverly hidden her state for months, as she thought that the child would be due in November.

After soothing her, Charles went straight to Roger and told him. It was not the type of problem for which he had been trained, and he was considerably shaken at the knowledge. Nevertheless he handled Mary's situation with tact and consideration. He ordered her to stop work at once, and sent her out of Bordeaux to another safe house for her security. He also saw that she had enough money for her needs, calling in weekly on his rounds of the circuit to see that she was well. At this stage, except for himself and the lady who was later to become his wife, all contact with the resistance was severed. Mary was in no state to risk being caught by the Gestapo.

Other problems also faced Roger. This was a bad time for the circuit. The Gestapo, aware of the arms drops, increased sabotage and Paris contacts of Bordeaux, were already busy in the Gironde, making arrests culminating in the discovery of Grandclément's wife and then in September, during an ill-considered visit to Paris, of Grandclément himself. The Gestapo managed to keep his arrest secret and, what is more, by some trick persuaded the man to act as a double agent for them in exchange for his wife's life, on their promise that they would not pursue his own special friends. Then they released him to do what damage he could. In October, the Gestapo also caught up with Charles Hayes, the sabotage expert they had long sought. He tried to shoot his way out but sadly failed. In between these events, arms dump after arms dump was discovered by the Germans and large scale arrests of ordinary members of the resistance began, over 300 being murdered by Grandclément's betrayal.

Roger early saw the hand of a traitor at work, and though without knowledge of what had really happened, felt that the finger of suspicion pointed directly at Grandclément. He was in a very dangerous position but he lacked proof. He thus countered it by cutting out his old contacts and making new, building up the nucleus of a new inner circuit which he hoped to leave in place to be revived after things had settled down. He even saw Grandclément and heard from his own lips a partial admission of what he had done but after Charles Hayes was lost, Roger knew that he must leave if he too was to survive.

It is greatly to his credit that among the many arrangements he had to make before his departure he found time to place Mary in a private nursing home to await the arrival of her baby. Through a contact of his fiancée who knew the matron, a place was found for her at La Valence, in a suburb of Bordeaux. It was not without its risks for his fiancée, who visited Mary regularly until she left the hospital, or to Roger himself paying his final call on 30 November in order to leave her with all the money he had been able to collect or borrow, on the day before escaping via the Pyrénées.

All passed safely, however, and in the first week of December 1943, Mary gave birth to a healthy little girl by Caesarian operation. Having a first child at her age was taking quite a risk, but just as risky was the chance that she might speak in English while under sedation and give them all away. She received the best of care and attention during her prolonged stay in the nursing home and the little girl thrived. When she was well again, Mary left, but by an intentional oversight omitted to leave a forwarding address. In fact she had laid her plans carefully, and unknown to anyone, she slipped away and took up residence in one of Lise de Baissac's flats in Poitiers, where she felt that she was far enough away not to attract German attention to her former work. Here she intended to sit out the war, living on the money Roger had left, and bringing up her child, comforted in the belief that Claude would return to marry her once the war was finished.

So the weeks passed quietly without event and Mary began a new life. Adept at disguises, she created a new persona and her money bought black-market ration books and papers to support her new identity and that of her child. Then early in the morning of 18 February 1944, she answered a knocking at the door. Pulling her dressing gown over her nightdress and with the baby wailing in the background, she looked full into the face of the Gestapo. She was wanted for questioning. Her heart must have quailed, but she reacted as any mother. 'But what will happen to my baby?' In the long hours that followed she found that not only she, but also all the other occupants of the building were under arrest. Somehow the Gestapo had found that Lise de Baissac had lived there. Soon the other occupants were cleared, and through the Gestapo's questions Mary realized that their suspicions eventually centred on her. Nor was this all. Shortly she found that they believed that she was Lise de Baissac. No greater irony could there be than that she, in reality the courier of another underground circuit, was not accused of that, but rather of being the sister of the man whose wife she would shortly be. What a tangle!

But through this, her first concern was for her child. Not only was she worried for her well-being, but also what would happen if she, Mary, should die in German hands. As far as possible she communicated her situation, the authorities mercifully took over, as they did in many other sad cases during the war, and the little girl was looked after by the French Social Services.

With her daughter's safety assured, Mary proceeded to weave an ingenious case for herself, using a cover story as Madame Marie Louise Vernier, a Frenchwoman from Alexandria in Egypt. Her knowledge of Arabic — she had a diploma from Cairo University — helped her to maintain it and she was able to fool her questioners, skilled as they were in probing for the truth. Whatever her knowledge and fears she kept them to herself and was also silent on the agonies of suffering she must have endured. No doubt her understanding of German, which she also spoke fluently, came to her aid. The outcome was that despite careful enquiries that took a few months and the conditions of harsh imprisonment meted out to all women civil prisoners, Mary was released just before Easter and went to live in a small country house near Poitiers, owned by the de Vaselot family who became lifelong friends. Then she reclaimed her baby from the orphanage and tried to pick up the pieces to put her life back together again. She had succeeded in the most difficult of circumstances; she had suffered and given nothing away, neither of herself nor of her circuit. It spoke much for her character that after her release, she again returned to the Poitiers prison to reclaim her watch and other items that had been taken from her. She was a very clever, brave and determined woman.

Thereafter she knew nothing of what was happening in the circuit, now renamed Actor, nor that Roger had returned in March 1944 and had enquired about her unsuccessfully. But now she was free from prison, it was June and news was sweeping the population that liberation was near. The Allies had landed in France and the Germans were retreating yard by yard. Now she must have wanted to be involved in what her training had prepared her for, but she still had to lie low, do nothing and only wait and hope.

Gradually the Germans were driven back, and in September 1944 Bordeaux was liberated. During these last hectic weeks, Lise, who had returned in April 1944 to a revitalized circuit in the far north, run by her brother, set out with Claude in a borrowed vehicle to find out what had happened to Mary. However, Mary's skill in covering her tracks from the Germans nearly defeated them, and it was only after some clever detective work that she was at last discovered. Then the full story could be told.

This was the first time that Claude learned of the arrival of his baby daughter, named Claudine after her mother's code name, and he was delighted. He thereupon collected mother and child and saw them safely back to England, himself rejoining them briefly in London in November 1944 when he and Mary were married. Then he had to go back to France, his work not yet over, as in 1945 he was to join the staff of General Koenig in the capacity of liaison officer to the Allied Command. Mary and her child therefore went to live at Moynes Court, with her father, moving after his death to a large country house near the Wye, where she saw Claude when he could manage the time to slip over the Channel to visit them. In 1947 he was finally released and the family were again reunited in London.

Mary had now all that she had hoped for — the husband that she had chosen and a baby daughter whom they both adored. She had also, for one dangerous year in the heart of France, made, with SOE, her own undeniably useful contribution towards the cause of French liberation.

5
Bang Away Lulu

Noor-Un-Nisa Inayat Khan

'Assistant Section Officer Inayat-Khan displayed the most conspicuous courage, both moral and physical, over a period of more than twelve months.'

Citation for George Cross, 'London Gazette' 1949

'Twice seen, never forgotten' said a friend of Noor-Un-Nisa Inayat Khan. Her oriental appearance and slightly foreign accent made her noticeable even among the French. Her speech was so shy and soft that she could hardly be heard and she was terrified of loud voices and heights. Her character was vague, timid and unworldly but marked by gentleness and great sweetness. She was a loner and surely the most singular and unlikely person to become an active agent for SOE. What outweighed everything, nevertheless, was that she was also excellent, and already trained, in her trade, which was why she was the first woman to be sent by F Service as a wireless operator to France.

Born in the Kremlin, Moscow, at the beginning of January 1914, she was the eldest of the four children of an Indian religious teacher and his American wife, who could claim the last Moghul Sultan of Mysore, an American senator and an evangelist in their families. She was eventually brought up and educated in Paris, with her home in the quiet suburb of Suresnes, which soon became the headquarters of her father's Sufi sect, a mystical branch of Islam. With such an unusual background,

Noor — her name meant 'light' — had few friends, except her eldest brother and some neighbours who pitied the solitary girl. She seemed afraid to commit herself to marriage, being engaged several times, but nothing further. In Paris she studied music, languages and child psychology, wrote poems and children's fairy stories and had some work published and broadcast.

War altered this promising career and she turned to nursing. This was interrupted by the German invasion of France, when, after many adventures, she and her family (her father was now dead) escaped through Bordeaux to England. Here her brother joined the RAF — though he was later to join the Navy when his eyesight prevented him being a pilot and Noor, disillusioned by the reality of nursing, joined the WAAF in November 1940. There the recruiting officer, not understanding her background, listed her as Nora and her religion as C of E!

In December 1940, after recruit training in Harrogate, she was sent to Edinburgh for six months' training at the GPO Morse School as a wireless operator, and her mother moved there to be near her. Irene Salter, a fellow trainee, knew her as 'a quiet, gentle girl who suffered badly from chilblains. For this reason she had to wear shoes two sizes larger than normal, and was unable to grasp the Morse key because of her swollen fingers'. Eventually she was posted to RAF Abingdon, where she shared a shift with Nora Wenman, who changed her Christian name to Wendy to save confusion, and became her friend. They had long philosophical conversations in the early morning watches and Wendy thought her very sensitive to the needs of others, though '...there was something "fey" about her. However, she was an efficient operator, despite the fact that her Morse key seemed to have a wide gap, and when she used it, there was a loud "clakketty-clack". This earned her the name "Bang-away-Lulu", at which she would smile unconcerned.'

In May 1942 she was posted to Compton Bassett for a further seven-week Advanced Signals and Wireless Course, bringing her speed in Morse to about 22 words per minute. At her next posting she was promoted to Leading Aircraftwoman (LACW) and Acting Corporal, but she became bored and applied for a commission in Intelligence. At about this time SOE had its attention drawn to her, because of her fluent French. In his first interview with her, Selwyn Jepson was impressed by 'the fine spirit glowing in her', while later Colonel Maurice Buckmaster noted that her motives were of the highest and that she fully appreciated the dangers of her work. In February 1943 she joined the Organization and later was granted an honorary WAAF commission.

Because she was already trained, her time at the clandestine wireless operators' school near Aylesbury was shorter than for the other 40 women who were the first intended for the field in this role and included

Yvonne Cormeau and Yolande Beekman. This may have cost her dear, particularly in her understanding of the sentence in her operations order that insisted that she must be 'extremely careful in filing her messages', as is shown later. She also missed out parachute training at Ringway because of an earlier operation in Paris.

And yet they were not altogether satisfied with her in training. She worked hard at Wanborough Manor, along with Yolande Beekman and Cécile Lefort, and won the accolade of 'exceptionally reliable and unselfish'. But at Beaulieu, the finishing school, her escorting officer found her interrogations 'almost unbearable', as she stood before the pretended Gestapo, white, trembling and inaudible. The overall opinion of her instructors, still on file, was that she was 'not overburdened with brains' and that she had 'some dislike of the security side of the course', but the most damning comment was on her 'unstable and temperamental personality' which made it 'very doubtful whether she is really suited to work in the field'.

Nevertheless, SOE was so desperately short of wireless operators in mid-1943 that the uncertainties were overruled and to the field she was sent. At her own request she went to the Paris area, despite the added dangers of being unexpectedly recognized, where the existing wireless operator was asking for another to share his duties.

Her first Lysander flight failed so that it was not until the night of 16 June that their pilots guided her, dressed in a green oilskin coat, with Cécile Lefort, Diana Rowden and a male agent, across the darkened airfield at Tangmere to the two waiting planes. This was Operation Teacher.

They landed in a moonlit field at Vieux Briollay to a reception arranged by Henri Déricourt, later suspected as a traitor, and when they

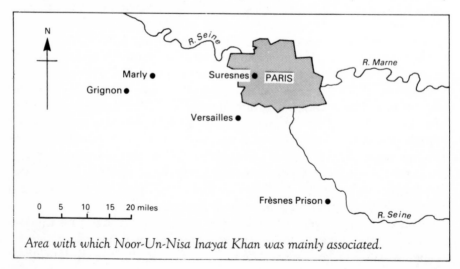

Area with which Noor-Un-Nisa Inayat Khan was mainly associated.

had climbed down their ladders to the ground, they were presented with bicycles with which to ride to the nearest railway station at Angers, seven miles to their south. From there they went their separate ways and Noor, with a fellow passenger and a guide, travelled cross-country to Paris and her first contact. Her two suitcases, containing her wireless equipment and clothes were parachuted later and caught up with her four days afterwards. Now she had taken on the character of Mademoiselle Jeanne-Marie Regnier, most appropriately a children's nurse, but her SOE code name was Madeleine.

When Noor finally arrived at the flat of Henri Garry, by some error she expected to meet an old lady, and she so confused the passwords that it was some time before they connected. There she met his fiancée and stayed overnight before meeting the rest of his circuit.

Francis Suttill, known as Prosper, had built up a large circuit in and around Paris. Sub-circuits had been added around Le Mans by Henri Garry, known as Cinema (which London changed to Phono on discovering his likeness to Gary Cooper, a name too near for safety), whom Noor had been sent to assist, and around Grigon by Professor Balachowsky. There were also several other sub-réseaux which met and used the Agricultural Institute in Grignon as their headquarters.

The next day Noor was taken to a charming house in the Institute grounds to be introduced to the Director, his wife, and others of the circuit and their wives. She got on well with them and Francis's wireless operator allowed her to make her first transmission to London with his set from a little greenhouse in the garden. For future transmissions she was to pass herself off as a student and live with the Director's family. She was warned, however, for making several mistakes, pouring tea and toasting bread in the English way, leaving her portfolio of codes from London in the entrance hall, and later, handing a map over to an agent openly in the street. As she was among friends she could learn from her errors in safety.

Then a week after she had landed, the sky seemed to fall in on her. On Thursday 24 June, Francis Suttill, his courier and wireless operator were suddenly arrested by the Germans in Paris, a prelude to a weekend of arrests of their supporters. Noor was advised to leave the Institute and Henri found her another room in a flat in Malesherbes Square owned by a shopkeeper. Nevertheless, Noor went to Henri's wedding on the following Tuesday and arranged to call on the newly wedded couple in their flat the next day, but this was not to be, because on that day the Germans descended upon it. Fortunately Henri and his wife were out when they came, and were stopped from entering by the *concièrge* who looked after the block, while Noor was warned in time when she called at the Professor's home. To make matters worse Noor was going down with 'flu and on returning to her tiny flat in Malesherbes Square she found she had to provide shelter for another agent who also had 'flu. It was a brief respite. Outside she knew the Germans were hunting for them.

Next day, ill or not, she still had to complete her 'skeds' (fixed times of sending and receiving messages), so she dragged herself up and cycled off to Grignon to transmit from the greenhouse. Leaving her bike propped up against the wall, she was about to enter the Institute when she realized that all was not well. When she saw the SS uniforms in the grounds she fled, leaving her bicycle and taking a passing bus to the nearest station, and thence back to her flat. Next day she phoned the Institute, a call luckily answered by a maid, and learned that the Director, the Professor and their families, had all been arrested. Almost the whole Prosper circuit had been annihilated, only she, the agent with her, and a few others, to at least one of whom by good fortune she had been already introduced, remained. It was her duty to lie low and hope that the Germans were not on her track.

How must she have felt in those terrifying hours, knowing her full danger? It says much for her courage that somehow within the next few days she managed to find another transmitter. Agents were usually supplied with more than one if possible, which they dispersed and hid against such an emergency. There she tapped out her patient Morse message to London, informing them of the full scale of the tragedy. London, knowing that she was the only Prosper operator surviving, in fact the only one of their wireless operators still left in Paris, decided to bring her back immediately. But it was for this very reason that she refused, because she felt it rested with her to try to rebuild a little of the circuit. Somehow she managed to persuade them to let her stay.

July then began the most perilous and lonely part of her work. Wearing dark glasses, with hair dyed red — surely more eye-catching than before — and carrying her suitcase transmitter everywhere she went, sometimes hidden in a large violin case — again asking for trouble — she trekked over Paris, even visiting her former friends in Suresnes, trying to find another flat and a safe place to continue her link with London. In this she took a great personal risk as anyone could have informed on her, but it says much for the courage of all those she contacted that they not only kept her secret (for no matter how little she told them — and she seems to have been pretty open about it in most cases — they must have had a good idea of what she was doing and the dangers they ran by even seeing her), but also they all tried to help her to the best of their ability. It was Noor herself, with her ever-present consideration and unselfishness, who sometimes rated their danger higher than the risk she herself took, and refused their offers.

One day cycling along, what she feared actually happened. A former neighbour thinking she recognized her called out her name on the street.

Occupied France

Above *On 24 October 1940, four months after the Franco-German Armistice, the Führer Adolf Hitler and Marshal Pétain, heads of state of Germany and France, meet at Montoire-sur-le-Loir to consolidate their agreement.* (Imperial War Museum)

Right *A Paris poster of Marshal Pétain, Chief of the Vichy Government in 1941, with symbols of the resistance chalked underneath.* (Imperial War Museum)

Inset *A stamp sold in the UK on behalf of General de Gaulle for funds towards the freeing of France.* (Author)

Above *Bookseller stalls along the River Seine in Paris with the Cathedral of Notre Dame in the background. In this circuit worked Noor Inayat Khan* **(Chapter 5)**. (Author's Collection)

Above *A view of the Bordeaux waterfront, where Mary Herbert's circuit was active* **(Chapter 4)**. (Major R. Landes)

Below left *Dijon: the tomb of Philip the Bold, a 14th-century ruler of the powerful Dukedom of Burgundy, of which mini-state Dijon was capital. Duke Philip's effigy — a wonderful piece of work — is in the Palais des Etats. During the occupation the city was used by a number of resistance circuits, including those served by Diana Rowden* **(Chapter 6)** *and Yvonne Baseden* **(Chapter 12)**. (Author's Collection)

Below *An aerial view of the vast, crowded spread of St Quentin, a hub of heavy industry in the north, with its railway, canal and factories. Yolande Beekman's circuit was centred here* **(Chapter 9)**. (Aerofilms Ltd)

Left *In occupied France, conditions for ordinary city people had become progressively worse with few clothes, scarcely any winter fuel and little extra food to supplement their starvation rations. Most French-produced food was sent to Germany. In this secretly taken photograph at 'Les Halles' — the famous, huge, covered markets in Paris — there is little for sale. On the empty tables are just a few potatoes and some lettuce. (Imperial War Museum)*

Below left *Armistice Day Parade, November 1944. In a Paris now freed from German occupation, the British and French symbols of resistance, Winston Churchill and General de Gaulle, head a procession walking down the Champs Elysées. (Imperial War Museum)*

Above right *Similar scenes occurred all over France, when the Germans shot hostages or members of the resistance. These men died at Lantilly in May 1944. (Imperial War Museum)*

Right *The widows of France mourn their dead. (Major R. Landes)*

Special Duties Squadrons

Above *The back part of Tangmere Cottage in 1943, where crews of Special Duties Squadrons and their SOE 'passengers' prepared for their secret flights and landings in France* **(Chapter 3)**. *(Mrs M. McCairns)*

Below *An atmospheric photograph of the barn at RAF Tempsford where agents — known as 'joes' and 'joesses' in Squadron parlance, where no names were used — collected their parachutes and last pieces of equipment before joining the planes which would drop them over France. Inset is a plaque marking the building today. (Group Captain F. Griffiths)*

Right *An aerial view of RAF Tempsford in 1943. (Group Captain H. Verity)*

Above *A Lysander of the Special Duties Squadron in flight. Notice the fixed ladder hanging over the side. This was an excellent aircraft for short hauls and secret landings in France. (M A. Deschamps)*

Below *Special Duties Squadron also used the Halifax bomber of a type similar to this, with its powerful, in-line, Rolls-Royce engines, for dropping men and supplies to the Resistance. (Flight Sergeant K. Hemmings)*

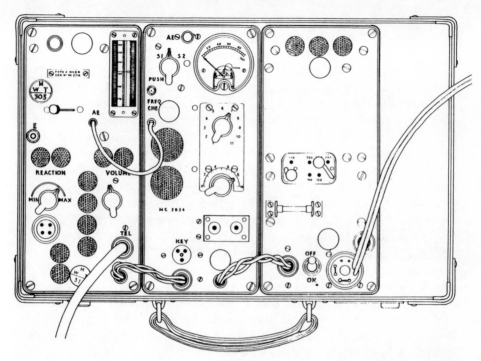

Drawing of an A Mark II transceiver — one of the earliest sets produced by the SOE
for its agents. In the suitcase can be seen, on the left, the receiver; in the middle the
transmitter, and on the right provision for the power supply. An extra container held the
headset, morse key, aerial, crystal, fuses and other spares. The contents of this suitcase
could be split into separate parcels. (Drawing by Lt Col P. Lorain)

Noor nearly fell off her bike in fright. The innocent, well-meaning
questions of what had happened to her, where had she gone and what
she was doing now, posed in a busy street with interested listeners, were
minefields fraught with utmost danger. Again she was in luck. After
some conversation it dawned on both of them that they were working
for the underground movement, and they arranged to meet later in a
café, where it was safer to talk.

Among the friends she contacted at this time was her former harp
teacher, M Benoist, and her father's doctor, Dr Jourdan. Dr Jourdan
was very helpful. He had two homes; a flat in Paris and a house in the
leafy suburbs of Marly, an ideal location because of the trees
surrounding it where she could string her aerial. The reception,
however, was distorted and weak but she utilized the house several
times. She also stayed a few days with the Benoist family in Paris. But
all the time she was still looking for another room in Paris, mainly as
a safe address where she could receive and send written messages, but
also where the occasional transmission could be made.

At length she found it in what might be considered in a sense an ideal spot, because although it was again fraught with danger it was in the least likely place the Germans would expect, on the Boulevard Richard Wallace, right in the middle of a block of flats occupied by German soldiers. The *concièrge* was ignorant of what it was to be used for, but in view of the strange men who called and the peculiar messages she was sometimes asked to carry for Noor, she might have guessed at one or two professions practised by her tenant. Blissfully ignorant of her effect, Noor continued very pleased with her new domicile, one room that was nothing more than a cupboard with a tiny bed for when she had to stay the night, and with a small window which looked out on to a solitary tree on the pavement outside. She was on the ground floor too, so at a pinch she could use it for transmissions, if she could rig the aerial to the tree without being seen.

One evening, as it was growing dark, she was struggling to loop the aerial on to the tree — she was not very tall, only 5 ft 3 in — when she heard a man's heavy tread behind her. She was discovered! She whirled around and could just make out in the gathering dusk the figure of one of the German officers who lived in the building. She was speechless! 'May I help you?' he asked, and then proceeded to loop the aerial very satisfactorily over the branches. What must she have thought at that moment? Were the Germans playing a game with her? And indeed, more puzzling, what did he think she was doing? Then he stood back and bowed politely to her. 'At your service, Mademoiselle.' With that he turned on his heel and left, and nothing else happened. She couldn't believe it. She had experienced yet another narrow escape.

But there was more. The Germans were now fully aware that there was one F Section operator still working for Prosper. In their Paris headquarters they received her messages loud and clear and knew she was nearby, but infuriatingly they could not pin her down, she transmitted from so many varied locations, as was the correct form for an agent who did not want to be caught. There was some confusion too, because in the first dreadful days after Prosper's arrest, and while she continued to search for a safe retreat to transmit, she had turned for help to another acquaintance, also in the resistance but working for de Gaulle. He had the great asset of owning a car, a rarity for the French in occupied Paris. It enabled her to be driven anywhere and have him stop in a quiet country place. She met him in the late afternoon and then sent out her messages in the fields between 5 and 5.30 pm. Her driver had lost his two wireless operators and therefore agreed to help her on condition that she passed messages to his organization as well as her own. In fact she was doing him a favour, as he was desperately in need of a large sum of money and this was the first message that she tapped out for him. On her side, arms and explosives were sent to the

Maquis on the parachute ground around Le Mans following her radio requests. However, the necessary switches of wavelength must have nicely muddled the patiently listening Germans.

Meanwhile Henri Déricourt struggled to put her and the agent who had stayed with her on to a plane back to London. Three times he tried and three times the planes were inexplicably cancelled at the last moment, so that the July moons were lost and there would be another long wait until the August moon. It was a stroke of sheer bad luck that during that period the Germans caught up with the Benoist family, and discovered in some papers found in their home at the time of their arrest the code name of the elusive operator — Madeleine, realizing for the first time that she was not a man, as formerly believed, but a girl. They were now much nearer discovering her. They put a high price on her head and advertised widely for information.

Their quarry was still restlessly hunting around for further transmission posts. One day travelling as usual with her suitcase on the Métro, she was stopped by two German soldiers. They eyed her suspiciously but seemed uncertain. 'What is inside your suitcase Mademoiselle?' asked one. Should she try to run away? She would certainly lose her wireless. Best to stay and try to bluff it out. She raised innocent eyes to her questioner and replied 'Cinematograph apparatus.' Back came the question she dreaded. 'May we see it?' Outwardly she smiled assent and with trembling fingers fumbled at the catch and lifted the lid, only sufficiently to show the top layer of equipment. They peered inside so long that, playing the innocent, she said crossly, 'Well you can see that it's bulbs and parts of the projector!' She caught her breath; would the pretence work? After a minute that must have seemed an age, they straightened up with, wonder of wonders, an apology. 'Sorry Mademoiselle. We thought it was something else.' Being ordinary soldiers they were obviously unfamiliar with wireless apparatus and took her word for it. What a good thing she had not run away.

The August moon arrived. The other agent and others returned but no order came to send her home. Had she again argued to stay? She was now the only British officer left.

Her former friend, Madame Prénat, agreed to let Noor transmit at her home, where she used their front room. Here for a short few hours she was able to relax. To her school friend Raymonde, she even explained her wireless and showed how to decipher messages. It could have been useful but she did not want to lay so heavy a burden on them. Nevertheless, what must they have thought when the loud clack of her machine sounded through the house, a terrible give-away to any nearby Germans, who had in fact requisitioned her old home, not far off.

Living and using her set at yet another neighbour's home, she again made a slip which could have caused disaster. Trustingly she left her code books open on the kitchen table overnight and forgot. They were found by her landlady next morning who scolded her soundly, but it hardly seemed to register. She shrugged it off with her sweet smile, and her landlady gave up.

In September Henri Garry found her a new flat as a letter-box and for occasional transmissions, in the Rue de la Faisanderie, near the Gestapo headquarters and under their very noses. Again she seemed to lead a charmed life. Hot on her trail, the Germans discovered her old room in the Boulevard Richard Wallace, but by now she had paid her rent and moved out. There was even a rather suspicious burglary on her new flat, but she was out when it happened and she had left nothing incriminating behind.

She had another narrow shave when trying to assist two Canadians whom London had instructed her to pass on to an escape network. They turned out to be German agents, who arrested their helper and, now knowing Noor by sight, set an ambush to trap her. She was warned of this in the nick of time by one of her new contacts, a most useful and unusual man called Monsieur Viennot. Outwardly very respectable, and often escorted by a picked group of brawny guards, he was a racketeer with many disreputable connections in the Paris underworld of organized crime, pimps and prostitutes, against whom even the Germans were helpless. He was therefore a wonderful source of intelligence which Noor duly passed on to London. She had met him originally when she needed someone to repair her wireless, and liking and perhaps admiring her, he took her under his wing. Saying that she still looked and dressed like an Englishwoman, he got her a new wardrobe from the smart Paris shops, and took her to a good reliable hairdresser, where her hair, unprofessionally dyed, first red, then blonde, then mousy, was changed to a light brown, which suited her much better. He also took her to task when he discovered that she was keeping her code books and exercise books with all the messages she had ever sent or received from London in cipher and clear. He wanted her to destroy them, but she refused stubbornly, saying that she had been told to do this by London. They wanted her to file the messages carefully! Had she misunderstood her instructions, certainly against the spirit, if not the actual fatal words, on her file? No arguments moved her, so at length he gave way. They were safe, as long as she was free.

Nevertheless her busy life began to tell on her. Her days were full of meeting people and sending messages and her nights of receiving messages, often after midnight, and then rushing around delivering them. She never walked when she could run, and always she arrived at her destination breathless. She was thinner and began to have a hunted look. She was still changing flats for transmissions and appears to have had little contact with Henri Garry, technically her boss, though now in hiding. At a friend's house she once burst into tears and said, 'I wish I were at home with my mother.' Her mind must have dwelt on the possibilities of capture, for to another she said, 'It is useless to strike a bargain with the Gestapo... They will shoot you just the same in the end.' One London message she received ended 'God keep you', which impressed her.

Like a cat with nine lives, she had lost too many to escape. She seemed almost afflicted by the fatalism of the east. At this time she may also have been involved in the shooting incident in Paris mentioned in her French citation. In early October, some other contacts, fearing that she was becoming a danger to herself and the network, put her on to a train to Normandy. They had themselves made arrangements for her to retire and lie low in a country farm there.

Another puzzling period then ensued, for two days later she reappeared in Paris. She resumed her contact with Viennot and told several friends that she was due to fly out on 14 October, something London denied. But she did not keep several appointments, one of her former landladies was arrested soon after seeing her and London lost contact with her for 10 days. She was also seen and perhaps recognized by two Gestapo men in a street near her flat — possibly by now she was being tailed — but her training came to her and she was able to melt away into the crowd. Nevertheless, the net was surely closing around her. Was she aware of it?

Then the blow fell. About 10 October 1943, a mystery Frenchwoman, only calling herself Renée, rang the German counter-intelligence Headquarters and gave them Noor's present address. Next day the woman met a representative of the Gestapo, showed him around Noor's flat, pointing out the transmitter in the kitchen as proof, and agreed to let him know when Noor was out. On about 13 October this happened, and it was arranged to leave a man inside the locked flat to arrest Noor when she returned that morning. Later Renée received and signed a receipt for the reward of 100,000 francs — a tenth of what the Gestapo were prepared to pay for the capture of 'Madeleine'.

Meanwhile when Noor arrived back in her flat, and the man left there tried to arrest her, she fought like the 'Tiger of Mysore', a name given to her ancestor Tipu Sultan. She fought so viciously, biting his wrists and clawing at his eyes, that despite his gun he was forced to summon more help from Gestapo headquarters. They also collected her transmitter and the all-important codes and note books in a bedside table. By threats of arresting the girl whose flat she shared, and who knew nothing, they managed to escort Noor quietly to their car which waited some distance away. So as not to draw any attention, they also wore plain clothes.

Confronted by a uniformed German officer when she arrived at 84

Avenue Foch, she glared at him and refused to answer any questions. 'I am Nora Baker' she told him — not *exactly* the truth as she had reverted to her mother's surname which she had used a number of times in SOE and the WAAF. (Later this was to increase the difficulties of those seeking her under her true name). 'You know who I am and what I am doing. You have my radio set. I will tell you nothing. I have only one thing to ask you. Have me shot as quickly as possible.' At this point it was the last thing her jailers wanted to do. She might be won over, or at the least supply them with very valuable information.

After an uproductive hour, her interrogator said that she might go to her cell until the afternoon to think. Meanwhile, seeking to soften her up, he asked if she wanted anything.

'Only a bath.'

'Well, yes, that can be arranged.'

Unfortunately she found that the Germans expected to leave the bathroom door partly open to forestall any attempt at escape, so she objected violently and refused to undress unless they closed it. Unused to this kind of prisoner, her captors agreed and the door was shut, but uneasy, one went to the window of a toilet that stood opposite the bathroom window. None too soon it seemed; for already Noor had wriggled out of her fifth floor attic window, and balancing herself on the guttering that ran around the square well on to which the building looked, she had started working her way around. As she passed by him, her captor caught her through his open window and pulled her in. Blaming herself and weeping, she was inconsolable, saying that she should have killed herself rather than be recaptured. So hysterical did she become that one of the other prisoners was called to calm her down before taking her to her cell.

That night Ernst Vogt, her interrogator, dressed in plain clothes, fetched her for dinner in his room, as she had refused all food. She took nothing except coffee and chain smoked all evening, but he used the opportunity to show her all he knew of her organization — hardly surprising in view of the material they had confiscated and her messages. This drew no information from her except that he saw she was shaken at the extent of his knowledge.

The next day, questioning went on. A radio specialist was called in, all to no avail, followed by SS Sturmbann-Fuhrer (Major) Hans Josef Kieffer, chief of the SD at Avenue Foch, who became so angry at her non-co-operation that he raised his hand to strike her, but was stopped by Vogt who warned him that such treatment would only make her more stubborn. Ernst Vogt then became her main interrogator and made sufficient progress with her over the next weeks that he was able to gain her trust and she became less frightened. She was even allowed to send for some clothes and belongings from her last flat, something that the astute Germans thought they might use to their advantage. Her interrogations sometimes lasted many hours, continuing throughout the day and night and depriving her of food and sleep, but neither then nor later, from her point of view under formal questioning, did she give the Germans any useful information in regards to her work, her circuit or her colleagues, as her captors testified at their trials after the war. Indeed, they all spoke with great respect of her coolness and courage, and at least one commented that she was perhaps the best human being he had ever met. If she subsequently said anything about herself and her home life, it was done in all innocence as of no value, although the Germans may have used this to answer suspicious questions from London, when their experts went on playing her set after her capture.

In all other respects she remained obdurate, but at night, after lights out, other prisoners could hear her sobbing in her cell. Among these were Colonel Faille, working for de Gaulle, and Captain John Starr, who because he was some use to the Germans was allowed more freedom during the day. Already Noor had communicated with John Starr, tapping out Morse on her cell wall. Now through written messages left in the lavatory, these three prisoners planned an escape together. This involved unscrewing the bars over the fanlights in their cells with a screwdriver filched by Captain Starr. At the last moment, on the designated night, Noor had unexpected problems removing her bars, and held up her waiting conspirators. The two men hauled her out and briefly embraced her. They were free. Then they set off, climbing around the roofing — a hair-raising venture.

They all carried their shoes around their necks and their blankets torn up to form a rope. Several times Noor stopped, frozen with fear and had to be pushed on by the men. Then just as they reached a flat roof leading on to the roof of a nearby house, the air raid sirens started to wail. The RAF was bombing Paris. Unfortunately this alerted the guards, who checked on their prisoners cells and the escape warning sounded.

During the pandemonium, the three managed to smash and climb through the third floor window of the nearby house. They crept down the stairs and out of the door, only to find they were in a cul-de-sac, at the open end of which they could see German guards forming a cordon. Keeping in the shadows they moved to the end of the street, planning to make a break for it. The first to go was Colonel Faille who was immediately captured. The other two ran back to the house they had just left and blundered back into the sitting room, where they remained in the dark, talking quietly until the guards at length found them. Though bitter disappointment and fatigue had left no fight in them, they were nevertheless beaten and knocked about by the guards before all three were lined up in front of Kieffer. After raging at them and demanding answers to his questions, he ordered them to be shot,

instantly. Expecting death any moment, Colonel Faille drew himself up
and said calmly, 'I have only done my duty.' This gave Kieffer pause and
a moment later he ordered them back to their cells. Shortly he visited
each of them in turn to demand that they give him their written word
not to try to escape again. Colonel Faille and Noor refused. Angered
beyond bearing, he telegrammed Berlin asking for these prisoners to be
transferred to a German prison.

Thus it was that next day, 26 November 1943, Noor was the first
British agent to be sent to Germany. After spending the night at
Karlsrühe, the Gestapo took her on to Pforzheim, a nearby prison for
political prisoners, where the governor was told that as a particularly
unco-operative and dangerous prisoner — although she was small and
scarcely weighed over seven stones — she was to be kept in solitary
confinement and chained to the wall day and night, her wrists in
handcuffs, fetters on her ankles and a chain between the fetters and
handcuffs. No one, not even the governor was to speak to her!

And so she was left. However, Noor's brave and cheerful manner
shortly won over the governor, already deeply concerned at this
inhuman treatment, and little by little, on his own responsibility, he
eased her conditions of imprisonment, including the removal of her
chains. In those long lonely hours she must have thought deeply about
her father's teachings. She also continued to practise what exercises she
could in her cell. Gradually, too, she managed to communicate with a
few other women prisoners, who sometimes sang the news to her or
scratched a short message on the metal food bowls.

This quiet existence came to an end suddenly in the early evening of
10 September 1944, when the Karlsrühe Gestapo fetched her for the
short car ride back to Karlsrühe prison. There she met again Yolande
Beekman, whom she knew in training and two other FANY agents who
had been imprisoned there. She may have been questioned again and
there were more formalities before the four women were escorted into
a reserved compartment of an early morning express train and given
some bread, sausages and English cigarettes for the journey. They
laughed and chatted happily, treating this more as a picnic than a
further stage of imprisonment. It was midnight before they at last arrived
at a little station, where they had to carry their luggage and walk up a
long hill to the prison where, in separate cells, they were to stay the
remainder of the night. They were at Dachau.

Next morning, 12 Septemberr 1944, they were taken to the courtyard
against the crematorium wall, where new sand covered the ground, and
the formal notice of their crime and execution was read to them. They
were then made to kneel in pairs, holding hands, and shot neatly
through the back of the head, their bodies later being cremated.

However, even at this critical stage it may have been that Noor was treated differently. An uncorroborated account relates that when the girls were separated on arrival, she was deprived of many of her clothes, badly beaten and then chained overnight. Next morning after the other three had died, she was shot alone in her cell, her final word being '*Liberté.*'

6
The Fearless One

Diana Hope Rowden

'Jeune fille Britannique volontaire pour des missions en territoire occupé fut envoyée en France... et continua avec courage a remplir ses fonctions de courrier.'

Citation for Croix de Guerre, 1946

Sans Peur, the Fearless One, the name of the family yacht, might also be applied to Diana Hope Rowden. Her background made her thoroughly bilingual. Born in London, she spent most of her early years in the south of France where her parents had a villa and yacht. By her mother's decription she was a turbulent tomboy, who spent her time out of doors racing around with her two brothers. This freedom came to an end at her age of 12 when her parents returned to Britain so that their children could have an English education. Diana hated it, becoming withdrawn and reticent, although appearing poised and sophisticated on the outside. Her education finished, her mother returned with her to France.

By now Diana had grown into a rather diffident, gentle, considerate and charming young woman. When war broke out she joined the French Red Cross and remained to nurse the wounded even after her mother escaped back to Britain in a coal boat from Bordeaux. During the next few months Diana's position as an Englishwoman in a German-occupied country became more serious, so she engineered her own escape through Spain and Portugal, arriving in Britain in July 1941. Now 26, this rather stocky woman of medium height, with reddish hair and pale complexion, looked around for work where her knowledge of French and France would be an asset. By the time something suitable appeared in September 1941, she had joined the WAAF and in the December of the same year was commissioned as Assistant Section Officer, doing Intelligence work first at Air Ministry and then at Moreton-in-the-Marsh, during which time she was promoted to Section Officer. However, she underwent a serious operation, which was later to prevent her being parachuted. In the convalescent home shortly afterwards, one of her fellow patients was a Squadron Leader from SOE, who immediately recognized her value. This realized her mother's worst fears, because she well knew her daughter's devotion to France and her urgent and often expressed desire to return to help prepare the way for its liberation. But despite her mother's opposition Diana went ahead and gained the necessary introductions, so that March 1943 saw her seconded to F Section of SOE.

She was to be sent to work for the sub-circuit run by Captain John

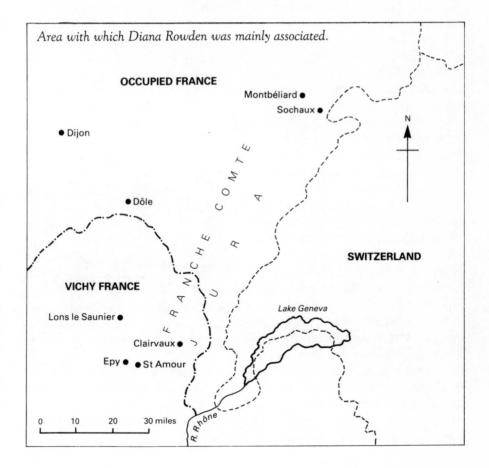

Area with which Diana Rowden was mainly associated.

Starr, codenamed Bob, the organizer of Acrobat in the Jura, a *département* of pastures and vineyards, stone villages, spruce forests and wild mountains. His was a part of the vast province of Franche Comté, where Captain Harry Rée of the Stockbroker circuit was in charge overall. Lieutenant Cuthbert Young, his youthful Scottish radio operator, had arrived by parachute along with John Starr in May of 1943, and they were impatiently awaiting their courier, who turned out to be Diana, code named Paulette. Her Lysander landed in the field near Angers in the early hours of 17 June 1943, on the same double flight that brought Noor Inayat Khan and Cécile Lefort. The girls had little time to make their hurried farewells in the dark, while other passengers were bundled into their places for the return to Tangmere. Diana had to make her way to the railway station from which she had to take the long journey to the east side of France. There, tired, dusty, and carrying her heavy case of clothes and belongings, she finally trudged up to the Hotel Commerce at Lons-le-Saunier. The manager was not too worried about entering every guest in his register, and she was given a dark, back, attic room.

It was here that she first met John Starr, a dapper little man with a pale face and silky moustache, who felt that although her French was excellent for an Englishwoman, it could still be recognized as foreign by the French. He therefore judged it best to give her living quarters in the Château Andelot at St Amour where he was based, together with Cuthbert his wireless operator whose foreign accent was even more marked than her own. It was remote, the Germans were not yet suspicious of it, and it was considered to be a safe house.

Diana may have expected to find herself in some unusual places but this medieval castle with its two round towers was beautiful and most comfortable. It had been owned by an American millionaire, but he had not occupied it since the war, and in his absence the only persons who lived there were the caretaker and his wife.

The Château of Andelot-les-St Amour, where Diana worked and lived for a short time. (M. Juniper)

Then began her work as courier, travelling long distances, often by bicycle with which it was easier to evade checkpoints, and sometimes by rail. Her journeys occasionally involved messages to other circuits, and took her as far as Montbéliard near the northern part of the Swiss border, Paris to the north-west, Lyon to the south and Marseilles, even further south on the Mediterranean coast. She had many narrow escapes. Once she was arrested at a checkpoint but cleverly managed to slip away while the soldiers' attention was diverted elsewhere. Again, on a long journey to Marseilles, she heard the police coming down the train doing one of their frequent checks on the papers of the passengers. Feeling uncertain that her forged papers would pass this test, she squeezed her way out and locked herself in the nearest vacant toilet. Fortunately she escaped their notice and was able to continue her journey undisturbed.

She also made contact with local groups of Maquis, for which the mountains of the Jura were a perfect hiding place, and whose members could sally out to sabotage or attack the Germans by night and then melt away in the darkness and be lost in the daylight. They knew the country like the back of their hands, having been born there, and knew how to live off it without help from the populace, who nevertheless often took the risk of offering it, since so many were related. Diana requested supplies and helped to find and pinpoint suitable landing grounds for these local groups, and was responsible for at least five successful drops. At several of these she helped to set out the flares to guide the planes, and then assisted in collecting and safely disposing of the parachuted containers of arms and ammunition. Among the successful coups achieved with these supplies was the sabotage, by Harry Rée's blackmail, of the Peugeot factory at Sochaux, resulting in three months' interruption in the making of tanks for the German army and an increase in the morale of the resistance.

On 16 July, Diana's organizer heard through a contact that Field Marshal Rommel's train was passing through their area, so the resistance set out to derail it. The train did not arrive and the attempt ended in failure. Worse, John Starr was captured elsewhere and Harry Rée, who had organized another derailment at Dijon, began to suspect a traitor among his informants. The best action was for the SOE agents to disappear. He sent word warning Cuthbert and Diana and after safeguarding as many in the two circuits as possible, he escaped over the mountain footpaths into Switzerland during August, returning in September to restore his circuit.

Meanwhile Cuthbert and Diana had split up, he to continue his wireless contact, using the sawmill at Clairvaux as his base, she to the little hamlet of Epy, only three miles from St Amour. There she found shelter in an apartment above a small café, even serving some of the customers herself, though the owner could see that she was not used to such work. During this time the Germans made a series of arrests, finishing off Acrobat as a viable circuit, and searching for the English agents. Through the work of Harry Rée, however, Stockbroker survived.

It must have been during this period that Diana first saw the inside of the German headquarters, for she was arrested on suspicion of helping the resistance. Her innocent-seeming replies and careful cover story, however, fooled the Germans who questioned her. Her slightly foreign French was not remarked by those whose French was even worse, and besides France housed people of many accents and races, especially near its borders. The Germans thought her one of the crowd, never realizing what a capture they had inadvertently made, and she was not passed on to more skilled questioners. Instead, after a day she was released, shaken but unhurt.

About three weeks later, leaving her hostess the present of a flowered headscarf, Diana felt it safe enough to join Cuthbert at Clairvaux. It was easier for her to be near him to maintain her contacts with London and the occasional message from Rée in Switzerland. The place where she sought refuge was ideal for the purpose. The sawmill was surrounded by woodland. It was not a single building but several, where different branches of the family who owned it lived, and the two agents lodged in the separate houses of the Juifs and the Paulis. The Juifs' home where Diana stayed looked like a Swiss chalet with a pretty wooden balcony overlooking a steep hill slope outside. Between the houses was a cobbled road. The Juifs liked Diana and were very kind to her, for seldom had her hosts met a girl of such calibre.

To help her disguise she changed her hairstyle, her clothes and adopted a new identity, calling herself Marcelle, a cousin of the Juifs, who was recuperating from a severe illness. It did not, however, stop her from wandering out in the woods nearby on her own at night to smoke her cigarettes.

From here she continued her contact with resistance groups and was a reliable and regular courier between Rée's groups,

The house of the Juif family at the Clairvaux sawmill. (M. Juniper)

now even more necessary after the breakup of Prosper's network around Paris. She also received a few more supply drops from the air. However, the organization still needed helpers, requested by both Harry Rée and Cuthbert, and in November, London told them that at last one was on his way. Great was the rejoicing at Clairvaux, and the two agents looked forward to the arrival of their new organizer.

Their new man, Albert Maugenet, was landed in another sector, but unhappily, as sometimes happened and as feared by all agents, virtually into the waiting arms of the Gestapo. He was immediately taken prisoner, his clothes, papers and bona fides borrowed, and a German agent sent in his place — surely the cruellest deception of all.

The imposter arrived in the Clairvaux sawmill on a fresh, dry, autumn morning at 7.30 on 17 November 1943, carrying a brown crocodile-skin briefcase. As he walked down the road between the houses to the Paulis, Diana peeped through the Juifs' lace curtains, curious to see what her new organizer would be like. At the Paulis' home, Cuthbert met him, and was handed his papers, amongst which were instructions written on cigarette paper and hidden in the false bottom of a matchbox, and a letter from Cuthbert's wife, correspondence which must have paled everything else into insignificance, so rare was such news from home after a long spell in the field. Then seeing all was well, Diana came across and was introduced to him. During their conversation the stranger said, 'I have left a suitcase full of explosives behind me in Lons-le-Saunier, and I would like to go and pick it up.' 'Good,' said Cuthbert. 'I'm sure we can arrange to run you there.' Diana too jumped at the chance of a lift, and suggested 'Perhaps we could have a drink together and it will give you a chance to meet some of our friends.' The new man was most agreeable. So the two of them squashed into the mill's van, driven by the younger son of the Paulis, and rode back to Lons. There they visited a café, and while they drank Diana's new organizer heard about the circuit and its work, information which she naturally needed to brief him about. 'How are things in the region?' he asked, and again, 'Are the Gestapo efficient here?' Later he enquired, out of curiosity, 'Doesn't all this frighten you?' She must have thought this was a strange question to ask, but she answered quite seriously, 'No.' Eventually they were joined by a resistance member in hiding and a man working for the local police. They spent the rest of the morning talking and then the stranger left and Diana went about her own visits while she was in the town.

Meanwhile, up at the sawmill Cuthbert became restless. He was uneasy about the new man's answers to several questions. The stranger had seemed too vague about the organization in London. There was nothing on which Cuthbert could actually put his finger, but it sounded suspicious. Prompted by his uncertainties, he decided to move his radio equipment, and did so several times, according to the Juifs who still had a good idea where it was. Then Cuthbert wandered around the Paulis' house moodily until late afternoon, when he went across to the Juifs' kitchen and began a game of chess with Monsieur Pauli while he awaited the man's return, no doubt ready to ask their guest some more searching questions.

It was now dark, and nearly six in the evening. The stranger escorted Diana up the road, she little knowing that behind his back the man was flashing his torch to indicate his whereabouts. They went into the Juif's house, where Madam Juif was now cooking their supper, and started to discuss where the new man should be lodged. Jean, another member of the resistance group, late for the meeting, rested a moment outside on the balcony at the back, unwilling to interrupt and perhaps a little nervous of his new chief.

Suddenly, three cars screeched to a halt in the yard outside, and out of them poured nearly 20 German Field Police. Some ran into the Paulis' house and dragged out Madam Pauli, whose family had never told her anything about her lodger. The others went straight into the Juifs' house, firing wildly. The first Diana knew about it was when the kitchen door was smashed open and the room filled with police armed with machine-guns. They immediately dragged her, Cuthbert and the stranger, out of the house into the waiting cars, with their wrists handcuffed behind them.

From there they were taken straight to the police station in Lons-le-Saunier where they all spent the night. There Diana heard poor Cuthbert being tortured to tell the location of his transmitter. It was in vain. Jean, on the balcony during the police raid, had jumped down unseen and sliding down the steep ravine outside, had escaped to warn his fellow resisters. Then returning with a bike to pick up the radio set, he rode off with it safely tied to his carrier. He was just in the nick of time, for the impostor, realizing that the radio had not been captured with the agents, came back and held up at pistol point the remnants of the shocked and confused sawmill families, while the Germans searched high and low for the tranmitter. They remained for the next few days, questioning, threatening, beating up the family and removing most of their possessions even down to the children's toys, but they never found the set for which they searched. Certainly its absence saved the lives of the rest of the family.

After their uncomfortable night in prison, Diana and Cuthbert· were taken with another captured member of the resistance to Paris, arriving at 84 Avenue Foch. Here another shock awaited Diana, one engineered with the greatest of pleasure by Josef Kieffer. 'Here is your chief', he gloated. Diana did not believe him until John Starr walked through the door, free and unharmed. At this time he was still employed by the Germans, who used him as a map-maker and tracer in their office and to shake the morale of the many agents brought to them. Diana, however, refused to be tricked and would not say anything that would help her interrogators who quickly recognized that they were wasting their time with this polite, serious, young woman. On 5 December 1943, she was packed off to Fresnes Prison.

On 13 May of the next year, looking white and drawn, she was sent by train, together with seven other SOE women handcuffed in pairs, to the women's prison in Germany at Karlsrühe, under orders from the Gestapo headquarters in Berlin. There they were all to be kept in 'protective custody'. Actually Kieffer had arranged this, since his family lived nearby whom he could visit under the excuse of calling in to further question the women, but he never did and the prisoners were no longer disturbed by him.

Diana found herself in an overcrowded prison, sharing a long narrow cell with two bunks and one high barred window, with two German women convicted of minor crimes. As time went on she struck up a friendship with her cell-mates who were much impressed by her cheerfulness and courage. She helped them with their laundry and shared their food parcels. During the exercise period in the prison yard, it was remarked that the SOE girls moved faster than the others and ran in the outer circle, where they were occasionally able to talk, though this was as soon noticed as prevented. Part of the morning and the afternoon the prisoners worked, But Diana must have endured soul-destroying boredom, especially after the active life she had led.

Then just as Diana was growing reconciled to this regime, a question was raised as to whether Diana and some of the other SOE girls who also were imprisoned there were in the wrong type of prison. As a consequence Berlin remembered about them and sent Karlsrühe a teleprint message ordering four of them to be removed. Diana was one of those named. On the evening of 5 July 1944 the wardress gave her back her belongings and she was told she would be leaving. Next morning early, she was wakened as just about four. She tied her short fair hair with a tartan-coloured ribbon, put on her grey flannel skirt and swagger coat and was escorted to the room where the Gestapo were waiting for her and three other SOE girls whom she did not know.

She left with them, probably first calling at the office of Karlsrühe Gestapo for a final interrogation, although this was of little use. Then she left with the others chained in separate compartments in a van, en route back across Germany to Alsace and the Natzweiler Concentration Camp, where she was told they were being transferred for argicultural work. It was a long gruelling journey of around 100 miles in supreme discomfort, through the heat of the day in a dark, breathless, coffin-like compartment, before she stumbled out, blinking and stretching, at her destination in the middle of the afternoon.

Natzweiler, however, was a men's camp, and there was much speculation when the men caught sight of four girls, as they were escorted up the paths to the administrative offices and from there to a hut called the Bunker by inmates, as it was used as a prison in the camp. Here Diana found herself in one room with the other three. When one of the others looked through the glass of the window, she saw the heads of two servicemen in the hut opposite, who by signs indicated that the window could be opened from the inside. This done, a hurried conversation followed, one of the men recognizing a girl with whom he had worked. Shortly afterwards the girls were removed and put two to a cell.

As the evening drew on some unusual orders were given to the men, who began to fear that something sinister was afoot and that it was connected with the four women. Everyone was ordered to be back in his hut by 8 pm and the black-outs put up, even though it was still daylight outside.

Around 10 pm Diana, having seen her companion taken out some 20 minutes before, was herself called out of her cell, she did not know for what purpose. She went down the path between two guards towards a large hut, which she assumed to be a hospital. She was taken through the gate down the corridor to a room containing eight empty beds where she was told to lie down as she was to have a typhus injection. She probably believed this. Instead the injection proved to be a massive dose of phenol from which she must have died almost immediately. Her body was later taken and burned in the crematorium attached to the building.

Thus briefly and without warning ended a very brave life. She was 29 years of age.

7
The Doctor's Wife

Cécile Margot Lefort

'She would have needed more courage than most to screw herself up to go to France.'

Francis Cammaerts

What could be more improbable than for the middle-aged wife of a respected doctor in Paris, very much in love with her husband and living in more than comfortable circumstances, to be willing to volunteer to return to France after escaping from the Germans, to face them again as a secret agent. Yet Cécile Margot Lefort did all this and more. She is also linked with Diana Rowden and Noor Inayat Khan in a number of strange ways. She loved yachting, as did Diana, and an incident in her life reads like a piece from the fairy stories Noor had written and continued to write during her imprisonment in Avenue Foch. As it happened all three were passengers in the double Lysander landings near Angers in the early morning of 17 June 1943.

Cécile was born at the turn of the century in London, in the household of the MacKenzies, a family of Irish descent, and she lived variously in England and Ireland. She grew up a tomboy, very fond of all sport and especially of yachting. In 1925 she married a wealthy Frenchman, Dr Alix Lefort, who had a flat in Paris and a villa near the fishing village of St Cast, on the north coast of Brittany, facing Devon. Here she was able to indulge her passion for sailing and became a

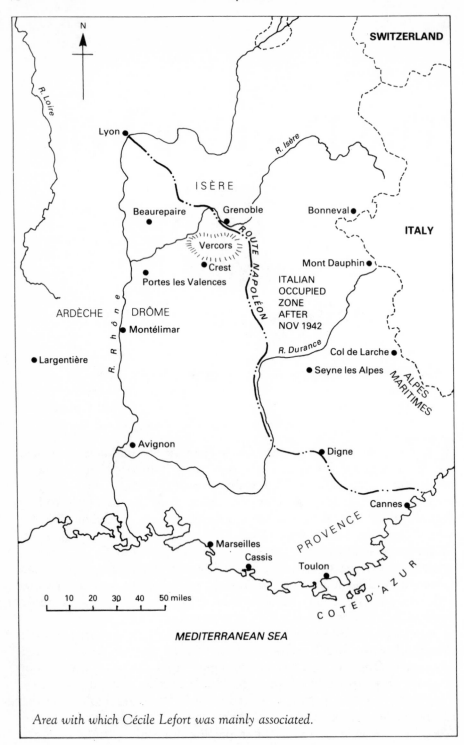

Area with which Cécile Lefort was mainly associated.

proficient yachtswoman, spending long holidays there with her husband, a like-minded enthusiast, and using the little beach below their villa. And it was here that what sounds like a fairy story in the best tradition turns up.

While in training for SOE, Cécile mentioned the place to a friend who passed it on to an agent who was looking for safe beaches to use as an escape route to England from the French coast. She also gave him an antique Irish ring which had been in her family for generations, and which everyone connected with her would recognize. Equipped with this the agent simply visited the empty villa and flourished the ring in front of the maid in residence to prove that he had indeed permission to use the place. Thus the Var escape line was set up, transfers being made on a rising tide after sunset on moonless nights from a rowing boat to a waiting gunboat. Though no one realized it then, this was not the first time that this secret landing spot had been used, for evidently it had served a similar purpose for the scarlet pimpernels of French Revolutionary days. Thus, for a second era, the place proved a successful escape point.

After the German invasion of France in 1940, Madame Lefort was advised, as were all British nationals, that it would be unwise to remain, and she therefore fled to England, leaving her husband behind in Paris. Fretting at his absence and for his safety, she joined the WAAF in 1941 as a policewoman, hoping that she could contribute somewhat to the overthrow of Germany. There her fluency in French was noted and eventually in early 1943 she was called to Baker Street and accepted for work with SOE. She was trained as a courier and hoped that she might be sent back to the Paris area which she knew well, and where of course she hoped she might see her husband again, though this was strictly against SOE rules.

But this was not to be. Fate decided otherwise. Instead, it was Noor Inayat Khan, who also knew the city well, who was destined for Paris and the ultimate disaster of the Prosper network. Cécile was intended for the Jockey circuit of Francis Cammaerts in the south-east of France. It was a network of small independent groups scattered from the Isère to the Maritime Alps, covering an area of 15,000 square miles, larger than two of the biggest British countries put together. There Francis Cammaerts was known as Roger and was well-loved by his supporters who would never betray him. By the Germans he was known as the great English devil, *le grand diable anglais*. The pressure of all his work, however, had compelled him to appeal to London for more help, and for this reason Cécile was being sent to him as a courier under the code name Alice.

Bunny Rymills, her Lysander pilot, was not very impressed by her French. To him, 'it didn't seem all that hot'. He also thought privately that she looked rather like a vicar's wife. But knowing her errand, he concentrated on being kind and encouraging, which may have been the reason why he accidentally left on his transmitter just after they crossed the channel into France. As a result, the following Lysander could hear, but not stop, his conversation with his passenger.

'Now madame, we are approaching your beautiful country — isn't it lovely in the moonlight?' Back came an answer in soft accented tones, 'Yes. I think it is heavenly. What is that town over there?' He replied, and continued pointing out all the local landmarks as they passed over them, a running commentary for which the listening Germans, if there were any, would have been most grateful.

Eventually the plane touched down safely on Déricourt's much-used landing strip at Vieux Briollay, and Cécile clambered down the metal ladder affixed to the plane, being assisted by the other passenger, a male agent, also going south. As the first part of her journey was to take her through Paris, she, Noor, and their guide set off together to catch the early train. When they reached Paris, it is more than likely that she managed to get word of, and perhaps see, her husband, although it broke all her security rules. Of this, nevertheless, she never spoke, and later no one liked to ask. At any rate, after a brief stop she again met her former Lysander companion and was fortunate in having his company for most of her train journey south, as she was making for Montélimar, famed for its nougat, where she would meet Francis and where she would be based.

In fact, she did not see the town very much after she arrived, for her work as courier sent her all over this vast territory. Francis recorded the places that he might see in one typical week, and there is little doubt that Cécile would have done much the same. It started with a visit to Toulouse, followed by one to Clermont Ferrand to see a circuit organizer. Afterwards he might travel on to Agen to see an agent, with a trip to Lyon on another errand, and then a further one to Digne to send or receive messages through his letter-box there. In between, he might call on a Maquis group or make sabotage plans with other members of the resistance which would not need to rely on the explosives they did not have.

Unfortunately, the south of France was less well served with supplies than the north because of its distance from Britain, as well as being considered less useful to the Allies when they would come to launch their invasion. In the middle of 1943, with the greatest of difficulty London managed to extract a few more large aircraft to step up supplies to France as a whole. Nevertheless the south still continued to come lower in the scale of priorities. Consequently, Francis only received 2½ planeloads of a total of 40 containers in the whole of 1943, so little that it made his task of encouraging the resistance even more difficult.

Cécile, acting for her organizer, carried out her errands conscientiously. She lived every day with the spectre of capture, whether in shelter or on the route, at rest or at work. She knew that any small slip of hers or those around her might give her away. She lived with fear. Timid by nature, she always bore in mind the risks not only to herself, but also those with her and the far wider network of helpers in her own and other circuits. Poor Cécile! How often must she have recalled her comfortable past. Did she ever regret her decision to take on such dangerous work? Was her love for her husband — still out of her reach — a sufficient motive? It was a hard and unforgiving life and at 43 years she was not as young and resilient as most of the others who undertook it. To her organizer she was a rather quiet, secretive, shy person, with a perpetually surprised look about her and to a young man she seemed old.

In the month after she arrived, the Allies invaded Sicily, and afterwards the mainland of Italy. London knew that helping the saboteurs to damage and distract the enemy in south-east France had become more important. So on the night of 13 August, Cécile was at the Beaurepaire dropping ground, which for long had been carefully reconnoitred and prepared for such a time as this. There, having arrived before curfew, and waiting for the dark on this moon-lit night, she was surrounded by members of the resistance — local farmers, footballers, shopkeepers and their devil-may-care younger sons, all merging in the shadows and praying for the promised loads.

She strained her ears for the thin whisper of engines far away. Bushes rustled, the grass was tinder-dry underfoot and all around was an unearthly silence. The messages had come on the BBC as prearranged and final confirmation had been broadcast at six. Now while she waited she could think of all the things that could go wrong. Had the aircraft chosen suddenly been found unserviceable? Was it raining at Tempsford in England? Was the cloud too low? Would the aircraft find its way? Would it get shot down? Were their torch batteries still working? Would the Germans discover them before the aircraft, or were they just lying in wait within earshot until it came, ready to swoop down and catch them all red-handed, so that their beautiful supplies would be lost and they would be lost too.

She half glanced over her shoulder into the brightening night. Then there came a ghost of a sound. Listen! It might be the hiss of someone's pent-up breath. There it was again, a thread of sound that throbbed louder by the second. Suddenly everyone was leaping from cover and they were all racing to position their torches so that the stiff paper tubes around their lights would make the pinpoints strong enough to be seen from the approaching low-flying aircraft in the form of the prearranged signal — a line of lights. Cécile carried the principal light, the one that gave the identification letter in Morse to tell the pilot that it was safe to drop his loads.

And so the plane came on. It sounded heavy. Perhaps it was heavily loaded? It circled and came lower. She flicked the torch on and off. The sound of the engines changed until it was almost on top of them. Then little grey puffs came tumbling out, mushrooming into silvery petals with long dark shapes slung below. The plane's engines roared into new life and it sped off, as if relieved that its burden was gone. Meanwhile, as one after another of the parachutes dropped and dragged its container along the ground, it was pounced upon by several men, who tamed the billowing parachute into a parcel-sized mass, and then hauled off the metal cylinder weighing perhaps 4 cwts. One or two were broken up into several lighter pieces. The whole load was then piled on to one of the steam-powered lorries owned by civilians, and in this case by a helpful town coal merchant, whose temperamental vehicle after a nail-biting pumping and delay, at last consented to take them to a neighbouring farm for the arms and explosives to be quickly and not so silently distributed. Finally the field, once a hive of frantic activity, shadows and low voices, reverted to reveal itself empty and innocent in the eye of the rising sun.

Cécile could congratulate herself that this drop had been most successful. She had counted seven cylinders and now they and their contents were all safely stowed away, while the local Maquis were rubbing their hands with glee at this bounty from on high. There had been no hitches and no casualties. Only the men, slower than usual at their work, were unable to divulge the secret of their sleepless night. She fortunately was able to return to her well-earned bed.

This was to be the beginning of a more active period of sabotage by the newly supplied resistance. Messages flew to and fro, and Cécile was on the road daily. As a result, bigger dislocations occurred on the Lyon to Valence and Grenoble railway lines, and to power stations and industrial targets. The largest and most damaging piece of sabotage occurred in the hydro-electric station near Largentière, in the valley of the river Durance. This supplied the power for factories in the area, producing aluminium used in the manufacture of German aircraft. Damage here took time to repair, thus considerably reducing production. Another effective piece of sabotage had more than the usual destructive results. This was at the railway yards in Portes-les-Valances, where steam railway engines were brought for their regular 100 mile servicing, together with much other rolling stock destined for Germany. Railway saboteurs were skilled in knowing exactly where explosives charges should be effectively laid to do the greatest damage, and one night's work set off a succession of explosions that put out of action over

13 locomotives and the railway turntable. The enormous destruction caused increased investigation by the Germans, who discovered the existence of a Roger and an Alice and set about tracing their whereabouts. Consequently Francis warned Cécile to avoid their headquarters in Montélimar as much as possible, in case the Germans picked up their trail.

The house of Raymond Daujat, where Cécile stayed.

In spite of his warning on 15 September 1943, Cécile called on Raymond Daujat, a corn merchant and leader of the local resistance at Montélimar. The constant strain and travel in Cécile's work were making her more tired than usual, and she asked if she might stay the night at his house, a fine whitewashed villa standing in its own grounds. She was carrying messages and instructions as usual, most of them in her head. In the early hours of the next morning, four members of the Gestapo banged on the door. Perhaps they were following a tip-off or had put together clues in their hunt for Roger and Alice. They roused Raymond from his bed, and three men went into the house, one staying on patrol outside to catch anyone breaking out. They arrested Raymond, who begged permission to dress. Watched by one man he went into the bathroom and was able to take advantage of a momentary diversion as the others searched his house to jump down from the narrow upstairs window overlooking the back yard, climb over an end wall and get clear away, while the guard outside was around the corner. Cécile was not so fortunate. She must have heard them as they drew nearer. What were her feelings at this time, knowing the almost certainty of what would happen if they found her? And find her they did eventually, in a dark little cellar beneath the house. The fact that she was hiding was enough admission of guilt. She was hauled out roughly, handcuffed, pushed into a waiting car and taken off to the Gestapo prison at Lyon, where she was so brutally interrogated that her answers were confused and her cover story did not hold. Then she was sent off to Avenue Foch in Paris. By now it was already too late for anything useful to be gleaned from her.

It is a peculiar fact that all three women who arrived on the June Lysander, to arrangements masterminded by Henri Déricourt, were captured by the Germans within five months. It is also strange that of *all* the WAAF who landed in this way, none survived. Were they betrayed before they landed and were they living on borrowed time before they were taken? Had the Germans first let them go, hoping to be led to more important agents? If so it was a foolish gamble and the German plans must have misfired, as they could not have realized the amount of harm that could be done by leaving the girls on the loose, added to which they almost certainly lost track of each of the girls for some time, although there was always the likelihood that one might later be recognized, as may have happened to Cécile. Noor and Diana were only caught by being betrayed. It shows therefore that either the German intelligence service was remarkably inept, or that the girls had learned their security drill in Britain very thoroughly to stay free for so long.

Eventually it was decided to send Cécile to a German concentration camp for women at Ravensbrück, 50 miles north of Berlin. It was built near a lakeland beauty spot, dotted with small holiday villas for the wealthier Germans, but on marshy ground, the breeding place for disease. Several smaller enclaves existed outside for working parties doing factory or heavy agricultural work in the community, as well as the Jugendlager or youth camp used for those too ill and unfit for any work. The main camp surrounded by high walls was built for about 6,000 prisoners. Inside were wooden huts for living quarters containing three tiers of bunks, a few brick buildings for kitchens, showers and a

Map showing the concentration camps to which SOE WAAF were sent.

concrete cell block. Cinder paths divided the huts in front of which bloomed flowers in profusion. But there all resemblance to cleanliness and proper conditions stopped. The place was in fact known to the French as *L'Enfer des Femmes*, the Women's Hell.

Nearly all the prisoners were civilians, both young and old, taken from conquered countries either as slave labour or on suspicion of involvement with the resistance, all being imprisoned without trial, though this did not prevent them being cruelly tortured during questioning in the camp's political department. During the war years over 50,000 women, at the lowest estimate, died in the camp from dirt, disease, overcrowding, squalor, starvation, overwork and ill-treatment, apart from those who were shot or gassed or sent away to die elsewhere.

When Cécile Lefort was admitted in 1943, she spent her first days in the quarantine hut, where new arrivals were kept for three weeks to ensure they brought no new infections to the camp. After being checked in, though weary from the long train journey, she had to stand several hours before being admitted to the bathhouse, where she was told to strip and her former clothes were taken away. Here she waited naked in the cold for a further few hours under the tiny hole in the ceiling where the shower worked, and that for only a few minutes. With a sliver of soap and a pocket hankerchief of a towel she had to clean herself. Again a long wait and then a shock. Two men came in, one to look at her teeth and one to give her a cursory medical examination, which revealed that something was amiss.

Then she was issued with prison clothing, thin and inadequate for the advancing winter, and dispatched to the quarantine hut. There, no one was to be allowed outside, though all were awakened well before dawn for bitter acorn coffee. Then they crowded at the window watching while the other women lined up five deep in front of their huts, in the freezing cold and rain, the living and the dead together, and stood for the hours-long 'Appells', where they were counted and appointed their work for the day. Some were detailed for gardening, some for sewing or knitting, some for corpse, rubbish or coal collecting, some for road mending, cleaning latrines, tree-felling or potato picking, women being used instead of horses to drag the heavy carts. Work went in shifts of 10 or 11 hours each, day and night, lights out coming at about 9 pm. Food, mainly vegetable soup and half a loaf of bread a day, was not sufficient for such heavy work. This was the life that awaited them when quarantine was finished.

But not for Cécile just yet. Suddenly she was summoned to the hospital hut, the Rever, for a further medical, and there what she had secretly worried about, was confirmed. She was found to have cancer of the stomach. Her German camp doctor was quite brilliant in his way and had certain theories, not only about the cancer removal but also the aftercare, and she provided him with an excellent opportunity to prove them. She had nothing to lose. So she was operated upon, and slept in a clean bed between clean sheets, and was fed on a special diet of thick vegetable soup and a type of porridge, on which she appeared to be thriving. This diet continued after she left the hospital block to join the other women, the doctor still following her case with great interest.

Conditions on the camp deteriorated in 1944, particularly after the heavy Allied bombing raids on Germany and the mid-year invasions by the Allies of France and Poland. The prison staff became more brutal, treating the inmates as scapegoats. Harder work was demanded of them and their food rations fell drastically. In addition the camp was now bursting at the seams, with six times the normal numbers, despite the mounting death toll. The clothing and mattresses of the prisoners were filled with lice, and the droppings of dysentery and Asian typhus seeped through the three tiers of bunks now housing five to six women to a bed.

Appells weeded out the weakest and increasing numbers of pink cards were handed out to take the bearers to the so-called 'convalescent' camp at the Jugendlager. Some time in about February of 1945, after around 18 months in these terrible conditions, Cécile's doctor heard that she had received a pink card and knew that the evidence of his successful treatment of cancer would disappear. Mary Lindell, a former escape line organizer, now a prisoner but working in the Rever as a nurse, on the doctor's information tried to get Cécile transferred on to a knitting group in the main camp. She was not quite soon enough.

By this time Cécile was at the Jugenlager with 1,500 transferees. Desperately, on her own authority and taking a great risk in doing so, Mary signed a form recalling Cécile with two other friends. The paper was delivered, but one of the three women was so worn down that she refused to return, and while Cécile was absent in her friend's hut trying to persuade her to change her mind, the group she should have joined left. What must have been Cécile feelings, when she eventually arrived with her friend, to find that they had been left behind. She was too late!

She never did return. It is believed that she died from an overdose of the white 'sleeping' powder, often issued by a fellow prisoner, who encouraged by the authorities, used her own extermination methods, or she may have died in the gas chamber. Whatever her tragic end, she died without trace and her body was cremated, yet another of the sad SOE victims taken by the Germans. Her husband, also involved in resistance work, survived the war.

Cécile's life had embraced both extremes, starting with the cloud-capped towers of fairy-tale happiness and prosperity, and ending with the vilest hell of any invention in degradation and death. After the outbreak of war few had much belief in their survival if they were on active service. From her organizer's point of view, Cécile never lost that conviction of despair. 'Tragedy seemed to hang over her like a cloud.' With such a prospect how much greater was the courage she displayed when she decided to undertake such doomed, dangerous work.

8
The Girl With Magic Fingers

Beatrice Yvonne Cormeau

'The question of not going didn't arise. I was ready to go. I'd steeled myself... There was constant fear, but you had to learn to live with it.'
Yvonne Cormeau

'**H**ow many Castelnaus?' asked the German officer in tones of disbelief. 'Eight, sir,' answered his junior uncomfortably.

They both looked at the bruised, shaking Spaniard who had given them the information. Being a foreigner in France, he obviously had little idea that that there was more than one village in that area named Castelnau. It was no use wasting further time on him or they would miss their quarry. 'Right. Show me the map.'

It was like looking for a needle in a haystack. Two would be enough, but to the German mind only a people like the French would be mad enough to call eight places the same! As his junior pointed out each in turn, the officer tapped it was a thoughtful finger. 'That one's big enough — electricity, good roads and a nearby railway... And this one! There have been several attempted sabotage raids near that little one, too.' And so he continued assessing the likelihood of each candidate. But one he dismissed out of hand. 'Much too small. No electricity for the girl to run her wireless transmitter. Besides, there's no water. The English love their baths. No Englishmen will live where there isn't any water for a bath. No use looking there.' They both agreed on this point. By a

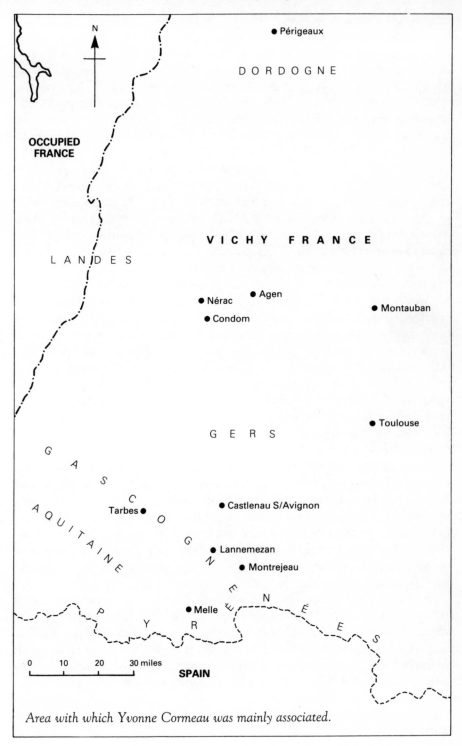

N

OCCUPIED
FRANCE

DORDOGNE

● Périgeaux

VICHY FRANCE

L A N D E S

● Nérac ● Agen

● Condom

● Montauban

G E R S

● Toulouse

G
A
S
C
O
G
N
E

A
Q
U
I
T
A
I
N
E

Tarbes ●

● Castlenau S/Avignon

● Lannemezan

● Montrejeau

P
Y
R
E
N
É
E
S

● Melle

0   10   20   30 miles

SPAIN

Area with which Yvonne Cormeau was mainly associated.

process of elimination they chose the villages and soon their cars, bristling with soldiers, set out to search them.

Thus the Gestapo hunted for the SOE agents in fiercely independent Gascony, on one of the rare occasions when all five were together, and missed them by looking everywhere but the right place. Among the agents was their dark haired, green-eyed wireless operator, Yvonne Cormeau, known by her code name Annette. She and those with her only later became aware that they had been betrayed, after hearing of the vain German searches of several larger villages.

Castelnau sous l'Auvignon hardly merited the name village. It was just a few houses on a plateau reached by a steep road, at the foot of which was a stream. A single well supplied drinking water. High above the rest rose an old tower and a church whose bell rang over the surrounding hills. It had remained unchanged like this for centuries, except that when daylight faded the cottages and farms were sometimes lit by acetylene flares and sometimes by candles.

Because it was such an unlikely place the SOE organizer, code-named Hilaire, made it his headquarters, lodging at the Mayor's house, but Yvonne, though living occasionally in another village house, rarely used it for her transmissions. She travelled far and wide, often acting as courier and messenger as well as wireless operator. Faithfully she followed the advice given her in England, so that she never transmitted from the same spot twice, either indoors or out of doors. When her travels took her into the Pyrénées, where the population was sparse, she would transmit on the edge of a wood, avoiding the leaves which deadened the transmission. Such a location made it almost impossible for the listening Germans to get a 'fix' on her.

Although she trained on the Paraset Mark 7, the first radio she used in the field was an A Mark II. Three had been dropped for her before she landed, but of these one broke on hitting the ground, one was captured by the Germans and only the third survived. With this last she managed to contact London on the day after her arrival — quite a record in itself. Her disadvantage was that, having only the one set, she was forced to take it everywhere with her for the next few months, despite the risks such action entailed.

This radio, used for sending and receiving messages and therefore called a transceiver, was one of the earliest types made by SOE for its clandestine wireless operators. Although its total weight was around 20 lbs (9 kg) in its suitcase, its range moderate and its signal rather weak, it was popular with agents because it could be split up into four separate parcels, easily hidden in small spaces of all kinds, as Noor Inayat Khan had found with her violin case.

Later in the year, Yvonne was sent the B Mark II set, better known as the B2 — an altogether stronger and more sophisticated transceiver,

Training

Above *A class of airwomen and airmen taking down Morse on a radio operators' course. SOE radio operators did separate, more intensive but similar preparation* **(Chapter 2)**. (Mrs G. Pritchard)

Below *A class at the Radio School learns about transmitters and land lines.* (Mrs G. Pritchard)

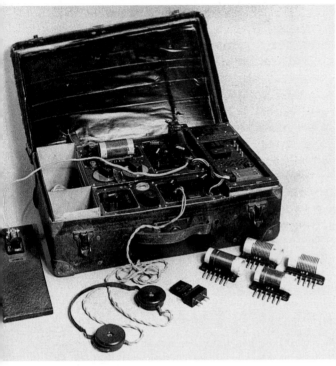

Left *B2 Suitcase transmitter and receiver, with Morse key, headphones and 6 pin interchangeable coils, used by the earlier SOE wireless operators. This link provided much of the French Resistance with supplies and organisers.* (J. I. Brown)

Below left *An A Mark III Transceiver suitcase set with headphones, used by the later SOE wireless operators.* (K. Melton)

Above right *Thame Park, where SOE wireless operators were trained. This shows the south front from the gardens. Some agents joked that their training centres suited the name SOE very well — the Stately 'Omes of England.* (Local Studies Library, Oxfordshire CC)

Right *At a Listening Station for SOE in Britain, wireless operators maintain a 24-hour cover for messages to and from their agents in the field. These secret stations, discreetly named 53A, B, C and D, were located at Grendon, Poundon, Bicester and Dunbar.* (Imperial War Museum)

Above *Arisaig House, the centre for guerilla training in Scotland. It had been burned down in 1936, but was rebuilt in the following year exactly as before. It is now a hotel.* (J. & R. Smither)

Left *SOE agents in training, trekking in the Scottish lakes.* (Imperial War Museum)

Right *An agent sees a warning from an object being placed in the window of a house. Maurice Southgate was captured* **(Chapter 10)** *when he forgot this precaution taught to all agents in their training, as seen here. Various other messages could be conveyed by this means.* (Imperial War Museum)

Left *Virginia McKenna in parachute training outfit while making the film* Carve Her Name With Pride. *Many agents learned to jump with this gear.* (Group Captain F. Griffiths)

Below *Early parachute training at Ringway, Manchester. The parachutist is doing a practice descent over the grounds of Tatton Park, another training centre.* (Group Captain F. Griffiths)

Right *Palace House, Beaulieu, the home of the Montagu family. Beaulieu became the finishing school for agents.*(National Motor Museum)

Below right *The House in the Wood, one of the houses used by SOE trainees in the grounds of Beaulieu.* (National Motor Museum)

Above *The ruins of the Abbey cloisters at Beaulieu where agents spent some peaceful moments when coming to the end of their training. Afterwards they would face the reality of their work with the resistance in German-occupied countries.* (National Motor Museum)

Left *The SOE memorial plaque in the Abbey cloisters, Beaulieu.* (National Motor Museum)

in its small four-compartment suitcase. Its disadvantage was that it was heavier at 32 lbs (over 14 kg) and quite a weight for a girl to carry around, although by now operators often had their sets transported by other members of the resistance and had several in different places. The B2 was none the less more powerful than her next set, an A Mark III, which was, however, much smaller and lighter at around 9 lbs (4 kg) in its suitcase.

The letters A and B were an indication of the power and range of the transceiver. 'A' sets were not expected to cover distances of more than about 400 miles, and thus from Britain to about northern France and Europe, although some exceeded this. 'B' sets could range up to 1,500 miles from base, and therefore easily covered southern France and could be used further afield as in Burma. Mark numbers then indicated the latest developments in the A or B sets. But there were slight variations in existing types, and there were other sets also used in France and elsewhere, quite a few made by different bodies.

In Yvonne's case, all three of her sets could, as necessary, be split up and used outside their suitcases, from the mains or batteries. The latter might be such as those used in cars, which, however, she had to find herself, cumbersome though they were. The crystals were supplied by courtesy of the RAF. Nearly always she used batteries because they gave her freedom of movement, so that while she transmitted she could see into the far distance and if anything suspicious moved there, she could be off and away, long before it arrived.

Beatrice Yvonne Biesterfeld began her adventurous life in Shanghai at the end of 1909. Her mother Olga was Scottish and her father Charles was a British consular official until his death in 1920, when the family moved around France, Belgium and Switzerland, where she received her education. She married Charles Cormeau in London before the war, but in 1940 her husband, now in the army, was killed in London on the last day of his leave, by a German bombing raid that destroyed their flat, leaving Yvonne, escaping with her life, a young widow with a two-and-a-half-year-old daughter. To safeguard the child from the bombs, Yvonne had sent her to a nursery school in Bristol, but when that was disbanded, afraid that during her own prolonged absences she might lose track of the little girl should the next boarding school be evacuated or closed in the prevailing conditions, Yvonne decided to place her in a country convent of Ursulines, near Oxford. Here she knew that come what may the nuns, and therefore their charges, would always stay together.

With her daughter happily settled, Yvonne joined the WAAF in 1942 as an airwoman, and worked on a bomber station in Operations and Intelligence before her fluent French took her into SOE in 1943. There she trained for five months in all, to be an F Section agent working in

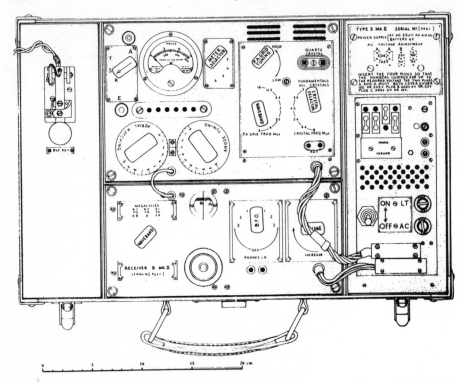

Drawing of the B Mark II (B2) transceiver. The suitcase contains four compartments: the left carries the accessories (aerial, morse key, headset, fuses, etc), the middle top part contains the transmitter and the bottom part the receiver, while the right houses the power fittings which could be used with a battery or the mains. (Drawing by Lt Col P. Lorain)

the field. Among other things she discovered how to spot people following her, how to contact other agents, how to answer awkward questions or interrogations, how to look after herself in dangerous situations, how to shoot with a Smith and Wesson pistol, a rifle, a Sten and Bren gun, as well as how to find good hiding places or spot those used by enemies, how to recognize who was lying or telling the truth, and who could be trusted or was likely to betray her.

At her first school, Thame Park, as well as plenty of keep-fit exercises, she was taught to be a good wireless operator in 16 weeks, a far from easy task in such a short time. She learned how to use and repair her radio, tap out messages in Morse using the codes and checks to verify her transmissions, becoming a highly skilled and technically efficient operator in the process.

Security was constantly dinned into her, pointing out the risks that she would run. During 1943, because of the increased skills and equipment by German Direction Finders, the average span of an F

Section wireless operator in France before discovery was only about six weeks. It was enough to frighten off all but the most courageous of potential agents. 'Playing the piano' as the French resistance called it, was the most dangerous work of any agent in the field. Noor Inayat Khan and Yolande Beekman trained with her in early 1943 and of the three only one survived. Yvonne Cormeau was so accurate, sensible and careful, that when her messages eventually started coming through to England, there was always rivalry among the FANY and others who worked in the home station, as to who was going to be the lucky one to receive her. Because her sensitive fingers were so vital in contacting London, no Frenchman in her circuit would allow her near them when they were setting explosive charges for fear of injury to her hands.

Finally she was ready and on the moonlit night of 22/23 August 1943, she dropped by parachute from an aircraft to a reception party of five Frenchmen in a field at St Antoine du Queyret, 75 miles from Bordeaux in south-west France. Although her landing went smoothly, her reception was far from so, possibly because hers was the first drop in that area. Everything seemed confused and noisy, from the crowd of locals who had gathered to greet the new arrival in the farmhouse to which she was taken, to their manoeuvres as they collected the many containers that had arrived with her. It was enough to alert any Germans within several miles of them. Fresh from her security training, she couldn't believe what she saw and was impatient to borrow a cycle and leave. It was with ringing ears and sinking heart that she set out with a guide to ride through the darkened lanes to the far-off town of Pujols, where her first 'safe' house awaited her. Here she learned the reason for some of the disorganization, as there had been many arrests in the area and her organizer had gone to ground after a close brush with the Gestapo. Eventually after a few days, she was summoned to the Pyrénées to join him. Up to the end of 1942 the area to which she had been sent to begin her work would have been much safer, since it was in the zone administered by Vichy, and therefore not occupied by the Germans. But those times had changed. Following the Allied landings in North Africa, the Germans had occupied the zone 'to protect the French', and were tightening their grip, being now not only afraid of Allied successes in North Africa but also the creeping menace of the Allies in Sicily and the falling apart of the Italian alliance. These gave the Germans a great deal about which to worry, as well as increasing the intransigence of the French population, scenting invasion on its own shores. The result was that German rule became harsher than before.

Yvonne arrived to become the wireless operator to George Starr, a quietly efficient agent, whose huge circuit — Wheelwright — covered ten *départements*. She was one of the few who could recognize him since she and her husband had been friendly with him before the war, which was fortunate as she needed to see him regularly for her work, and luckily they got on well together. He was a small man, balding and living on his nerves, but trusted by all who came into contact with him. Soon, however, they realized that the Germans knew who they were and what they looked like, as there had been an informer among those at Yvonne's reception. She therefore started her work with this

dangerous threat hanging over her like a sword. It was thus essential that she never remained static. In such a large circuit, with its centre in the Gers *departement*, her travels could take her from the Dordogne to the remoter areas of Gascony or up into the Pyrenees. For this purpose she had several disguises, such as a children's nurse, a cow-minder for a very short time, or a district nurse. She travelled on trains and buses but, when the Germans stepped up their random checks on public transport, she fell back on the more frequent use of her bike, on

The lower Pyrénées. Yvonne moved her radio around such areas knowing that it was difficult for the Germans to detect it there.

some days cycling up to 60 miles (around 100 km) through all kinds of weather, starting off early in the morning and arriving before the nightly curfew, her radio set perched on the carrier behind her, covered with vegetables or other innocent-looking objects. Often in later months her radio was transported by local people who would attract little suspicion and knew the hazards of their area better. Then the little silk slips used as keys to her codes travelled in the false lining of her briefcase. Despite her weapons training, she never carried her pistol knowing it would be her death warrant if, at check points and road blocks during personal searches, it was found in her possession. 'You had to be very steady, You couldn't afford to feel exhilarated. After I'd come through a difficult check, I would feel washed through. I felt the strain — I couldn't help it.' She made for farms or homes known to the resistance as 'safe' houses, and thus found herself lodged in everything from the bedroom of a private house, the backroom of a shop or café, a loft, a barn or an outhouse. Sometimes she had to lie hidden for hours and was often most uncomfortable, but accepted whatever she was offered gratefully, because she knew the terrible risks those sheltering her took. Like Diana Rowden she used attics but also the vine wires in the vineyards to extend her up to 70 foot long aerial. Through all her wanderings not once was she refused a bed or betrayed, although there was a heavy price on her head

— five million francs (it was 10 million for her organizer, George). On her side she never prolonged her visit for more than three consecutive nights.

When she landed in August 1943, she was sending her messages about three times a week, some indoors and some out, but they became more frequent, increasing to as much as three times a day during the critical months of 1944. It was her good fortune that instructions were shortly given from London to the effect that the former fixed times and wavelengths of messages that all operators had been instructed to keep and called 'skeds' (schedules) were to be made far more flexible and varied, so that the German detectors would find it harder to focus on any regular pattern of signals. Incoming messages were also grouped at night, a practice that was far safer if more disruptive of sleep. Additionally, agents were instructed not to transmit for longer than 15–20 minutes — shorter if possible and never more than 30 minutes at the maximum. In the early days many operators had been caught beside their sets because of the long, wordy messages upon which their organizers had unwisely insisted. Yvonne had shorter material and she did not start putting it into cipher by the double transposition method until an hour before her call. The key for her cipher was drawn from a sequence of figures, cut from a jumbled assortment printed on a silk handkerchief, which she preferred to use rather than the one-time pads, as these were both bulky and difficult to hide and transport. Silk slips and messages were then burned as soon as transmissions were completed, so that nothing remained if she were subsequently discovered. The same went for any incoming traffic, which she promptly decoded

A street in Condom.

and passed to her organizer or gave the instructions to those concerned. She was meticulous about the security of her messages, her set and her location, her care paying dividends.

One day London received a message with an aggrieved passage, sent through Yvonne. Evidently the RAF had dropped leaflets in the vicinity of the town of Condom on the previous night — it may have been intended, or as a blind for other activities. Whatever the cause, George objected strongly and wanted to ensure it did not happen again, though he had his reasons: 'Ordered by Boche to clean up leaflets from our best parachute ground. Spent all Sunday picking up. Lumbago very painful. Tell RAF to drop pamphlets in sea, next time.'

Of course weapons and ammunitions were also dropped, for which leaflets provided a diversion or cover. From the 400 or so transmissions made by Yvonne during the next 13 months, over 153 successful drops of arms, explosives and supplies arrived at the co-ordinates and arrangements given on her radio. Although she was often exhausted and weary from her work and her journeyings, she kept up her punishing schedule, even finding enough time to recruit and train two local wireless operators, ready to take over in case she was ever captured, for this was ever in the forefront of her mind, no matter how successful she might be. These men were a French butcher and a former radio operator in the now disbanded French Air Force. They sometimes practised on her set but they did not have her ciphers or other secret material.

It was Yvonne's additional task to monitor the long lists of personal messages, broadcast daily on the BBC French service which she could hear on an ordinary radio. These rather odd jumbles of words might sometimes contain a particular phrase or sentence agreed on by her group, and which she had earlier transmitted to London in one of her communications. To recognize this, whenever broadcast, was to confirm that an arms drop for her resisters would take place that night. However, almost inevitably there were often delays of many days or even weeks between her request and the broadcast of her message, pinning her to the radio for long sessions and thus increasing her dangers, but saving the resisters from their vulnerable receptions on nights when the drops would not take place. Such messages could also be used for other purposes. Late in December 1943, instructions came from London to try out the effectiveness of the resistance. Consequently there was an outbreak of sabotage all over the South of France, showing London that its work and supplies were well spent. Afterwards the flow of supplies began to increase.

In common with other operators, she had many narrow escapes. Once her messages to London warned that the Gestapo was on her trail and that for a time she would have to lie low. On all other occasions she conscientiously maintained communications, whatever occurred. Her regular cycling kept her physically fit, but this kind of lifestyle kept up over a prolonged period, together with a lack of good food and sleep, ultimately affected her health, so that her weight went down to 87 lb (just over 6 stones, less than 42 kg) and she began to suffer from insomnia.

Then on 1 June 1944 came the long-awaited 'A' messages, broadcast by the BBC. In the evening Yvonne heard the first line of the poem by Paul Verlaine, slightly misquoted but selected to give a general alert to the French in her area — *Les sanglots lourds des violons d'automne* — followed by the second line on the evening before the landings — *Bercent mon coeur d'une langueur monotone*. Afterwards came about 300 other action messages to the resistance all over France. From her air traffic also, Yvonne knew that an Allied invasion was imminent, but not where. The Germans aware that something was about to happen, stepped up arrests of suspected resisters, forcing many circuits to alter very quickly arrangements of parachute fields and caches of arms dumps. Yvonne's area was one affected by this greater German vigilance, but the changes meant more messages at an already busy time. The 'B' radio messages gave orders to cut railway and telephone communications, thereby increasing German difficulties in encountering the Allied landings. Everyone in France seemed to know when these occurred, but Yvonne knew that F Section wanted to hold back the French from rising too soon or the Germans would be able to pick the resistance off before the allies arrived and their support would be lost.

At this critical time Yvonne again moved her set to be nearer to George's headquarters in a farmhouse, so that she could be close to him in emergencies. Her establishment had also been increased, as SOE had sent her another wireless operator to assist her in handling the enormous number of messages which were now passing through her hands. George had formed a Maquis group of Frenchmen with a few Spaniards at Castelnau sous l'Auvignon, which became so overcrowded that many young men had to be turned away since their work would be more valuable on the land, farming the supplies that fed the resistance. His Maquis took part in several local forays and then was caught up on the peripheries of bigger actions happening elsewhere.

On 7 June 1944, the 2nd German Panzer division, christened *Das Reich*, was ordered to join the German troops in Normandy, where their arrival during the difficult early days of the Allied invasion could very well have swung the battle in favour of the Germans. The main part of its force after leaving Russia was based near Toulouse, at the eastern end of the Wheelwright country. Foreseeing such a move, George had already marked down and now proceeded to blow up all its accessible petrol supply depots, forcing the Germans to turn to the trains for transport. Being a panzer division, *Das Reich* was heavily armed, well-equipped with tanks kept on trucks near Montauban against such an emergency. A neighbouring circuit now ensured that all the trucks seized up when required. Therefore alternative transport had to be summoned and this was located at Perigueux, some 100 miles distant, leaving it wide open to ingenious sabotage tactics along the way. Impatient to be gone, the soldiers were forced to set off on foot and march north, not only delaying them but also laying their stragglers and scouts open to sniping and forays by guerilla resistants, who melted away as soon as the Germans stood still to fight, only to return to buzz around the rear, hampering the troops every step of the way. Once the division had passed through George's circuit, the attacks were taken up by the men of the next circuit, giving the troops no peace as they wearily trudged onwards.

It was at this time that the German troops in George's region decided
to attack the Maquis headquarters at Castelnau. The men had warning
from their reconnaissance patrols and women, children and old folk
were evacuated from the village. Yvonne stayed as long as she dared but
eventually, carrying her precious radio set, she had to leave, as it was
vital that she keep London informed of what was happening. As she
hurried out of the village she was joined by a doctor, another resistant,
going in search of more medicines. He helped carry her case and together
they raced as far away from the battle as possible. They twisted and
dodged, using what shelter they could find, with their hearts in their
mouths and expecting any minute to be stopped by German soldiers and
shot. By now the firing grew intense and about midday they heard an
explosion which shook the ground, followed by a great cloud appearing
around the top of the hill. When it cleared one of the village towers had
vanished. By this they knew that the resistants must have destroyed
their arms stores to prevent capture by the enemy, and that the village
was now in German hands. Aware that she could not risk being seen
working her set, yet desperate to inform London of the position, she and
the doctor eventually took refuge in a farmhouse by the roadside, where
he was known, and Yvonne managed to send out her message. Then
they set off once again and reached safety. Later the Germans pillaged
and then levelled the village of Castelnau as a warning to future
resistance. The battle involved about 800 Germans and 150 Maquisards,
out of whom the losses were 240 Germans and 20 French.

The Maquis remnants withdrew to join another group, and Yvonne
accompanied them with her wireless as George had become one of their
leaders. She lived uncomfortably with them and became inured to
taking risks, since whenever there were Germans about, sporadic fighting occurred. Where they travelled she went also, her radio their
invaluable link, not only in planning operations but also more
particularly in arranging the vital drops of supplies of all kinds for the
Maquis.

August brought the invasion by the Americans and the Free French
on the south of France, west of Cannes. These forces quickly drove
north eventually to join up with the northern forces near Dijon in
September. Caught in this maelstrom, Yvonne became busier than ever.
At one time, she was on the plateau of Lannemezan during a German
attack. Despite the battle raging around her and being machine-gunned
and strafed from the air, she kept her head and continued sending her
messages as long as it was possible. She never took any unnecessary risks
but her coolness and courage saw her missions through successfully.

In late August 1944, when Toulouse was finally freed, Yvonne and
George rode in the place of honour at the head of the Maquis army of
over 1,000 men in a cavalcade of vehicles and people, as they swarmed

to the town square to celebrate their liberation. Suddenly in one of the side streets, amidst the cheering, a loud bang rang out from the middle of the procession. Immediately everything stopped, men fell flat on their faces or scattered in all directions, running for cover. An eerie silence fell on the once hot and crowded street. After a long pause, when nothing else happened and it became clear that this was not the action of an enemy sniper, men started to return, red-faced that they had been caught out. Then the cause became apparent. A bald tyre had burst on the vehicle carrying Yvonne and George! Laughing and shouting in relief and making jokes at their reaction, the men lifted the car bodily and the two SOE agents were swept into the square on the shoulders of their army. Thus was the city of Toulouse liberated. This must have been a great day indeed for Yvonne, to see all her efforts vindicated. At last she was free to return to England. This could have meant a long journey back, but as luck would have it, one of her last messages instructed her to meet the Chief Test Pilot from Farnborough, who was flying across to Bordeaux. She was to help him find and bring back the black box and a wheel from the latest German Heinkel Bomber — a reminder that the war was, of course, far from finished. With her help and those of her circle of friends, the parts were located. She was thus able to accept with alacrity the proffered lift, and George and she arrived back in England on 23 September 1944, along with the required spare bits and pieces.

There she was reunited with her daughter Yvette, whom she found well and happy, and that would have been the end of her story. But her service was not yet over. She had one more task to perform. In November, she accompanied the F Section Judex mission to her circuit. This consisted of a convoy of four vehicles, manned by senior members of SOE and a French liaison officer, which toured the main centres of France over a period of several months, mainly to investigate the work and fates of its agents and the French who had helped them. It was also to recover any equipment which might be needed for the Japanese war and to compensate those who had suffered badly for helping its agents. As the war was still continuing, however, its efforts were hampered by the fact that the names and decorations of those still held prisoner by the Germans had to be kept secret for fear of reprisals. Thus many who deserved the most gained the least, and others disliked the attention paid to latecomers who had sat on the fence until they saw which side was winning. Nevertheless the tour had its share of public ceremonies, though it may not, as had been hoped, have increased the goodwill for England built up by SOE and the RAF.

Yvonne, however, was pleased by the results in her area, where from a centre set up there she helped to identify those who had suffered most, and whose distress gifts of money, clothing and, particularly in agricultural areas, farm implements and seed, would serve to alleviate. After a few weeks of this work, she was able to slip away and return again to her daughter in time for Christmas, her task finally accomplished, home to safety and England at last.

She left behind her many friends and an enviable reputation. Of her work in France, Colonel Buckmaster said, 'She was always incredibly precise in her activity. She sent about 400 coded messages under conditions of great strain *without a single miscode.*' Few could match such a record!

Yvonne Cormeau

9
Still Waters Run Deep

Yolande Elsa Maria Beekman

'... a Swiss woman of thirty-two, as steady, as reliable and as unforgettable
as himself (Gustave Bieler). In the words of one of their helpers, "They
were both of the finest stuff imaginable..." They made up in steadiness
anything they lacked in fire.'

'SOE in France', M. R. D. Foot (HMSO)

Her mother described her as a gentle, quiet, self-effacing child with
a core of steel. This was the young Yolande, daughter of Jacob
Unternährer, a business man of Swiss extraction. After some years in
Paris, where Yolande was born and spent a happy uneventful childhood,
the family moved to London where Yolande had her schooling in
Hampstead Heath, and then went to a finishing college in Switzerland.
She therefore became fluent in English, German and French, which she
spoke with a slight Swiss accent; for instance it was noticed that she could
not pronounce 'huit' as a Frenchwoman would. This cosmopolitan
background produced a young girl who was good-humoured, kind and
rarely ruffled, but with a surprisingly homely English appearance. In
training she endeared herself to the men by darning their socks. She was
perhaps not such an unexpected choice for SOE — a very nice
unexceptional person, already past her 21st birthday when Hitler came to
power in Germany.

In 1940 she joined the WAAF where her dexterity fitted her for the long training as a wireless operator. Afterwards, she was posted to several Fighter Command stations before she heard about the work of SOE and volunteered for it, starting her training as an agent in February 1943. Even wireless operators, although fully trained, had to undergo further training in the more secret aspects of their work. It was at this time that she met Noor Inayat Khan and Yvonne Cormeau, who went into the field as wireless operators before her. Then just before her training finished she married a serviceman called Beekman, but marriage did not shake her determination to go into the field. However, she did not want to jump by parachute, and she got her way.

Accordingly, on the moonlit night of 18 September 1943, her Lysander set her down to a double Lysander reception arranged as part of Operation Milliner by Henri Déricourt on the same field on which Noor Inayat Khan, Diana Rowden and Cécile Lefort had earlier landed, north-east of Angers. She was intended to join the circuit of Captain Trotobas at Lille, so her first mission was to make the dangerous journey cross-country, eastwards towards the Belgian border, alone, carrying her transmitter and radio equipment with her in two suitcases.

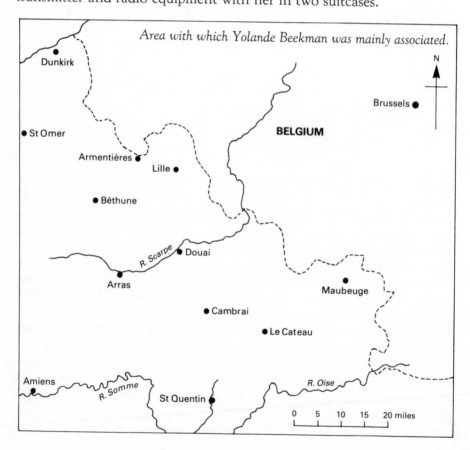

Area with which Yolande Beekman was mainly associated.

She travelled under the alias of Madame Yvonne de Chauvigny, a war widow. Nevertheless, despite her carefully tailored French clothes, her dog-eared cardboard suitcases with their terrible secret and her London forged papers, it must have taken both nerve and courage to complete a train journey in heavily occupied France with Germans all around, when newly out of training. However, her tact and patience were to be tested even further, for on arrival at her destination she was handed a signal from Baker Street, instructing her to leave Lille and carry on to St Quentin where a radio operator was needed by a new chief, Captain Gustave Bieler.

Guy, as he was known, a huge, rugged, unflappable Canadian, had broken his back when he had parachuted into France at the end of 1942, and so it had taken him some time to get his circuit, called Musician, effectively started, but although he was slowed down by his injury, he nevertheless had established a very active circuit by the time Yolande joined him. His greatest disability until her arrival was that he had to use the services of the Lille and Paris operators for his messages. Now with his own operator the wires soon started to hum.

St Quentin was an important industrial and railway centre and lay in the heart of the canal system of a large area. Through its locks and down its waterways flowed barges carrying submarine parts to the Mediterranean and engineering equipment to French and German factories making tanks, guns and aircraft. It was a gift to saboteurs, but the Germans knowing this had it very heavily policed.

On her arrival Yolande, code named Mariette, was assigned a lodging with a schoolmistress in the Avenue de la République in St Quentin. She did not remain long through fear of incriminating her hostess, and moved first to a farm and then to rooms above a café. Her transmitter, meanwhile, was lodged in the attic of a member of the local resistance in the Rue de la Fère, where she appears to have continued sending messages from October to December. For such a sensible careful operator this was a strange thing to do, as it went against all her training, and laid her open to easy detection in an area so packed with Germans. The only excuse for such a practice was that either Yolande or her chief must have considered that it was safer to keep to a known and secure place, rather than risk betrayal when seeking for new ones. This was of course a densely packed city, not a widespread rural area.

At any rate, Yolande's arrival signalled an upsurge in requests for and deliveries of explosives and arms and the havoc raised by the use of them. Railways, telephones and petrol-storage tanks were damaged, and at one point in the autumn Yolande was able to report that with the abrasive grease which would be syphoned into the lubrication points of engines, ten locomotives had been put out of action at once. The main railway line between St Quentin to Lille was also cut at least once a fortnight.

Yolande was not only involved in negotiating the demands for supplies, she was also present in the reception parties of over 20 parachute drops. Included in the consignments were Sten guns, bazookas, ammunition and magnetic limpet charges for the barges and lock gates. When these were finally and most damagingly used, free passage on the canal was stopped for several weeks. In addition she saw to the distribution of the materials, since there were several well-trained and, ultimately, well-armed Maquis groups in the Musician circuit.

At one point the circuit at Lille appealed to Musician for help when their area became too dangerous for a wireless operator. On her own initiative Yolande offered to help them, and then in even more substantial form, told them that they could use the services of a young Frenchman whom she had trained for herself, and who could use the radio whenever they needed him, since she could give him the necessary codes and had cleared him with London. The result was that the Lille circuit received the arms it so much required, dropped by the RAF to a pre-arranged ground near Paris and then brought on to Lille by lorry as part of the loads of drivers recruited for this task by the resistance.

The changes to her 'skeds' not yet having reached her, Yolande still observed the set schedules of transmissions that SOE expected in early 1943, messages being sent three times a week, at certain times and wavelengths. In the country, by constant movement, these would have been more difficult for the Germans to trace, but in the smaller area of a town it was tempting providence. To help secure her set, Yolande left certain parts of it with various friends. At the house at Rue de la Fère she would joke with the family, telling them that she would come back after the war, wearing her WAAF uniform. As she was always in ordinary clothes this would be a great treat for the family, and she would describe it from the peaked, soft-topped blue cap with its RAF winged badge, to the blue jacket and skirt, brown leather gloves and black shoes, and perhaps she would tell them some of the stories of her life as an airwoman before she joined SOE and became an honorary officer. They would laugh and she would promise that they would all celebrate the liberation together.

She was always laughing in those days, seemingly without fear and absolutely sure that France would soon be free. She was solid, reliable and seemed to have no nerves, ready to cheer the family if things were difficult for them or if, as occasionally happened, a member of the resistance was picked up by the police and there was the possibility that others might be endangered if torture made him talk. And of course there was the constant fear of German reprisals, not just for the death of one of their number but for acts of sabotage, which were increasing and so infuriating the Germans that they redoubled their efforts to find the lone pianist. Fear was always lurking in the background of the minds of most members

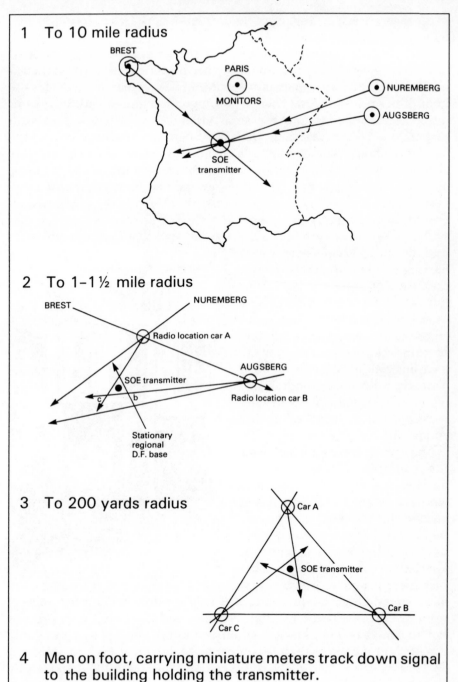

1 To 10 mile radius

BREST
PARIS
MONITORS
NUREMBERG
AUGSBERG
SOE transmitter

2 To 1–1½ mile radius

BREST
NUREMBERG
Radio location car A
AUGSBERG
SOE transmitter
Radio location car B
c b
Stationary regional D.F. base

3 To 200 yards radius

Car A
SOE transmitter
Car B
Car C

4 Men on foot, carrying miniature meters track down signal to the building holding the transmitter.

Stages in the narrowing down of SOE radio signals by German direction finders (DF). (With thanks to Lt Col P. Lorain) of the resistance, but despite her task, Yolande appeared to be untouched by it.

In the cold little attic where she worked there was a wide divan, covered in brown velvet. There she would lie, her head cradled in her mittened hands, looking down and quietly reading a book, while she waited for the hour of her transmission. Then at the appointed time she would lay out her set, throwing the end of the aerial out of the little window, and begin tapping out her messages, her dark head bent in concentration. As the lady of the house worked in a local chemist's shop, whose members were also resistance sympathizers, the house was often empty. At such times, Yolande would let herself in with a key she had been given and go up alone. This happened even on Christmas Day, usually celebrated in France, as in England, with great festivities. But this was a bleak and solitary day, made more menacing by the news that German direction-finding vans had been seen moving slowly along the streets in the neighbourhood. Worse was to follow. In the week before New Year's Day, while she was again transmitting, her hostess saw one of these closed-in vans actually pass her house. She ran to warn Yolande, who immediately broke 'off her transmission with her warning sign and packed up her equipment.

The two women hurried with the suitcases to the house of another friend of the resistance who was willing to take the risk of harbouring the set. As a further precaution however, Yolande set up another radio post in a farm at Fansommes. She also bleached her hair blonde and took on a new

A country café.

alias. In St Quentin, however, she still continued her thrice-weekly transmissions. Now the German listening and interception service was hot on her heels. They knew she was nearby and it looked as if it was only a matter of time before they caught her if she remained static for long. On 12 January 1944, men in heavy overcoats, their earphones hidden by their high turned-up collars were seen in the street outside the very house where she was transmitting. Warned by the resistance who also had eyes everywhere, she again prepared to move.

That evening before curfew, Yolande pedalled her bicycle through the frosty streets of St Quentin to the outskirts of the town, almost in the open country, to an ugly, grey-brick building standing near a canal bridge. This was the Moulin Brulé, the Burned Mill, a small, wayside café where she was now lodging. Inside coffee and drinks were served at marble-topped tables. The next day Yolande came downstairs and joined Gustave Bieler, a local mechanic and the husband and wife who owned the café. Doubtless Yolande needed to discuss moving her radio, but there were many other things and the Germans were becoming more vigilant. As they talked, two cars drew up outside. Wiping her hands on her apron, the lady of the house rose to greet her new customers, only to be confronted by the levelled pistols of the Gestapo, who immediately handcuffed all five and dragged them into the waiting cars.

It was by a strange quirk of fate that Yolande had been captured not through her work as a wireless operator, but by the information of a traitor, or maybe not even that — perhaps a man driven past endurance by torture. He belonged, probably, not even to the St Quentin circuit but to that of Prosper in Paris, which was now almost totally destroyed and had brought down so many other circuits with it. Patiently piecing the clues together, the Germans had arrived at the café on this cold January day and at one swoop caught not only the organizer of the Musician circuit but also its wireless operator, leaving it headless.

Gustave and Yolande were hurried to the Gestapo headquarters at St Quentin, where they were tortured. The Germans knew who they were and concentrated on these two. They also knew a great deal about their work and asked searching questions without getting any answers. Gustave so enraged them that he was executed within a few weeks. When Yolande was questioned she also refused to give any information and was subjected to much brutal treatment. She was also badly knocked about the face, as was observed by the chemist for whom her first hostess worked, when she was brought into his shop a few days later to ask if he knew where certain large sums of money belonging to the circuit had been hidden. Fortunately for him, he was able to convince the Germans that he was totally ignorant of the matter, and Yolande was roughly dragged away.

Her arrest was followed by those of many others in the area, a dozen or more being taken on suspicion. The day after her arrest the chemist's assistant, her first hostess, admiring her courage and taking a great risk herself, tried to get some food to Yolande but was told that she was held in an underground cell. Then a plan was drawn up by the resistance to help her escape but this was foiled at the last minute when the Germans decided to send her to Paris to the dreaded Avenue Foch, as they could get nothing out of her by their methods at St Quentin. Still refusing to co-operate she was taken to Fresnes Prison to be put into solitary confinement, and on 13 May 1944 she was sent in the convoy of

eight SOE girls, including Diana Rowden, handcuffed in pairs, to the civil
women's prison at Karlsrühe. Here crowded into a cell for two but
occupied by four women, with a spy hole in the door, Yolande had to face
a different life. At least she was free from the cruel questioning that she
had undergone and need no longer fear that by a chance word she might
betray something or someone in the resistance. Here she was treated as a
common criminal, which must have grated on her sensibilities, but she
knew that if she could attract no attention and survive the deadly
monotonous routine of the days — rising with the bell at 6.30 and going
to bed without lights at 8 pm, with only a little work, exercise or food,
mainly acorn coffee, bread and soup — she might have a chance of seeing
the end of the war after all. It must have given her hope, as well as the time
to recover from her ill-treatment. The roots of her hair, untreated, now
began to show dark beneath the blonde, and without dye she could not
cover it up in her once a fortnight shower. There was also the possibility,
on the daily exercise hour when they circled the courtyard, that she might
steal a word with one of her other SOE compatriots, and this might have
brightened the occasional day.

It was only to be a brief respite, as an interfering chief wardress one day
discovered that her SOE women were political prisoners, and were thus
being held in the wrong type of prison. As the prison was overcrowded
and she was outraged at this flouting of the rules and regulations, she
immediately raised the matter with the governor, who passed it on to the
authorities in Berlin. Consequently orders came down for the transfer of
the women. Diana Rowden had already left with one group of four in July
for Natzweiler, and now two months later Yolande was in the second
party to be sent away.

Thus on the evening of 10 September 1944, the chief wardress called at
the cells of each of them. When she reached Yolande she returned all the
personal possessions which had been confiscated when Yolande arrived
at Karlsrühe. Yolande also was informed that she would be called next
morning to be transferred to another prison. At 1.30 an elderly male
warder on night duty called her out of the cell and took her down to the
reception room, where she saw two other SOE FANY agents and Noor
Inayat Khan, who had just arrived from Pforzheim prison.

Their papers were signed and the four handcuffed girls were handed
over to three Gestapo officials — one of them a woman — who escorted
them by car to the nearest railway station. They were put into reserved
compartments of the early morning train to Munich, given window seats,
food and allowed to speak freely, their German guards having changed to
ordinary soldiers who saw nothing wrong in this. Consequently, the girls
laughed and talked, enjoying the relaxation of these precious few hours.
Late in the afternoon Yolande and the others arrived at Munich and
changed trains. Held up by an Allied air raid, the train eventually

covered the 12 or so miles to its destination by midnight.

Everything was quiet and dark as Yolande picked up her suitcase and trudged with the others up the shadowy hill to the walls of her new camp. The only movement was the searchlights sweeping row upon row of huts silent as the grave. She must have been wondering what type of agricultural work she had been allocated, as that was what she had been told she was to do, and she must have been nearly dropping with fatigue after such a long, eventful day. The handing over of the prisoners, arriving at such an untimely hour, was fortunately brief and she was given a small windowless single cell like the others. She must have thought it a great relief after the overcrowded life at Karlsrühe. But there was little time for thought as sleep soon claimed her.

At dawn next day, she was awakened brusquely. In short order she again joined her companions as they were marched out to a small sand-strewn courtyard, a smoke-blackened building with a large chimney along one side. When she saw the waiting German officers, smart in their uniforms, she must have immediately realized the reason for all this ceremony. One stepped forward and read out the formal notice of their execution. There was no doubt or delay. Taking her nearest companion's hand in her firm clasp and showing no sign of fear she walked forward and then knelt as she was instructed. The shadow of her executioner fell on the sand before her and she shut her eyes. This was the end. Then all was silence.

Even the officers present at the executions were impressed by the cool courage of the girls as they met their fate. They died, holding hands in pairs, from a single shot through the back of the neck. Then their bodies were removed to the crematorium behind them and reduced to ashes. The day was 12 September 1944, the camp was Dachau, and Yolande was 32 years of age.

It is quite likely that even while she died, her executioners knew that their own days were numbered. The Allied armies were almost at the German frontier and large parts of France, Belgium and Holland had been freed. For those Germans who looked at the war realistically, it was only a matter of time before their ultimate defeat. That may be the reason why these women had to die so late in the day, when it might be thought that their hostage value could have been greater and more reason to keep them alive. It could have been that the authorities in Berlin or the retreating Gestapo in France feared these girls who had all been part of or in contact with circuits penetrated by German intelligence. Some of their radio posts were still controlled or worked by the Germans who hoped not to be unmasked because of the amount of misleading information they could feed to London. These women were therefore in possession of information potentially damaging to German intelligence. Was this the reason that they had to die — that they knew too much?

10
She Who Must Be Obeyed

Cécile Pearl Witherington

'... Le vivant exemple de l'abnégation et du plus pur patriotisme. Toujours
sur les routes, exposant sa vie sans cesse.... elle a été par son calme et son
sang-froid, un bel exemple pour nos combattants du maquis.'
                                            Citation for Legion D'Honneur, 1946

It was like some absurd guessing game.
'Do you know Jean?' Pearl asked the man in the hot, tiny room
upstairs.
'No.' His eyes half closed.
'You must know André.'
'No.' He wasn't trying to help her at all.
'What about Octave?' He was a well-known local farmer, active in the
resistance and she was sure that he would be known, but she couldn't
seem to get through to this man.
'No.'
At her wit's end, Pearl could sense hostility and suspicion coming
towards her in waves. She felt the hair on the back of her neck begin to
prickle with a warning of danger. Surnames are not usually mentioned
but she took a chance and blurted out.
'But you must know him — Octave Chantraine. He was imprisoned
shortly after I landed on his dropping ground.' She was getting frantic.
Suddenly the man's face changed, and she realized he must be Robert. He

took a deep breath, then he raised his voice: 'Ah Chantraine! Yes I do
know him.'

There was a scuffling in the room beyond and suddenly four armed
young men spilled into the room, and started shaking hands. It was then
that Pearl realized how close to death she had come, for if her last
question had failed, they would all surely have shot her as a German spy.
She had never been in greater danger than here, from her own people of
the resistance.

It had been a difficult assignment from the beginning. She had been
handed a task — a most delicate one — of fetching money from people
who neither knew her nor she them, in an area where she was a stranger
and therefore a suspect. All the information she had been given was to say
that she had come on behalf of 'Robert'. Not much help!

Sometimes money was needed by the resistance. It could bribe, buy,
pay back or help a clandestine organization in many different ways.
Though SOE members handled large quantities, they rarely used it for
themselves. On 5 April 1944 three agents had landed with a large sum
that had been urgently requested by Pearl's organizer. As they had come
down outside his area and were destined for a circuit even further away,

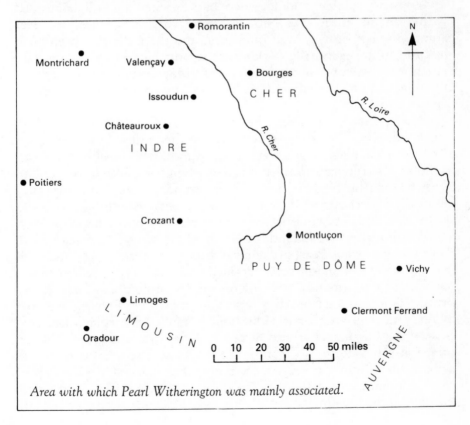

Area with which Pearl Witherington was mainly associated.

they had no time to see him, and therefore had left the money with a contact in a safe house for someone to collect, but they had neglected to give a password.

Having duly arrived at the country café where she had been sent, Pearl had come face to face with a woman who told her that 'Robert' was in another town just then, but would be back if she called again next day. Sure enough when she returned as appointed, she was shown into a large room occupied by another man. The peculiar expression on the face of the woman who showed her in, had prepared her for trouble. After a few unsatisfactory questions he had led Pearl up a little twisty staircase at the back of the shop into an upstairs room. This was when the questions had begun, each trying to establish some contact with the other without any success until Pearl's final question and its result. That sort of work could be given to a courier, though this had been more tricky than usual, but then Pearl was no ordinary courier.

Cécile Pearl Witherington was one of the notable successes of the WAAF sent to France, in that she far exceeded what was expected of her. This should not have been perhaps so surprising of a girl from a family whose ancestor had distinguished himself in an earlier age of hand-to-hand combat and long-ago battle, when he still continued fighting on his knees after both legs were cut from under him. Her parents, though British, lived in France, and there she had been born and brought up, eventually working at the British Embassy in Paris. Her French was therefore impeccable. Then in May 1940, the normal tenor of her life was rudely shattered by the lightning advance of the German panzers into France.

Too late, London ordered the evacuation of the Embassy and all British subjects. They only served to swell the endless mass of French and Belgian families in cars, carts and on foot, who blocked the roads to the northern ports, a target for enemy bombers, and an obstacle to the manoeuvring of their own armies. At Cherbourg harbour, they found themselves stranded, overtaken by events. Anything that could sail or steam was at Dunkirk ferrying the remains of the fleeing French and British forces to mainland Britain. Nothing was left to rescue them. After a useless wait, Pearl broke away from the official party and with her widowed mother and sisters decided to find a port elsewhere. They struck out for Normandy, meeting on the way a number of bewildered British soldiers cut off from their units and stranded in France. Sheltered by one and then another friendly French family, the women not only escaped the Germans but also helped to hide these stragglers. Though comparatively safe in Normandy the family still sought to return to Britain, and finding no transport there, they took the risky step of crossing France, north to south, to the port of Marseilles, right across the path of the invading armies. With incredible luck they survived and found a safe place to take cover while they tried to find a boat to take them to Gibraltar.

Marseilles had always been a busy harbour, running legal and illegal shipping, which it suited the German book to continue for its many uses. Here, too, the earliest French resistance groups had begun to form, and it was Pearl's good fortune to contact one in her search for help. Eventually with their connivance, she and her family escaped and trekked through Spain and Portugal before they at last found a boat to take them to Britain, landing at Greenock, in the far north near Glasgow, seven months after they had left Paris.

From here Pearl went to London and in 1941 was given a post as the personal assistant to the Director of Allied Air Co-operation and Foreign Liaison at Air Ministry, where she still felt her talents stifled and longed for more active work. All this changed for her one day, however, when a former school friend, Flight Lieutenant Maurice Southgate, also

Map of Europe, September 1940.

at the Directorate of Allied Co-operation and Foreign Liaison, decided
himself to go to work against the Germans in France and applied to
SOE. Inspired by his example, Pearl worked her way through the
hierarchy of Air Ministry requesting her transfer and met with a blank
refusal. Her services were more valuable at home. At length, she took
matters into her own hands and approached Baker Street direct. No
doubt they were immediately struck by her experience, her fluency and
her determination — she was a natural for their work — and they agreed
to take her. Gleefully she returned to Air Ministry and won her release.
It was June 1943.

Missing out the period in Scotland, she did the rest of the normal
training of a courier, except that she also did the special explosives and
weapons course. When she was ready she was prepared to be sent to the
province of the Auvergne in the centre of France. Here she faced a
difficult two-fold task, to be a courier called Marie to the organizer of
the Stationer circuit based at Clermont Ferrand, and liaison officer to
a touchy French Colonel commanding a sizeable Maquis group in the
Puy de Dôme *département*.

When everything was ready, she
had the bitter disappointment of
boarding her aircraft, flying over
her dropping zone — so near and
yet so far — waiting for the signal
to drop out of the aircraft, and
then feeling the plane turn again
and head for Britain. This
happened not once but twice,
each an aborted sortie, until she
must have felt that nothing would
go right. But on the 23 September

*Montrichard. A typical town in Maurice
Southgate's circuit, where Pearl worked
in her earlier months.*

1943, on the third attempt, she at last heard the command 'Go', and felt
the wind whistle past her face as her parachute opened above her. Even
so, this landing was not quite according to plan, as security conditions
had forced her to be dropped in another zone of a different region.

Now, finally, she came face to face with the organizer with whom she
was to work so closely during her time in France. He was in fact the man
she already knew, Maurice Southgate. Known as Hector, he was
developing a circuit from the Indre, almost to the Pyrenees, and forming
good relations with the Wheelwright and Scientist circuits. Another
unexpected friend ready to welcome her at the farm to which Maurice
now took her was Henri Cornioley, whom she had known in her Paris
days. Since then he had soldiered against the Germans, become a
prisoner of war, escaped and now led an underground camp loyal to
de Gaulle in Maurice's sector. Maurice was willing to provide help to

any who opposed the Germans, whatever the type of person or his political motives. But just now the meeting of two young people, who had lost one another for four years, had nothing to do with politics and everything to do with delighted reunion.

Pearl soon found that Maurice was constantly on the move — not surprising with such a far-flung circuit to maintain. He also inspired enthusiasm in everyone with whom he came into contact, expecting as much commitment and hard work from others as he did from himself, giving little thought to his own safety and welfare. He already had one reliable courier, a woman who had parachuted in with him, followed a few months later by a wireless operator, the unflappable aristocratic-looking Amédée Maingard from Mauritius, a French-speaking British island in the Indian Ocean. Now Pearl came to make up a quartet of SOE agents.

One of her first tasks was to win over the French Maquis Commander by a mixture of charm and ability. These forces, numbering about 1,000, were mostly ragged and unarmed, with more patriotism than discipline, mainly young men avoiding forced labour drafts and with few arms save for RAF weapon drops. Part of her work was to carry messages for London to send supplies and another was to restrain the men from unwise actions and foolhardy bravery. Seeing her wheeling her bicycle into their bleak camp kept up their morale and made them feel that they were not forgotten by the outside world.

Her journeys became longer and took her over large areas. One of the big coups of her early days was in progressing the signals flurrying back and fore between Maurice and London, pinpointing and arranging for the destruction of the huge Michelin rubber and tyre factory at Clermont-Ferrand by a massive RAF bombing raid. Yet another role was to work out co-ordinates for suitable sabotage targets and the all-important dropping zones for supplies and agents. Then of course there was the delicate work of collecting groups of supporters to form reception parties, so that they would reach the places at the right times and have the means to spirit away whatever arrived, very often under the very noses of the watchful Germans. Her work — their work — was extremely dangerous and not always successful. The penalties for discovery were deadly.

On 17 October, less than a month after she arrived, she watched Maurice climb on to a plane taking him back to Britain. Baker Street had insisted that he return home for a rest and rebriefing. Pearl and her circuit were left headless to carry on as best they could. It was then, imperceptibly, that the reins of leadership seemed to slip into her hands. Busier than ever, her cold train journeys increased and at other times her bicycle wheels seemed to fly over the lanes. Winter closed in. Mud froze in ruts, pools iced over, the wind cut like a knife. There was sleet to drive against her labouring pedals, and snow to block her wheels. It was a hard, bitterly cold winter and she suffered for it. But still the momentum kept up. More supplies started to fall from the skies. Food, clothes, and some arms for the Maquis and the waiting French saboteurs. She plotted with Henri Cornioley, now often by her side, the best places to blow up railway lines or cut telegraph wires. Then off she would go to warn this group or that what to do. When some escaped airmen were passed along to her area, she made the arrangements to hide them from the Germans until they could be passed safely to an escape line. There was no time for rest and little for food, which was in any case scarce.

Then in January 1944, rested and refreshed, Maurice Southgate returned, very pleased at how things had run in his absence and bursting with news and new ideas. Though no dates or places were known, the invasion of Europe was a certainty and that not too far ahead. Sad to say also, the rising tide brought to the fore political disagreements and quarrels amongst the French. Pearl had her work cut out trying to pacify and conciliate the complicated protagonists. Perhaps someone of less tact, steadfastness and personality would not have succeeded, but she did.

While these negotiations were going on, Pearl already knew that other negotiations were being carried out with London, which had ordered Maurice and his first courier to return to England. With the long-awaited D-Day drawing near neither wanted to miss it, and they pleaded hard with Baker Street to be allowed to remain to see their work to fruition. At length SOE agreed to allow Maurice, as Organizer, to stay, but the Gestapo were hot on the trail of his first courier and she must return. So on the moonlit night of 9 April, the same Lysander that brought Philippe de Vomécourt for the Ventriloquist circuit, picked her up, leaving Pearl and Amédée Maingard as Maurice's chief courier and wireless operator, for by now he had others to help him, though not from SOE.

But recruiting for the resistance, however careful, could not eliminate the risk of infiltration by a German spy or V man — a paid, reliable, French collaborator. Thus it was that only three weeks later, Maurice Southgate, hurrying to a meeting at the house of an assistant wireless operator in Montluçon, forgot that simplest of precautions, to check for a danger signal, and was picked up by the Gestapo, ending up at Buchenwald. On that day Pearl and Amédée should have also attended, but Pearl slightly concerned at Amédée's tired appearance, and herself feeling far from well, suggested that as it was a beautiful sunny first of May, they should take the day off and go for a picnic. This uncharacteristic but well-earned few hours of leisure saved them. However, they were now faced with again running the circuit alone and at a most crucial time. They therefore very practically decided to split up Stationer's large area, leaving Wheelwright to look after the far south entirely. Pearl took over the northern half of the Indre, covering the Indre, Loire and Cher Valleys, calling her circuit Wrestler, while Amédée took over the area south-east of hers and called it Shipwright.

Having made the arrangements, she set off on several very dangerous journeys over the length of the old circuit, with several narrow escapes from Germans flushed with the success of Maurice's capture, to warn members of what had happened and of their new plans. Only after this major upheaval had settled could she start furthering Maurice's ideas and developing them. It is to her credit that matters continued so smoothly.

A view of Crozant in Pearl's later circuit.

More agents for all parts of France arrived in her dropping zones. Indeed F Section sent in 16 agents to her reception parties in April and May 1944 alone. Weapons and supplies had already been sanctioned by Churchill at the end of January 1944, so that the RAF and USAAF were able vastly to increase the tonnage of their parachutages. She was now receiving more explosives for her local saboteurs, and arms and money for her local Maquisards.

Strangely, she was almost caught napping when the Allies invaded Normandy. On 5 June 1944 she knew from BBC messages broadcast on the radio that D-Day was about to begin, but she was without any detailed instructions since her only local radio operator had been forced to go into hiding after being nearly caught by the Gestapo. She and Henri rightly concluded that the best they could do to hamper the defending German troops most at this stage was by cutting all available road, rail and telegraph communications in her sector. Though she only had a working handful of men, her efforts were so successful in slowing down reinforcements that the Germans put a price of one million francs on her head, and her face, with its obviously English looks, decorated placards everywhere. They recognized that she was now the organizer of her circuit, but no one ever betrayed her, although the price the population paid for her men's acts of sabotage was wretched. So effective were the rail dislocations caused by Pearl and Amédée in their areas that they could claim no less than 800 separate hold-ups on the system during June alone. This was important as the main lines from Bordeaux and Toulouse to Paris and therefore the Normandy battle area lay through their territory, and so also did access to the bridges over the river Loire, many destroyed by the Allied air forces, that might have been used by

German divisions marching north. One such, the *Das Reich*, mainly based at Toulouse in the south, was ordered up to Normandy after the Allied landings. The journey north to south should have taken about three days, instead of the nearly three weeks it actually took. This was the division which will always be infamous for the dreadful massacre of the villagers of Oradour-sur-Glane. It was no doubt venting some of its frustration at its men and tanks being held up by railway sabotage, and its final enforced march north being subject to incessant guerilla attacks.

On 11 June 1944, Pearl and 150 men — hastily armed civilians — were caught in the woods at Taille de Ruine, near Romorantin, by a force of 2,500 German troops, tanks and artillery. Fighting for their lives, mainly in concealed pockets, Pearl's forces resisted heroically throughout the long day, themselves losing only 24 men to the Germans 86. At one point Pearl, like all good commanders involved in the strategy and planning but not herself taking part in the fighting, was herself cornered, and dived into a field of ripening corn. There she was forced to remain for many hours, burned up by the scorching sun, while the Germans fired hopefully into the field which they imagined contained a number of her forces. She hardly dared breathe, knowing that her position would be given away by the swaying corn around. Instead she turned this to account by moving with patient and agonising slowness towards the other end of the field, in co-ordination with the breeze as it stirred the heads of the corn above her. Her patience paid off and she escaped. After many hours the Germans broke off the action and prepared to move on, but she had achieved her object of holding them up, inflicting casualties and diverting their route. On the other hand, they took heavy reprisals in the district.

Nevertheless the Germans had succeeded in badly damaging Pearl's group and she had to work hard restoring its shaken morale. German reactions, however, had roused such hatred around that more Maquis recruits flowed in than Pearl could manage. Soon she found herself responsible for supplying and arming over 2,000 men, whom she used in continuing guerrilla attacks on other German columns as they passed through her area to the battle front.

She recorded, 'It was not my official mission to command guerilla fighters, but events were beyond me and I had to make the best of my modest capabilities.' Modest *she* might be, but not her capabilities! She split her Maquis into four groups. She saw to it that they were well organized with their own territories of control, their own officials being responsible for different duties, such as sabotage, supplies and reception parties, and with a sub-commander who reported directly to her. Henri Cornioley was in one group as reception specialist and he organized over 40 successful parachute drops. She also found that some of the weapons they received were new and unfamiliar to the men, so she had to act as their instructor. She also played an active part in their work, even going with the men to lay charges against the sides of the railway sleepers and bridges, mainly on the Toulouse-Paris railway line, to show them by example. This did her no harm, as she was soon seen to be so competent that her local standing grew, the men laughingly calling her Lieutenant Pauline. In all these varied duties Pearl showed exceptional ability. She was an excellent, clear-headed organizer with such powers of leadership, personality and skill that she could, for the most part manage most situations to her advantage. This was no easy matter for a foreigner, and a woman at that, to control the troops she in effect commanded. But apart from the willing support of Henri Cornioley, she also could rely on the French Colonel of the Maquis if there were any difficulties. For the rest her wisdom carried her through what would have been for any a trying period.

Not satisfied with her other actions, she also ensured that one of the five signals regiments in France, based on Orléans, was never able to restore its telephone communications with its High Command. As fast as they were repaired, they were sabotaged, and in fact it never restored the link before it withdrew to Germany, forcing it to resort to wireless contact, easily picked up by its enemies. In late June, Pearl was able to bring her wireless operator out of hiding and resume her contact with London, which produced 26 more parachute drops by mass formations of planes and eventually, at the end of July, sent a French regular officer to take over the command of her Maquis, which had now expanded even further to 3,500 men.

By mid August, the Germans in her area and some tank units of crack troops were trying to withdraw eastwards towards their own borders, being between the advancing allied troops to the north and the newly invaded south. As they crossed into her circuit they were attacked by the Maquis, notably at Valençay, and their petrol supplies were destroyed by Allied bombing from information supplied by her own men. Eventually on 11 September 1944, this hammering by the combined forces of the Maquis from various areas brought about the surrender at Issoudun of one German army of nearly 20,000 men who, however, preferred to hand themselves over to the Americans rather than risk falling into the hands of the avenging French. This was Pearl's crowning achievement, and she was proud to have made her own contribution towards it.

After the war Pearl became Madame Cornioley and settled to a quiet family life in Paris, but she left golden friendships and memories behind her, of the days when she fought with the Maquis of the Indre and helped to drive the Germans out of France.

11
The Lucky One

Anne-Marie Walters

'Things were not so easy as during the first days... In Dordogne, the Fourth Republic had fallen, and the population suffered pitiless reprisals... People were getting discouraged and morale dropped lower than at any time during the days of the underground. This was not peculiar to the Dordogne alone. The fighting on the distant beaches of Normandy seemed to make no progress. The airborne landing in the south-west was definitely not going to happen. The war in western Europe seemed to threaten to be a long one.'

'Moondrop to Gascony', Anne-Marie Walters (Macmillan)

Everything seemed to finish well for Anne-Marie Walters, from the flight of the first Halifax bomber that was to take her to France, from which she escaped after it had crash-landed in the fog in a field in Kent badly bruising and shaking all but her determination to try again, to the second flight which went smoothly. The same happened in France with many imminent disasters that were averted at the last moment. As sailors at sea believe that some captains and the ships they sail are born lucky, so it seemed to be with Anne-Marie.

She was born in Geneva of a family part British and part French. Her father, an Oxford don, worked for the League of Nations, ultimately becoming Deputy Secretary-General at the beginning of the war. Her education at a boarding school in Paris gave her a pronounced accent of

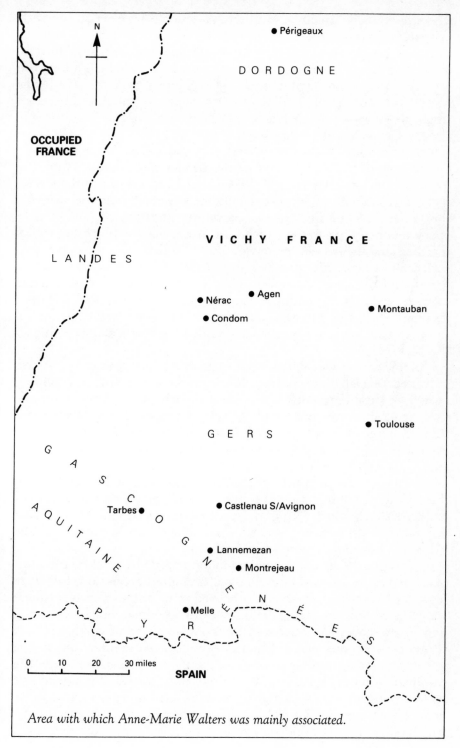

Area with which Anne-Marie Walters was mainly associated.

that area, but she usually spent her long school summer holidays with her parents in the south of France, playing on the sun-drenched beaches with her young sister 'Sissi' and other children, her days happily unclouded by the advancing shadow of war. Back in Britain during the war, she became an airwoman in 1941, entering SOE in 1943. After nearly five months of training she was ready to join George Starr's circuit in south-west France as a courier, where Yvonne Cormeau was already George's wireless operator.

She and an explosives expert landed by parachute in a marshy field on the edge of the wooded area of the Landes some distance from the town of Condom on 4 January 1944. As she came down in the star-lit night, surrounded by 23 assorted containers swaying from their rigging, she found that the lines of her parachute had tangled, and it only opened properly just in time for her to land safely. Among other things that her aircraft had delivered earlier were leaflets and carrier pigeons, each with its own little parachute to its box. The reception party, when they found her, greeted her with glee. 'But this must be Mademoiselle Colette. We've been waiting for you for so long.' They took her to a decrepit farm, deep in straw and manure, for hot acorn coffee and a snatched nap, while a two-oxen cart trundled patiently along picking up the packages.

The tide of war was not turning everywhere in favour of the Allies. Italy had officially surrendered although there was still stiff fighting ahead, and the longed-for landings on French soil to help the people throw off the German yoke had not yet taken place. In his Wheelwright circuit George Starr was amassing and secreting vast stores of arms and explosives against that day, as well as conducting useful sabotage forays, and collaborating with the secret army in an advanced state of organization under a French officer. Anne-Marie was to help connect all these vital activities, acting as a link with all the widespread members of the resistance which George did not have time to reach. Another vital role was to help escapees to reach the Pyrénées, so that they could be led across by guides to the safety of Spain.

At daylight she set off, partly by foot and partly by truck to the town of Condom, in what seemed almost a triumphal procession. Everyone seemed to know that she had just arrived from Britain and everywhere she stopped she was asked in for a drink of wine, which she felt it impolite to refuse. She arrived in Condom at lunchtime on the cobbled streets between the high old houses, white in the midday sun, feeling rather drunk and needing to sleep off the effects. A few hours later she wakened to meet Le Patron, as George Starr was locally known. He spoke in broken sentences and the state of his fingernails showed that he had been tortured. Chain-smoking himself, he gave her a.lecture on not smoking in public and warned that he never expected her to make

Above left *Colonel Maurice Buckmaster was the head of SOE's F Section from November 1941 and was based in London.* (Weidenfeld & Nicolson)

Organisers

Above right *Major Claude de Baissac —* **David** *— was organizer of the Bordeaux Scientist circuit for which Mary Herbert* **(Chapter 4)** *worked as courier. He later organized the Scientist circuit around Chartres to which Phyllis Latour* **(Chapter 15)** *was wireless operator.* (Mrs C. Pappe)

Below *Major Roger Landes —* **Aristide**. *As wireless operator of Scientist in Bordeaux, Roger worked with Mary Herbert* **(Chapter 4)** *in the early days of her mission. Later he returned to revive the circuit, renamed Actor, and is here seen planning and giving instructions to leading members of his resistance group on the day before D Day, while Mary was still in hiding.* (Major R. Landes)

Left *After the war, Claude de Baissac, with his wife, former courier Mary Herbert* (**Chapter 4**)*, their young daughter Claudine, and Lise de Baissac, Claude's sister and organizer of Artist, an interconnecting circuit based at Poitiers. Later Lise assisted Claude and his wireless operator Phyllis Latour* (**Chapter 15**) *with the new Scientist circuit in the north.* (Mrs L. Villameur)

Below left *Major Francis Suttill —* **Prosper** *— organizer of the Paris circuit. One of his sub-circuits around Le Mans was organized by Henri Garry* (**Cinema** *and later* **Phono**) *to which Noor Inayat Khan* (**Chapter 5**) *was sent as wireless operator.* (Weidenfeld & Nicolson)

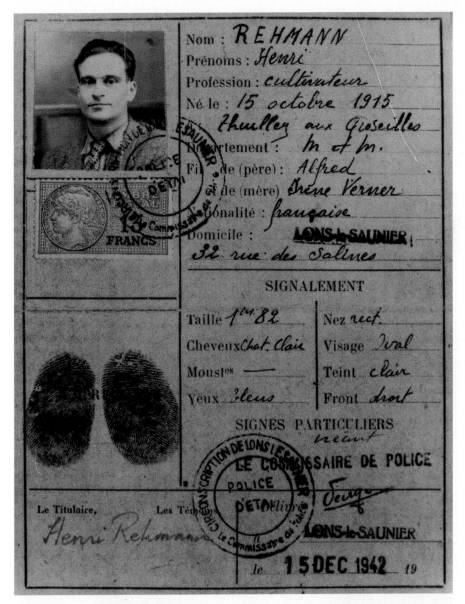

Left *Lieutenant Colonel George Starr* — **Hilaire** — *organizer of the vast Wheelwright circuit stretching from the Dordogne to the Pyrénées. Yvonne Cormeau* **(Chapter 8)** *was sent to him as his wireless operator and Anne-Marie Walters* **(Chapter 11)** *as his courier.* (Weidenfeld & Nicolson)

Above *Captain Harry Rée* — **César**. *This is one of the forged identity cards used by Harry Rée in France, where he was organizer of Stockbroker in Franche Comté. Here he poses as Henri Rehmann, a farmer from Alsace. Diana Rowden* **(Chapter 6)** *worked as courier to Acrobat, one of his sub-circuits led by John Starr* **(Bob)** *in the Jura.* (Weidenfeld & Nicolson)

Above left *Captain Gustave Bieler —* **Guy** *— organizer of the Musician circuit. Yolande Beekman* **(Chapter 9)** *became his wireless operator.*

Above right *Squadron Leader Maurice Southgate —* **Hector** *— organizer of Stationer in the Auvergne, to whom Pearl Witherington* **(Chapter 10)** *was sent as one of his couriers.*

Below left *Major Philippe de Vomécourt —* **Major St Paul** *— organizer of the Ventriloquist circuit in the Sologne. Muriel Byck* **(Chapter 14)** *became one of his wireless operators.*

Below right *Lt Col Francis Cammaerts —* **Roger** *— organizer of the huge Jockey circuit in south-east France. Cécile Lefort* **(Chapter 7)** *and Christine Granville* **(Chapter 18)** *were both sent to act as his couriers.* (All photos, Weidenfeld & Nicolson)

Imprisonment

Left *84 Avenue Foch, the five-storey building commandeered by German Counter-Intelligence. Part was used to interrogate British SOE agents, who were kept in cells on the fifth, attic floor.* (Author's Collection)

Below *SS Sturmbann-Führer (Major) Hans Josef Kieffer (ringed, left). Chief of the SD IVE at 84 Avenue Foch, he controlled the interrogation of all British agents brought there. He sent Noor Inayat Khan* (**Chapter 5**), *Diana Rowden* (**Chapter 6**) *and Yolande Beekman* (**Chapter 9**) *to prisons near Karlsrühe. SS Sonder-Führer Ernst Vogt (ringed, right) a former bank clerk, part Swiss, was employed as Kieffer's interrogator and interpreter because he spoke both French and English. He was greatly impressed by Noor Inayat Khan's goodness* (**Chapter 5**).

Left *A small solitary confinement cell with leg fetters on the floor and grille in the door through which food was passed to the prisoner. It had no direct light.* **(Chapter 5)** (Imperial War Museum)

Top right *Part of the Concentration Camp at Dachau, in Bavaria, north of Munich. In common with other Concentration Camps, it had its usual accompaniment of searchlights sweeping along the rows of serried huts, electrified barbed-wire fences, concrete walls, watchtowers with machine guns, as well as crematoria. Its inmates were usually worked to death.* (Wing Commander M. Turner)

Middle right *The crowded sleeping bunks in a typical Concentration Camp hut.* (Imperial War Museum)

Right *The crematorium ovens at Dachau (with memorial wreaths).* (Wing Commander M. Turner)

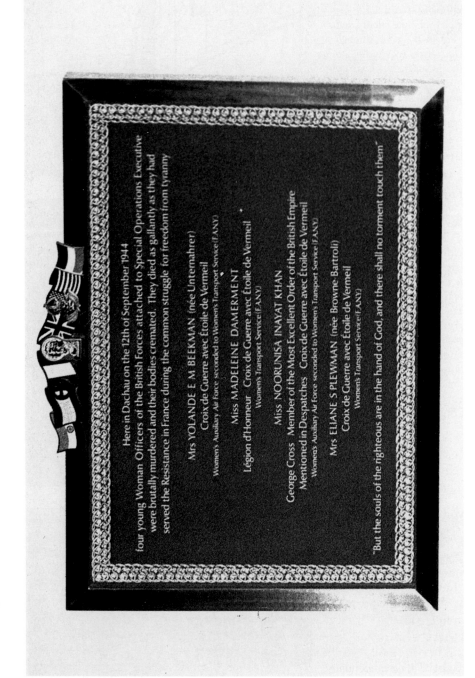

The text on the plaque reads:

Here in Dachau on the 12th of September 1944 four young Woman Officers of the British Forces attached to Special Operations Executive were brutally murdered and their bodies cremated. They died as gallantly as they had served the Resistance in France during the common struggle for freedom from tyranny

Mrs YOLANDE E M BEEKMAN (née Unternahrer)
Croix de Guerre avec Étoile de Vermeil
Women's Auxiliary Air Force seconded to Women's Transport Service (FANY)

Miss MADELEINE DAMERMENT
Légion d'Honneur   Croix de Guerre avec Étoile de Vermeil
Women's Transport Service (FANY)

Miss NOORUNISA INAYAT KHAN
George Cross   Member of the Most Excellent Order of the British Empire
Mentioned in Despatches   Croix de Guerre avec Étoile de Vermeil
Women's Auxiliary Air Force seconded to Women's Transport Service (FANY)

Mrs ELIANE S PLEWMAN (née Browne-Bartroli)
Croix de Guerre avec Étoile de Vermeil
Women's Transport Service (FANY)

"But the souls of the righteous are in the hand of God, and there shall no torment touch them"

Memorial Plaque at Dachau. (Wing Commander M. Turner)

the same mistake twice. Shown her identity papers he rejected all but two, saying that new ones must be made, but she must watch that she did not carry two sets with different names at the same time in case of searches.

Next day she walked self-consciously around the town, thinking that she had British agent written all over her face, a feeling that it took three weeks to overcome. In the afternoon the Patron sent her off by car with a reckless driver to her future lodging in a farmhouse where, because of her accent, she was to pose as a Parisian student recovering from pneumonia. Everything in the house was thoroughly waxed and new, except there was no toilet, bushes behind the hen house having to serve instead. Otherwise her bedroom with its frilly curtains and yellow eiderdown was comfortably not to say luxuriously furnished and the family — a typical Gascon farmer and his wife, grandmother and son of Anne-Marie's age — made her one of themselves, discreetly avoiding awkward questions. Meals were generous, despite prevailing rationing. She had been lucky again!

The following days were a whirl, trying out her new black-market bicycle, going to the Saturday market with the family, where she purchased some sabots, and visiting with the Patron various contacts and leaders of the resistance movement in several towns. Here she saw her first German soldier, whom she thought very sloppy, plain clothes men whom she recognized as Gestapo, and a film-star-like mink-coated woman who headed the Agen Gestapo and was notorious for her tortures. She also heard of the arrest of a suspect by the Gestapo, a 17 year old boy, who had died of their treatment that day, a frightening reminder of her own danger!

Soon her work as a courier began. She learned to drive in the hair-raising French style, mainly in vehicles with charcoal-powered 'gazo' (or gazogène) as the French mockingly nicknamed any makeshift power source which they were forced to use for their transport, since only the Germans had petrol for their Citröens. She used cars, trains, her bicycle and crowded local buses. She sometimes had to chase far afield after busy members of the circuit to deliver and pick up her messages. She met people of all kinds, shapes, sizes and walks of life who were members of the resistance — a butcher, a spare parts shopkeeper, a womanizing spiv, a communist, a second-hand-clothes dealer, a wine merchant, a girl whose husband had escaped to England and a Jew.

Back in Condom she made friends with the Agen bus driver, who may have guessed her work as he always let her off before the bus stop where there were often Germans inspecting papers. He kept her a seat beside him, thus avoiding the crush in the bus but giving her a hot rear from the engine and a cold nose from a broken window.

She spent several nights away from the farm on errands and then, as if in support of her cover story, she went down with a hacking cough and

high temperature. The doctor was called and the family nursed her
devotedly. In four days she was up but took several more days before she
was well. The Patron visited her almost daily to keep her informed of
what went on in the circuit, to put her in the picture and help outline
the scope of her work, but he gave her very little opportunity for
personal initiative and freedom of action, something which was increasingly to irritate her. It was at this time that she learned about another
facet of her duties, helping in the escape routes of prisoners on the run.

Just recently there had been a mass break-out from the prison at Eysses
paid for dearly by the shooting of a number of French hostages, some
being members of the resistance. When George heard that some of the
escapees were members of SOE, he sent Anne-Marie to Agen to arrange
transport and then to travel the hundred miles to Tarbes to alert guides
to take them over the Pyrénées. There were difficulties. The guides were
already escorting a party of Americans over and would not be able to
take the new party just yet, which meant that George would have to find
the escapees safe houses around Fourcés for much longer than usual.
Another difficulty arose when news was received that a trainload of SS
had arrived on the previous day to find and eliminate the resistants in
the district. Evidently communists had killed a number of German
soldiers on the streets of Agen by daylight, but the consequent heavy
reprisals harmed the resistance more than the communists.

The Germans intended setting up road blocks to all the town
entrances, and the only way to avoid them was to move the escapees
through the town before the barriers were set up. Anne-Marie was sent
on her bicycle to meet the truckload of prisoners on the road near Nérac
to make sure the way was clear of Germans and then cycle ahead into
the town to warn of any roadblocks. Fifteen minutes later, when she
rejoined them, her bicycle and four bags of charcoal were loaded onto
the truck, Anne-Marie herself being squeezed into the back with the 15
men to cheer them up and relieve the tension. Just before reaching the
bridge that spanned the river out of Agen, they were warned that the
French police had set up a barrier and were searching all cars, but that
evening they were to be replaced by Germans. 'Okay,' said one of their
two drivers, a policeman with a chubby pink face, 'I can deal with
them...' The ex-prisoners did not feel so certain! However, with half an
hour to the German hand-over, their policeman driver got them
through the barrier in two minutes.

When everyone could breathe again, Anne-Marie swapped stories,
hearing about their harsh prison life and the fear of deportation to
Germany that had made them prefer the risk of escape, although already
over half their number had been recaptured. The gazo had its limits
however, and on the next hill came to a halt until everyone climbed out
and pushed it. 'Won't it be fun if this happens in a town,' observed one

of the prisoners. He was right, it did, on a hill in Nérac, but their driver did Trojan service with the gears and they moved like a snail to the top. All seemed well until they saw Milice at another roadblock to the suspension bridge out of the town. They were waved down and the police driver tried his guile again, but the Milice checking them wanted to examine his cargo. As the guard stepped away to consult a colleague, the driver put the van into gear and moved off. 'Stop!' yelled the Milice. 'Lie flat,' shouted their driver. As the van gathered speed they heard a few scattered shots behind them, but the Milice had been caught by surprise and the van got away.

At Fourcés, Anne-Marie retrieved her bicycle and rode ahead to check

the way and their destinations and learned that they had just missed a troop of Miliciens. An hour later they parked at a lonely barn on a hill, where they could eat and sleep. Anne-Marie left them next day, when they would be dispersed to safe houses until ready to proceed to the Pyrénées, armed with special road licences brought by Anne-Marie on her ever-ready bicycle.

The old bridge at Nérac, the town where Anne-Marie nearly lost her prisoners.

Later she again joined the men on the road between Lannemezan and Montréjeau, this time in a covered truck with a powerful petrol engine. Their driver assured his men that all would be well as he carried some hand grenades to manage any troubles. Their next hostess saw them fed and properly clothed for their long mountain trek before Anne-Marie left them, her mission done. With her bicycle on board, her driver raced the 75 miles to Condom in one and a half hours, the grenades bouncing merrily in the back and chickens scattered over the road, as he zig-zagged around corners. They discovered the truck was wonderful except for its defective brakes!

Another escape mission was to accompany a French police inspector to the Pyrénées. He had worked for the resistance in Paris, Grenoble and Agen, but now the Gestapo net was closing around him, so he had to be sent to safety as he was endangering not only himself but also the circuit. On the way to the railway station he confessed to concern over the fact that he carried a gun and two identity cards. One was a false civil card to show the Gestapo, the other was his true police card allowing him to carry arms, which he could use at French police controls. In their first train he dozed and all went well, but in the second from Toulouse to Montréjeau, sitting opposite each other in an empty compartment, they were interrupted by a ticket collector. Before looking at their shared ticket he started asking Anne-Marie searching questions and then studied her companion's civil papers. From where she sat Anne-Marie saw the policeman grow pale and she remembered the incriminating revolver. She grabbed her bag and started fumbling in it, drawing the ticket inspector's eyes to her. Still looking at her he handed back her friend's papers and left the compartment without another word. As she relaxed, the policeman warned her to be still and slipped his gun behind the seat. Then two men in turn passed along the corridor, watching them out of the corner of their eyes, a frequent trick of the Gestapo who hoped to catch suspects relaxing and taken off their guard. The police inspector's brother had been caught like this. Nothing more happened, however, the journey was completed, and the policeman was delivered to a safe house ready for onward transmission to the Pyrénées guides.

Shortly afterwards instructions came through from London for the demolition of the Empalot factory at Toulouse. This was the third biggest powder factory in France and heavily guarded, but with inside knowledge and help it was planned to take the explosives into the office of one of the engineers and set them in strategic places at night. Anne-Marie helped an agent make up the explosives near Montréjeau and then with another helpful police inspector, the three of them took four loaded suitcases by train to Toulouse. As they came to the exit barrier at Toulouse station, a policeman tapped the inspector on the shoulder and took him to a waiting room for questioning. He was carrying two cases. Anne-Marie and her friend hurried on, uninterrupted, with one suitcase each. They stopped a few streets away and to their delighted relief were joined a few minutes later by the inspector who had shown his interrogators his inspector's card before being questioned or having to open his cases, and they had apologized and let him go. After a meal Anne-Marie left them. Eventually she heard that the demolition had taken place.

This was not the only time that she carried a suitcase of armaments on a train. On another occasion waiting with an agent and two suitcases on the railway platform before the train to Tarbes came in, she noticed four Germans acting rather suspiciously. 'Go away,' she told her friend. 'Hide until the train comes in.' It was just in time, for the Germans started to stop any able-bodied men on the platform, who did not have papers of exemption, to herd them off to Germany on forced labour. Finally, the two of them got onto the train together safely, and while the man stood with one suitcase in the corridor, Anne-Marie found a seat in a crowded compartment and put hers on the rack above her head. Some time later a member of the Gestapo entered their compartment and asked for their papers. Anne-Marie passed over her forged documents and answered her questions innocently enough and her luck seemed to hold. Then the Gestapo agent barked out 'Open cases', and Anne-Marie's heart nearly stopped. She wondered if she could jump from a speeding train. She saw her companion in the corridor feeling for his gun. She slowly took down her case. What could she do? Then she heard the woman at the end protesting at being asked to open her many parcels all tied with string, with her two babies climbing all over her. After a squabble, the German only asked to see her big case and then losing interest in them all asked to see two more cases, 'This and this.' He then left without examining Anne-Marie's. That was a journey to remember!

In addition to these sort of tasks, Anne-Marie also found that she had to help train members of the resistance in the use of the British and American arms which were new to them. She did not find this easy as the men did not like being instructed by a girl. Another of her tasks was to help in reception parties for parachute drops, sometimes of arms and sometimes of other agents. Occasionally she met the frustrating and disappointing night when the plane arrived but left without dropping its load, once because the batteries in the Eureka she carried were flat.

On 16 March, she had her 21st birthday party near the Pyrénées, at which Yvonne Cormeau was one of the guests. It was made more memorable by the appearance of a beautifully decorated cake with 21 lighted candles, impossible to obtain in occupied France, but it had the unexpected result of quickly emptying the room, as the lovely candles turned out to be pieces of detonating fuse, helpfully painted pink by their explosives expert!

Another notable journey she made was to Paris to pass messages from George Starr to another organizer, whose wireless operator had been captured. George had radioed London for him and now she was to carry the very important answers back, then go on to Tours to pass a message to another wireless operator. These she memorized and burned before setting off. The long train journey was dangerous and uncomfortable because of Allied bombing and resistance sabotage. Her contacts in Paris were inhospitable and shifty, and the organizer was away, though they could contact him in about a week. Meanwhile Anne-Marie found a lodging with a family friend.

By chance she met another member of the Agen resistance the next day, who had been looking everywhere for her. He had been sent to stop her going further, as the radio operator at Tours had been caught and the circuit of the organizer to whom she had been sent was now breaking up. She therefore had to return without accomplishing her mission. So again chance had saved her.

Now the A and B notices in preparation for activities just before D-Day arrived to be memorized and carried to all areas of the Wheelwright circuit. What was more, due to a careless leader of one of the resistance groups, shot by the Gestapo with a copy of the messages carried on his person, all the messages had now to be changed by London, new ones issued and distributed once more. On 1 June the A messages were broadcast on the BBC. Hopes rose that the invasion would come immediately, but they were dashed by the delay that followed. Instead German arrests in the area intensified. The police had also been asking questions in Condom about the fair-haired, blue-eyed girl who lived nearby, and Anne-Marie was warned to stay on the farm. George Starr started a Maquis group in his village. Then came the invasion in Normandy. In her area of the south-west, Anne-Marie found the people disappointed that their area had not been the one invaded but they were still ready enough to fight. She herself was summoned to the Patron's village to help with the Maquis.

Life became dull for Anne-Marie, who thrived on excitement and disliked being engaged on the mundane tasks of doing washing or typing reports. This came to an end when the Germans attacked the Maquis in the Patron's village. Anne-Marie acquitted herself bravely filling grenades, but the fighting was confused and soon a retreat was ordered. She was given the records of the Maquisards to hide or destroy if there was any danger of them falling into German hands, as they would incriminate most of their supporters in the region. She also rescued a Sten gun, some magazines and some of the SOE money from the Patron's house but she did not manage to collect her valuable identity cards, since the houses around her were being blown to pieces. Fortunately they were handed to her later. She ran some way after the men and then found an ancient cave below the village church where she buried the documents, covering them with stones and then jumping on them to make them look natural. Then she followed the retreating Maquis through the firing and the carnage. As she left she heard the arsenal of the village blown up by the rearguard to prevent it falling into the hands of the enemy. In a nearby farmhouse, she saw and tended some of the wounded and then late in the afternoon accepted a lift into Condom where the remnants of the Maquis were joined by another group of Maquis under a French officer. In the evening they set off to regroup, singing, excited and feeling like heroes, despite their losses.

She stayed with the Maquis in the Armagnac Battalion, receiving parachute supplies and several commandos. But she ran too many risks, and at length for her own safety the Patron told her to return to England over the mountain routes that she had sent so many others in the past. She was bitterly disappointed that she could not stay to see the Germans' final defeat in her circuit but she probably realized herself that her time had run out. Escorted by a New Zealand pilot, she went with five others, all prisoner of war escapees, of whom three were American.

They started on 1 August 1944 and accomplished the journey to the mountains by car. Anne-Marie wore a man's rubber shoes and a warm tweed skirt. The guides met them and gave her a long smooth stick to help in the rough parts of the journey. At four in the warm afternoon they stopped for a rest and water, 8,000 feet up the Pyrénées. Later they stopped again while the guides went on, but they had lost the way and it was two hours before the guides found the path. Then they all had

to be silent as they crept downhill near Boutx, as they did not want to alert the German Garrison there. Near the bottom of the valley there was a white road which they had to cross and then a small river, which they did safely in Indian file. It was now nearly midnight and the air was cold. The party stopped to eat briefly and sleep a few hours, but started again at five the next morning to avoid the Germans and their dog

The Pyrénées over which Anne-Marie escaped.

patrols. Again they got lost and then refound the route. In the afternoon they rested in a shepherd's cottage until dark. The next part of the journey was downhill and easier. At 10pm they were at Melle and had to stop until the German guards passed so they could take the bridge across the river. They fought their way through thorns and undergrowth for a further hour before sleeping, but they found they were again lost and discovered that they had just missed a precipice. As they climbed higher, fog surrounded them and the ground grew wet and slippery. At the top of the slope they faced a further five hours along the mountain crest. Anne-Marie was now walking like an automaton, but suddenly the mist rose and she saw a valley in the midday sun. Bitterly disappointed they realized that it was still France — they had been walking in circles. One of the Americans had a pilot's silk map and compass, so they decided to use this and let the guides return. Then the party tried again, heading south towards the Spanish border. The sun scorched them and they forgot to hide or beware of German bullets.

At six that evening they crested the last slope and saw their first Spanish village below them. As they came down the hill, Anne-Marie saw an old woman coming towards them. 'Is this Spain?' she asked, her heart in her mouth. She was answered in Spanish. They had arrived!

After Anne-Marie went back to England the Patron and 1,000 Maquisards marched from Gers on Toulouse. In the battle that followed, the Germans could have been quickly expelled but for the rivalry between French factions and parties. Finally, however, Toulouse was freed. Later, on 28 October, General de Gaulle, fearing the risk to the safety of the state by such private armies, ordered the Maquis to disarm.

12
Only One Way Out

Yvonne Baseden

'Another wartime Christmas was over, the Christmas of 1943. It had been a blacked-out Christmas, with no turkey, no ham, no crackers, few carols and even fewer soya-bean sausages. But it had been more than a day in the calendar. It was a day on which one had to pause and look both backwards and forwards... We all knew what the future would hold. There were those among us who wouldn't see another Christmas — or if we did, we would see it through the bars over the window of a cell... I suppose I thought I would be one of the lucky ones who would get away with it. It's somebody else who is run over by a tram... But I said my quiet prayers all the same.'
Yvonne Baseden, from 'Moon Squadron' by J. Tickell (Allan Wingate)

These were the thoughts of Yvonne Baseden when she was coming to the end of her training for SOE. She had started by becoming an airwoman clerk in general duties as soon as she was old enough to volunteer at 18, after which she found herself stationed at Kenley in late September 1940 during the hot, busy, dangerous days which saw the end of the Battle of Britain and the onslaught of the blitz on the cities, especially London. There she met and admired the men who flew and the men who worked on the planes, and when the Free French pilots formed their own squadron, she was asked to help them with their technical English. Although she spoke French fluently, being born and brought up in Paris, with a French mother and an English father, this was not as easy as it seemed, since she had to learn the technical terms herself before she could teach them. But she did her best and in the following year found herself commissioned as an Assistant Section Officer in the Intelligence Branch. Her special skills finally took her into the Directorate of Allied Air Co-operation and Foreign Liaison. Pearl Witherington was on the staff there too, already involved in highly confidential work, and it was from her efforts to get permission to be released to join SOE that Yvonne first learned of the existence of the organization. From there on Yvonne was sure of what she wanted to do. She applied to SOE and after a number of interviews, she was accepted in May 1943, a month ahead of Pearl. Her training, however, took much longer as she was to take on that most risky and skilled of occupations, a wireless operator.

That was how in late February 1944 she came to be in a car racing up the Great North Road from Baker Street to Tempsford with her future organizer, Baron Gonzagues de St Geniès, codenamed Lucien, in the back seat. They spent the night in a house used for agents in waiting,

Area with which Yvonne Baseden was mainly associated.

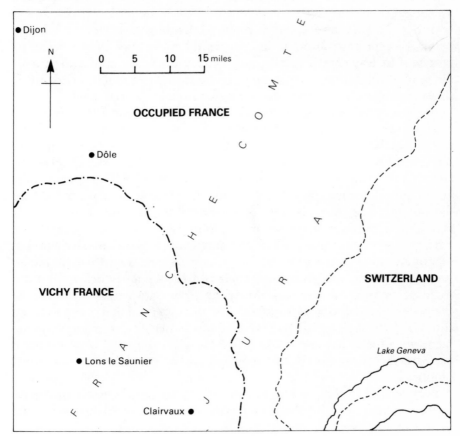

serviced by FANY's, and then in the evening of the next day were driven to Tempsford airfield, where they were equipped and checked. Yvonne's money — 500,000 francs in banknotes — made a cushion for her back under her parachute harness, and her handbag hung by a string at the front. She also had her wireless crystals, a revolver and her lethal tablet, which turned the feeling of adventure into a more solemn occasion. She decided to leave the last item in case she was ever tempted, and this proved right. Then they boarded the aircraft, not to sit on seats but to lie on the hard metal floor.

The pilot was friendly, the despatcher cheerful, the cold intense. During the flight Yvonne thought much about her future work, acting as a link between the two countries she loved. When they reached the dropping zone the dispatcher hooked the parachute on to the static line and opened the hatch. Yvonne sat with her toes dangling into space as the plane began to circle their field. There was no doubt about it being the right place but there were no lights, no signals. The plane circled a few minutes in case the reception party was delayed. Nothing happened. With a sick feeling Yvonne thought of the men who would have welcomed them but might even now have been taken by the Germans and shot. The plane returned to England, landing at dawn and Yvonne had to accept that another month would go by before she went to France. On leave until recalled, she and Gonzagues dined around in different restaurants and patronized London shows, killing time until they were again summoned to Tempsford on 18 March 1944.

This time they were to land in a different place, near Toulouse down in south-west France, and their plane was a large Halifax. The flight went smoothly, there were no snags and soon they were hanging suspended in the midnight air above their new landing field. Despite the fact that Yvonne was encumbered with three wireless sets for her use, and that her mother was still living near the place where she landed, she did not stop nor reveal herself. Now apart from her code name, which was Odette, she travelled under the disguise of Mademoiselle Marie Bernier, a young secretary. She and her organizer had to make their way separately north and east to the mountainous ridges and valleys of the Jura department, the progress of their trains constantly delayed by the work of French saboteurs — frustrating but satisfactory evidence of the value of air-dropped supplies. On one stage of her long journey she boarded a train going to Dôle and found herself sharing a compart-ment with four German soldiers. This was getting local colour with a vengeance. She sat quietly and demurely and no one asked any awkward questions.

Yvonne and Gonzagues had been sent to set up a new circuit called Scholar, almost on the Swiss border, to help two overlapping circuits in the area, one of which had been encountering difficulties in communication. In addition they were to provide a new base for the safe parachuting of supplies of all kinds. These were much needed by the local Maquis in particular, who were very strong in such a mountainous area, having grown greatly by taking in young men anxious to avoid the forced labour levies being raised by the Germans for work in Germany.

When they finally arrived, Gonzagues soon discovered that a reason for the lack of communications from one circuit had been the arrest of its organizer, and therefore he set himself to try to pick up the pieces and re-establish the organization — contacts, safe houses, and resistance members to help in reception parties, the circulation of arms and storage places. Yvonne thus found herself carrying messages around the circuit by day and contacting London by night.

The Jura region where Yvonne worked.

Work became quite frantic after the Allied landings in early June, when there was a great influx of agents and supplies. It also became more dangerous for members of the resistance, as the Germans, with large troop movements through most areas, were becoming more nervous of and frightened by the havoc a well-armed resistance could create. London was also aware of this and decided to arrange a large scale drop of armaments to Yvonne's area, such as could not be supplied by the normal night operations. This required much planning and Yvonne's radio set was in constant use for weeks. For the last 24 hours she herself had to remain in the dropping zone — a dangerous practice in itself — sending frequent crack signals throughout the preceding night, reporting on conditions and readiness. Then when the aircraft took off in Britain she was in constant touch with them, her signal directing and ready to warn them away if the Germans appeared in her vicinity.

This was to be the first mass daylight drop mounted by the American Eighth Air Force and it was given the operational name of Cadillac. In the grey morning of a Sunday in mid-June 1944 the sky seemed to shake with the roar of powerful engines as 36 huge Flying Fortresses swept in to the target area and dropped their vast load of over 400 containers to the hundreds of waiting Maquis who, armed and ready, guarded the dropping zone below. The sky was darkened and then filled with tiny white parachutes, which were each chased by a group of Maquisards who retrieved them and then carted them off quickly and safely to their mountain hide-outs before the Germans could stop what had taken place. At last Yvonne was able to tap out her mission successful message to London and then relax. She was a first class wireless operator and had certainly proved her worth that night.

As Yvonne, her organizer and several members of the resistance drove away from the site, a student in their close group volunteered to transport Yvonne's radio by a different route to their destination. This was a large cheese depot, sometimes known as a factory, at Les Orphelins in Dôle. German road blocks and patrols naturally increased following the visit by the American Air Force, and it was by one of these that the youth was stopped as he was cycling through a nearby village with the radio on his carrier. The radio was discovered, he was arrested and taken to the

The Château Vougeot surrounded by its fields of vines, one of the many Châteaux in Yvonne's region.

local German headquarters. This brave young man was severely beaten and after suffering terrible injuries forced to reveal the details of his destination.

Meanwhile at Les Orphelins, Yvonne, her organizer and six of their group were having a special lunch to celebrate the success of such a huge operation. They were just drinking their coffee, when there was a hammering on the door below them. Their hostess went to the window overlooking the door and gasped with horror. 'Germans!' In a minute the table was swept clear of dishes and the eight people dispersed to the several hiding places in the huge factory, these having been long agreed in case of such a situation as this. Yvonne's place was in a narrow gap in the middle of a pile of planks. Gonzagues hid in the space between the floor boards of the room upstairs, which held the drying cartwheel-sized cheeses, so that he was lying on the ceiling directly above the kitchen where they had just been eating.

While this was going on, the woman threw open the window and shouted down, 'What do you want?' Back came the order: 'Open up.'

'If you want some cheeses, I'll come down and help you,' she said, playing for time before she went down and opened the door, but she was very frightened. The Germans came in and went everywhere looking for the suspected agents but they could find nothing. At length, puzzled and annoyed, they assembled outside, each with a large piece of cheese given by their hostess to sweeten their tempers. Their sergeant finding that he alone had been missed went back to claim his slice. With shaking fingers she cut him a piece. Glad to see her so impressed by their actions he repeated his warning that those who helped the resistance would be shot. She seemed visibly frightened and to impress her still further, he raised his pistol and fired into the air. Then he marched out. 'What was that shot?' demanded the officer in charge. The sergeant explained. 'She certainly looked frightened!' he licked his lips. Not satisfied, and feeling there was more than they had discovered, the officer returned to the kitchen. There he saw the woman slumped on a chair and above her head blood was seeping in a wide stain over the kitchen ceiling. By an incredible mischance the bullet had hit Gonzagues in the head.

His body was hauled from its hiding place and he was thrown down to expire in the yard below. Then one by one the others were hunted down in their hiding places, cheese by cheese. Yvonne heard the boots of a German mount the pile of wood where she lay. He looked down, saw her in her grey skirt and blue blouse and roughly pulled her out by her dark hair, striking her unconscious with a blow across her face. Everyone was taken in a horse-drawn wagon, handcuffed in pairs, to the German military barracks in Dôle. There each was interrogated and Yvonne's training in how to stand up to questioning and torture was put into practice. The Germans did all they could to break her spirit without result. At length unable to extract anything useful from her, they sent her to their area headquarters at Dijon prison where there were more expert Gestapo questioners.

Here she was subjected to some of the cruellest interrogation she had yet encountered. For one whole day without food or drink, two men hurled their questions at her, seeking to trap or trip her up. In the evening, still unsatisfied, they threw her into a windowless underground cell, running with moisture and vermin with only a plank for a bed. There she lay for the whole of the next day, hearing the groans and shouts of the other prisoners and fearful of what might happen to her. She waited without food she had no idea how long, growing more weak and disorientated. When she was again summoned for questioning, her guard gave her no helping hand and she had to crawl on her knees up the stairs from her cell. In the Gestapo office the questions began again, and again she refused to give way. She was threatened and then one of the men stamped on her bare toes. The pain became so unbearable that she fainted. Later when she was returned to her cell, her guard had to drag her. At this time she must have regretted her decision to leave behind her poison pill, which would have given her the power to escape from her misery.

But this was not the end. Her interrogators had one more card up their sleeve. If she did not give them the information they wanted, they threatened to shoot her. They reasoned that to a young girl life would still be sweet, but perhaps they had driven her too far. In any case, she would not co-operate. So they staged a mock execution, propping her against the wall and pointing their pistols at her. When they fired, Yvonne must have felt it was a happy release. But this was not to be. A minute later, she realized that she was still alive. They had not killed her after all.

This seemed to be their last attempt to wring information from her. Following this, she occupied a different cell and was allowed food but kept in isolation, with only her own thoughts and fears for company. During this time she carried out the physical and mental exercises recommended by her trainers, so that she might gather strength and keep sane during the long weeks alone. In both these objects she was successful, the Gestapo having nothing further to gain from her.

Dijon prison was vast. It housed both men and women, kept on separate floors, many awaiting execution or onward transport to Germany. The solitary confinement cells were tiny, but they contained an iron bed with army blankets, a shelf with a bowl and jug of water for washing and drinking. This was bliss after what she had endured. Once a day prisoners were taken to a little exercise yard where they walked around in circles. Silence was the rule but at this time Yvonne made contact with another prisoner in the yard behind hers, when she heard the other whistling *There's A Long Long Road A-winding*. Her companion in misery turned out to be Mary Lindell, also British, who had been helping in the escape networks. Shortly Yvonne found that they were only a few cells away from one another, enabling them to sing and recite to each other at night, though they did not discover one another's identity until by happy accident they found themselves together in the same air-raid shelter during one of the Allied raids. Eventually the Allies advanced so far into France that their guns could be heard far in the distance at night, and the Germans decided to shoot or send away many of their prisoners.

Thus it was that Yvonne found herself sharing a train compartment with Mary bound for Germany. They immediately planned to escape, and would have done so but they became separated when an Allied air raid brought the train to a stop in a tunnel. When they made contact again in the darkness, there was a guard under their door so they could not get away unobserved. In the evening they reached Saarbrücken concentration camp, badly bombed and peopled by walking skeletons, some of whom the German guards took pleasure in drowning in a nearby pool when the mood took them. In the crowded hut to which she was assigned, along with fleas and dysentery, Yvonne met five more members of her organization, though they were moved away a few days later. At last she and Mary were sent on their gruelling way to Germany, standing jammed into cattle trucks with other women and no food or water.

The train stopped at irregular intervals, when the sliding doors were opened for the distribution of soup to keep them alive. At length they came to Fürstenberg station and their final destination. As they were hustled onto the platform they left behind the many corpses of those who had died en route and joined the straggling mass of women who had survived, carrying their meagre suitcases into Ravensbrück concentration camp. Here, Yvonne spent her first night in the open air, sharing a blanket with Mary. Next day, she followed, with the other prisoners, the proper procedure for being accepted as a prisoner at Ravensbrück. First, she went with the other women to what was called the shower room. Here they lost all their previous belongings, which were replaced by the clothes of those who had died before them. Yvonne received a pleated red skirt and sailor boy's shirt, but she was allowed to keep the ski-boots she was already wearing. She and her companions laughed at the appearance they must have made. This was perhaps the only ray of humour in the dark days that lay ahead.

After some weeks in the quarantine hut, Yvonne was transferred to her permanent hut where she was allotted a bunk which she shared with another woman in one of the three tiers which filled the room. There were 800 women in her hut, together with accumulated filth and fleas, and there were even little children and pregnant women among their number. Every morning they were awakened at three and given bitter-tasting acorn coffee, then they shuffled outside to line up in five straight rows in front of their hut, hands on the shoulders of the women ahead, for three hours at a stretch during Appells. Here they were counted and checked by their SS women guards. Afterwards came the fiercely hard manual work with only a 20 minute break for a bowl of carrot or mangold soup and a little bread. Food became scarcer as the months went by and the deaths in the camp and Yvonne's hut began to mount. The struggle to stay in existence took Yvonne's energy and, as she saw the chimneys of the camp crematorium working overtime, she remembered the words of one of the camp doctors when they arrived. 'The only way out of here,' he told the tired and scared women, 'is through the crematorium chimney.' He had thought it was a great joke but no one else was amused. Life was grim.

Punishments were enormous even for the most trivial of offences, the SS guards, both men and women, taking the greatest of pleasure in causing pain and suffering to the hapless individuals in their camp. One day Yvonne, while helping unload some pillows from a truck, accidentally let a feather from a seam, blow onto the uniform of one of the guards. He immediately raised his whip and felled her to the ground with a blow, which might have killed her but for the watchfulness of a fellow prisoner, who deflected it by pulling her partly out of the way, so that it fell on her thigh and not her head, but she was badly kicked as a consequence. To her sorrow, she early lost her friend Mary who was taken to be a nurse at the camp hospital, a much desired privilege.

As a result of the harsh life at Ravensbrück, Yvonne found herself diagnosed as having tuberculosis with a spot on her lung. Instead of being sent to the hospital block, however, she was told to report to a convoy that was being collected to be taken to Belsen. With her was a friend who was also far from well. As luck would have it, the news came to the ears of Mary Lindell in the hospital block, who intervened and, with the assistance of a girl she had previously befriended, managed to have the two names taken off the list. Then to make the hut numbers right, she admitted them into one of the eight hospital blocks as patients. In this place, Yvonne spent her 23rd birthday.

Christmas 1944 had come and gone. Water in the camp had frozen, and so had many of the inmates in their flimsy summer clothes. Women began to fight one another for scraps of food. The Allies were advancing on the Rhine and Germany. With foreboding the women saw the Germans bringing drums of oil into the camp and began to fear that they might be burned alive so that the Germans could cover the evidence of their war crimes. To the prisoners it was a race between death and the advancing Allied armies — Russians on one side and British and Americans on the other.

Even in prison-camps rumours spread, whether with or without foundation. As winter moved into spring, a rumour began to circulate that the Red Cross were being allowed to make an exchange of German prisoners for those of the Allies. It was said that Count Bernadotte had got Himmler's agreement to the plan. The camp began to hope again, though the idea seemed too good to be true. Then it happened. Outside the camp a fleet of snow-white Swedish buses and ambulances appeared, resplendent with big red crosses. Lists of women were written out and summoned, before being checked and cleared through the gates, while the other inmates gazed wistfully after them. Gradually the sad little groups departed. One of them was to contain the American and English women on the camp. Yvonne was in this party but after she had counted the women through the gates, having marched them up with Mary Lindell, she turned around only to find that her friend had been barred exit. There was nothing they could do about it and they both burst into tears. Unwillingly they embraced for the last time and then Yvonne was taken up by the convoy, to explain what had happened. None would stop to enquire further and hold up the evacuation at this point, but the man in charge promised to see what he could do. It was 28 April 1945.

Yvonne was driven north to Denmark and then shipped to Malmö in Sweden by the Swedish Red Cross. There she was relieved to hear that Mary had been able to join the next convoy from Ravensbrück and had also got away.

Yvonne herself returned safely to Britain and into the care of a British hospital, where she remained for many months, recovering from her ill-treatment and the many privations she had suffered. She was not ready to report back to work at the Air Ministry until the end of that year. She was, however, one of the fortunate ones who had done something few had achieved. She had been to hell and come back.

13
In Dublin's Fair City

Patricia Maureen O'Sullivan

'Though handicapped through imperfect technical knowledge and the consequences of a serious illness, she nevertheless by patience, perseverance and devotion to duty, made a success of her work.'

Vera Atkins

On this day Paddy O'Sullivan was forced to take her radio set with her on one of her journeys in France. Riding along a quiet lane she suddenly saw that the Germans had set up a snap check point, where there was usually none and she had received no warning. She must have been furious that this was the one time she could be caught red-handed with the set on the carrier of her bicycle. The hedges round about prevented her swerving away to the side of the lonely road, and in any case she was in full view of the waiting Germans who would immediately become suspicious and run after or shoot at her if she were to disappear suddenly or turn around and go back in the opposite direction. That way they would be sure that she was involved with resistance and take no time in discovering her set. There was only one chance. To try to bluff it out.

So putting on her most sunny and beguiling smile, she rode boldly up to the two men, one of whom liking the look of her advanced some way up the road to meet her. She stopped and leaning on her bike, chatted animatedly with him. Flattered by her friendly attitude, he asked her to meet him for a drink that evening when he came off duty. After some more chat she agreed if he could suggest a suitably quiet place where she would not be recognized. Satisfied at last he let her past him, no doubt already contemplating his night with such a charming companion. At the road check, the other German awaited her, and while he examined her papers, she laid herself out to be just as delightful to him, consequently so bemusing him also that he completely forgot to examine her case, while excited by the notion of making his own assignation with her for that same evening. Laughing, she pushed her bicycle through the check post and rode off waving happily to her two erstwhile suitors, with neither of whom, needless to say, did she keep her appointment. But it had been a very near shave, only carried off by consummate acting and the brazen use of her charms. Never, she vowed, would she carry her radio set with her again. She could not expect to get away with it twice. Nor did she.

Patricia O'Sullivan was born in Dublin, the daughter of a newspaper editor there. That city has therefore cause to be proud of this young woman. Coming from Ireland and with a name like Patricia, it was a foregone conclusion that she would be known as Paddy. She was pretty and attractive which often helped to get her out of scrapes in the French convent where she was educated, and she remained bubbling with the high spirits which made her most eager to throw herself into the life of the French underground, treating it all as if it were a great game. By that same token she was willing to run the risks of that most vulnerable of agents — the wireless operator.

Then she joined the WAAF in June 1941 at the age of 23. While she was at RAF Gosforth she met and became friendly with Sonya Butt, another future SOE recruit, but she did not know about the activities of SOE until quite late in 1943. Nevertheless to hear was to find herself immediately drawn to the type of work it would involve. She was, however, recovering from the effects of a serious illness so she had to wait until she was again fit before joining the organization.

She embarked on the arduous training given to all agents. She had passed her selection course at Wanborough and had partly completed at Thame Park the special course given to wireless operators, when she was hastily summoned to Headquarters.

'We have a circuit in France desperately in need of a wireless operator. Will you take it on?' She knew enough of the work to manage, though she knew that she still had a lot to learn. But she was always ready and willing to rise to any challenge and she could not resist this one. She had been aching to go, ever since she had heard of the organization. Her only answer therefore was 'When?' 'The next moon period.'

Time was short. She had to master in quick succession her cover story, details of the region to which she was being sent and the all-important

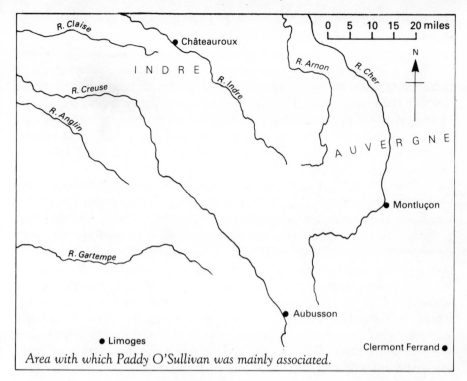

Area with which Paddy O'Sullivan was mainly associated.

information on her secret ciphers.

By late 1943, the year before Paddy was due to leave, most operators in France had been using the B2 transmitters. They had a powerful 30 watt output with a very wide range, transmitting between 3 to 16 megacycles, but tuned only to their home receiving station by their quartz crystals usually carried in a separate little box. Because of security inter-communication between circuits was prohibited, such messages having to be carried by courier. This kept wireless messages from one circuit independent from those of another and, as each operator had a different cipher from the rest, the Germans who broke one cipher were no nearer breaking any other. However, sets could both transmit and receive and worked on a 6 volt battery merely by throwing a switch. Thus they were isolated from the electric supply, something that in the past had helped the Germans track down a set. Such freedom made detection more difficult.

In addition, operators now used a complicated cipher based on a 'one-time' pad, peculiar to that one agent, the second copy being held by the decipherers at the receiving station. No further copies existed. On a single silk page was printed a random selection of figures or letters. Turn over and the next page was a different selection and so on. Once used, the page was burned. Added to these precautions, the sender also had three checks to send with her message for the home station: a bluff check, which could be wrung out of her if caught by the Germans, a true check, never to be given, and a random check. Then there was the individual fist, which was supposed to be recognizable and individual in the type of Morse-tapping by an operator, and, in theory at least, so long as the Germans did not capture the operator in the act, they would waste long hours trying to imitate her work. The person of course was more easily caught and when she had a little suitcase weighing 32 lb it was soon recognizable, each looked so alike. It also used a 70 ft long spread of easily discovered aerial.

By 1942, SOE had got over its initial problems of competing for equipment with other agencies. Formerly, the intelligence-gathering SIS, had been deemed of far greater importance than a little ad hoc, late-arriving, body like SOE, and SIS therefore had monopolized the lion's share of all special wireless equipment. But now SOE was at last able to take over the experimentation and making of its own sets, which it was soon able to produce in numbers sufficient to give each operator in the field several.

Such advantages meant that not only could the sets be widely scattered over a circuit, increasing German difficulties of detection, but that operators need no longer carry their sets around, as did poor Noor Inayat Khan, and breakdown of any part was not the major disaster it had been, driving an operator off the air for long and perhaps vital

A page from a 'one time' pad, consisting of a series of letters, often printed on uncrushable silk or rice paper. Wireless operators found that enciphering messages by this method was a vast improvement over double transposition. It was easier, faster and more secure — advantages in the field, which could make the difference between life and death for the agent, far outweighing the extra burden of the pocket-sized, microfilmed, random keys list, used with it. (Lt Col P. Lorain)

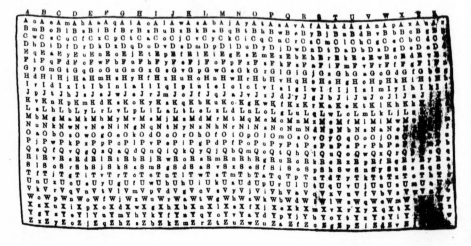

periods or else making her take unacceptable risks in obtaining a new part elsewhere. Smaller sets, too, were now on their way.

The picture was therefore much brighter for Paddy when she took to the field, although on the reverse of the coin the skill of the Germans at catching operators had proportionately increased. What had also changed in favour of the SOE circuits in France was the attitude of the populace to British agents, who were now generally seen as the heralds of liberation at the least and at the most as the producers of manna from on high, in the form of badly needed supplies of all kinds for the resistance. For this softening of attitude the Germans had themselves been to blame, for the heavier their impositions and treatment of the French citizens, especially their conscription of men for forced labour in Germany, the greater became opposition to their occupation. Even those Frenchmen who preferred to stand aside in the early years of Vichy rule, now found themselves opposed, albeit clandestinely, to the Germans, while there were areas particularly in the southern or mountainous parts used to their independence from whatever government existed where the whole population was solidly for resistance.

Paddy's task was thus already smoother on 24 March 1944 when she waited for her code name to appear on the blackboard in the transit house, to call her forward for her flight. Quietly and hardly noticed, she slipped away from the other expectant groups to join the car which whisked her away in the darkness to a hut on Tempsford airfield where the process of preparation began, checking clothes and belongings, adding last minute articles including her crystals, and donning a rubber helmet, a jumping suit and parachute harness under which were her bulky rolls of French bank notes. Then she joined her aircraft, looming in the dark like a gigantic bird, bade farewell to her escorting officer and the engines began to throb, pulsing along the cold floor where she squatted, senses alert, ready for her journey to France. Soon she was airborne and the heavy aircraft droned its way to a dropping zone in Maurice Southgate's great Stationer circuit in the middle of France. The flares were there and the Morse signal flashed to confirm that the reception party was ready.

Paddy leapt out into the night sky, feeling that at long last she was starting on her great adventure, a feeling that soon evaporated when she realized that although she had done all she had been taught, her parachute cords had become tangled and her parachute would not open properly. This was the great fear of all parachutists, as falling from such a height was almost always fatal. Her descent became swifter and she was almost losing consciousness as she struggled with the lines trailing above her. Now, short of an unexpectedly soft landing, she was doomed before she had begun. Seconds became hours, when suddenly her fall was halted by a great jerk, as her parachute flowered out high above her.

With the ground only a short way below, it had opened just in time. Even so she made an awkward heavy landing, rolling as the ground met her, suffering a bad shaking and bruising as her parachute dragged her along, working now when she had no need of it. When her rescuers managed to catch her and release her from her harness, she was lying with all the breath driven out of her in the middle of a field of cows. Indeed, she declared afterwards that apart from her rubber helmet, she owed her life to the bundles of French banknotes she carried wrapped around her like a cushion. She spent the rest of the night resting her bruises, before setting off next day on a borrowed bicycle to meet her organizers.

In this way Mademoiselle Simonet arrived to act as wireless operator to Percy and Edmund Mayer, codenamed Maurice and Barthelemy. The brothers had come, as did many successful SOE agents, from the French-speaking British colony of Mauritius, and had landed just over a fortnight before her to see the situation and work out just where they could be most useful. Once they had decided, they needed only the arrival of their wireless operator to go into action. With Paddy they moved to Limoges and set up a small circuit which became known as Fireman. Its extent was modest, covering an area in the triangle roughly bounded by Limoges, Montluçon and Châteauroux. Stationer was crumbling around them as they set to work, beset by many arrests, finally culminating in the arrest of its chief Maurice Southgate. Fortunately his able assistants, Pearl Witherington being one, continued his work but split his circuit into more manageable sections, with Pearl to the north forming Wrestler, and Amédée Maingard — another Mauritian — taking the middle part as Shipwright to the north of the Meyers. Eventually Salesman, of much longer foundation, became a viable southern neighbour, so that between them they would become a formidable team when the day of liberation would dawn.

Meanwhile there was the ordinary daily work to be done and the situation was dangerous. Paddy was lodged in a farm in most squalid conditions, its discomforts being outbalanced by its safety. Despite this she rarely complained and her messages went through to London promptly. As

A Limousin farmhouse in Paddy's circuit.

time passed with the opportunity to improve her technique, she even managed to recruit some local men whom she succeeded in training although by now she was far from well. Such training was not easy, when the implications of keeping even a small circuit well served are considered. In order to deliver and collect her messages, as well as do some of the work done by a courier, she had to cycle from 20 to 30 miles every day. She had to keep a watch for road blocks and German checkpoints and have her cover story ready to fit the occasion when she did get stopped. This was the time when she charmed the two German guards.

There were other instances of being nearly caught by the Germans, but Paddy seemed to thrive on these, breaking the rules set down by her SOE trainers and getting away with it. 'Never', she was told, 'use a telephone or a taxi for your work. The operators and drivers are often in the pay of the Germans, and will report anything they think suspicious.' But of course, Paddy did.

One day, not feeling too well and being in a hurry, Paddy took a taxi to a faraway destination and carried her small wireless set in its battered suitcase with her. It would be needed for messages once she had met the contact whom she was going to visit.

The wooded countryside of Limousin where Paddy worked.

Giving a place not exactly at, but near, where she wanted to go, she leaned back on the worn upholstery and prepared to enjoy this unusual luxury. It was a long country run and she did not expect to pass through any controls or roadblocks, but she had miscalculated.

The taxi wound its way along roads and rough lanes, through the Limousin countryside with its woodlands of beech, oak, flowering horse-chestnuts and fruit trees, and shining stretches of water. The gentle sunlight made her feel sleepy — did all radio operators who worked day and night always feel so tired? She was jerked awake from her pleasant doze by a screech of brakes as her driver stopped. A quick glance outside showed her that they had met with a German check point. Had her driver brought her here to betray her, had he taken a different route or was it a snap control — these were growing more frequent, especially where there had been recent sabotage attacks, of which she was well aware from her daily air traffic. The first possibility was ruled out, as her driver, grumbling, pulled out his papers for the soldier's examination. Next the German turned his attention to the passenger. Now Paddy was in extreme danger from the incriminating suitcase beside her, even allowing that her forged papers would pass his scrutiny. He opened the door and poked in his head. He was quite young and rosy-cheeked — an increasing tendency among recent recruits, showing how deeply Germany was drawing on her reserves. When he saw the shy young girl with frightened eyes, he flushed and mumbled, 'Mademoiselle. Your papers please'. Silently she handed them to him and prayed inwardly. Acutely embarrassed, he averted his eyes from her and hardly glanced at the papers which were obviously in order. 'A relative... very ill... there isn't much time...and I need to hurry,' she appealed to him, words tripping over one another in her nervousness. He looked uncomfortable. 'Sorry to delay you, Mademoiselle.' He slammed the door quickly and waved the driver on.

Paddy sat back in her seat and felt weak. He had not even noticed her suitcase, far less searched it. She decided that he was quite a nice young man and hoped he would return home safely when the war ended. And me too, she thought. I hope I get back home safely! Now there was the next mission to complete and her work to carry on. Each crisis left her shaky but elated. She was certain of the Allied invasion and only impatient for it to be soon.

The situation in her circuit became more difficult in April when Stationer had its spate of arrests, and in May when the Germans became more frantic in their attempts to track down all those in the region connected with resistance after its organizer was arrested. They also had more captured information so that eluding them became more difficult. Paddy thrived on the excitement and enjoyed playing her part, no matter how dangerous, but her work-load of air traffic increased enormously as D-Day approached and the circuit geared itself to the expected invasion. Finally it arrived and Paddy was kept at her set day and night. In all, during the short period between April and August 1944, she was responsible for transmitting about 300 messages.

The circuit under Percy and Edmund continued its quiet but efficient way, despite having so colourful and flamboyant a wireless operator. It had less astonishing feats to its credit than some of its neighbours, but it joined in the harrying of the panzers moving north to reinforce the German troops facing the Allied invasion, forcing them to frustrating delays.

Because of disagreements between the leaders of the communist and Gaullists on the one hand, and the Gestapo and the garrison Commander on the other, the surrender of Limoges was held up but finally effected on 20 August. Here the Fireman group merely backed it up. Nevertheless, Fireman had played its part in late August by making the withdrawal of the German troops from Aquitaine and Limousin eastward a veritable morass of attrition, whereby the hidden French cut off stragglers and impeded German movements by road or rail. Together with the German troops from Provence trying to draw out northwards ahead of the American troops, who were now threatening to cut them off as they advanced swiftly up the river Rhône, they were finally cornered and forced to surrender near Limoges. Their number must have amounted to nearly 100,000, and their surrender was the result of constant guerilla and Maquis action, although to the fury of the French, the Germans finally only surrendered to the Americans, leaving the circuits and their supporters baulked of their true victory.

This brought to a virtual end the operations of the circuit. Clearing and mopping up in the thousands of small towns and villages, was left to the French themselves.

Thus Paddy O'Sullivan, well-loved and remembered by the individual French men and women amongst whom she had been known and worked, sadly saw the shores of the land she had loved and been prepared to give her life for, vanish out of her sight, as she flew back home.

14
A Cross Against Evil

Muriel Tamara Byck

'She was a small, dark, pretty, little woman, earnest and serious... Later we girls thought of her with awe at the enormity of the task she had taken on... I always shudder when I think of those vast empty fields of France and how they must have looked to a young woman dropped into enemy territory.'

Audrey Ririe

Shortly before the D-Day Normandy landings, SOE sent a flurry of agents to help the French weaken the Germans and prepare risings when the Allies arrived.

Among several radio operators destined for the western Loire and Cher area, a land of smiling pastures, sleepy ancient towns, ornamental châteaux and thriving industries, was Muriel Byck. Muriel was to work in the Ventriloquist circuit with her organizer, Philippe de Vomécourt, whose personal choice she had been. Unusually, she arrived ahead of him, since he landed by Lysander on Maurice Southgate's ground, being unable to parachute because of a torn leg muscle.

At that point, Muriel may not have realized how lucky she was in her chief, a man of great experience, who had previously operated successfully in France and was again returning. This showed in his meticulous checks before she even left Britain — on her cover story, her papers and her belongings, right down to the new leather compact, her fiancé's gift, from which she would not be parted and which he returned suitably dog-eared. Nor was he so busy as not to be concerned with the daily welfare of those working around him.

To an onlooker, Muriel might have seemed too fragile for such a mission, hardly built in a heroic mould. However, her pretty, chubby, tiny and almost childish appearance masked the maturity and resilience of a 25-year-old woman. De Vomécourt said, 'She looked so young, but I had seen enough in France to know that courage knew no barriers of age.' Her shoulder-length dark hair could be arranged in a variety of styles useful for disguise and she had the appropriate photographs to support these identities. Born of French parents, Luba and Jacques Byck, now naturalized British citizens, she spoke perfect French. She became an airwoman in 1942, working in the Records office before joining SOE. She was intelligent, cheerful, a most capable and resourceful radio operator and a Jewess, this fact alone guaranteeing her unwavering hostility to the Germans.

On the day intended for her to leave England, she arrived at Tempsford airfield with the other radio operators and made ready for her flight, but at the last minute the weather closed in and it was cancelled. Twice more this happened on consecutive nights. It almost seemed as if the heavens themselves had conspired to thwart her mission. It is hard to imagine the mental and physical torment she must have endured, each time winding herself up to keep at bay her fears, of the dangers of night flying, of the act of parachuting and then of landing in a country where a relentless enemy would immediately start hunting her down. It was only on the fourth attempt that she and the others with her finally took off.

Over France the lights below flashed their signal, and one by one they leapt into the dark. She felt her parachute jerk and fill as she swung between earth and heaven. Then the ground rushed up and swallowed her and she was surrounded by voices, purposeful dark shapes and torches.

'Are you all right, Mademoiselle Michèle?'

This was France at last, the real language and her new code name! Rough hands helped divest her of the cumbersome parachute and patted and hugged her in welcome, and, since it was the beginning of Easter Day, the 9 April 1944, one of the reception party pressed into her hands as a keepsake a small gold cross and chain — a kind of talisman against evil from which she was never to be parted.

It was her organizer, Philippe de Vomécourt, now known to the resistance as Major de Saint Paul (a reminder of his prison days in Lyon) and to London by the code name Antoine, who took Muriel to a safe house in the small town of Salbris, where she was to lodge. The owner was Antoine Vincent, a reliable member of the resistance, who also

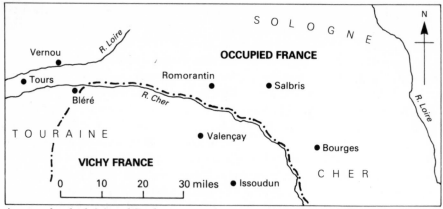

Area with which Muriel Byck was mainly associated.

owned the garage alongside his house where the Germans came to get
their vehicles repaired.

On her first day, while she was just getting to know them, Vincent and
Philippe, partly to tease her, took her for a meal at a restaurant just
outside the town. She looked around her and her eyes widened with
fear. She would have run back out, had she been able. 'We can't stay
here,' she whispered. In the smoke-laden atmosphere she saw that the
place was filled with German soldiers and to her horror she realized that
she and her two companions were the only French people there. Indeed
it was a favourite eating place for *Les Boches*. Vincent barred her way,
he wouldn't hear of it. It was his method of getting her used to the sight
of Germans. He knew that it was fine to think of them in the abstract
from the safety of England but quite another to see them around her
every day. Quietly he insisted that they sit down and proceed with their
meal as if nothing were wrong. Muriel could hardly swallow her food.
It wasn't very good anyway after what she had eaten in England,
rationing was much fiercer in France. However, it was an object lesson
in accustoming herself to the situation in occupied France and one meal
she would never forget.

From the time she landed, Muriel was kept very busy night and day.
By this time the A Mark III wireless transmitters and receivers were in
use which could not only work on batteries but also were much smaller.
They were thus easier to hide and transport from place to place. In
addition, the former fixed times of sending and receiving messages, the
'sked' given to every operator, had for some time been altered, as had
the wavelengths. Once she had changed the words into cipher, Muriel
could therefore tap them out in Morse during the day, at odd times,
places and frequencies. By now operators were instructed that such
emissions were not to exceed five minutes in length. Moreover, she was
now able to receive most London calls at night and decipher them when

she was locked away safely in her bedroom.

These changes had been instigated to safeguard the operator, for as SOE's arrangements and equipment became more sophisticated, so had the Germans' skill in tracking down the source of these messages. Banks of cathode-ray tube displays, resembling television screens, in the German radio-location centre of the RSHA (Reichssicherheitshauptamt) kept a 24-hour watch for such calls. A good direction finding station could narrow a signal down to about 20 miles and small canvas-topped detector vans, filled with equipment, to a further three or four. After this, men on foot, wearing hidden portable sets strapped to their waists and reading information on wrist dials, could pinpoint the exact place. However, men and vans could only work while a signal continued and a good resistance organization could recognize and take precautions against intruders. Operators now fully understood German detection methods.

The strain of working and watching night and day told on many operators but it seemed not to trouble Muriel. With a laugh and a quick wave she would pedal off on her old bike to deal with her 'telegrams', and when she returned, with a cheery smile she would quietly disappear for a short time secretly to decipher and later pass the 'telegrams' to her chief. On occasion, too, she helped out other regions with problems, nor did she mind acting as courier when the situation warranted, cycling off to deliver Philippe's messages to local resistance groups or taking information to alert sabotage teams.

Philippe was SOE's organizer of resistance in five counties. By this time more agents were available and London was able to give him several radio operators, both men and women, of whom Muriel was one. Nevertheless she was located in the house in Salbris which he usually used as his headquarters when he was not cycling or driving over this vast area. This was a far cry from three years before when there has been only one operator and one set in the whole of France. Not only that, but also Muriel herself had not one but four transmitters, which she kept in various places within a 10 mile radius of Salbris. One was in a village attic, another in a country house, one in a woodland shack and the last in a shed attached to a scrap yard near Vincent's garage.

She was here one day, sitting on a box amidst the tangled wreckage of old cars, tyres and rusting metal, tapping out her message to London, when she suddenly had a feeling that she was being watched. Still tapping away as if undisturbed, she ran her eyes quickly over her surroundings. She thus became aware that the knot-hole in one of the wooden planks of the shed wall had become alive. An eye was watching her. Her message changed to include a danger signal. Where was the man who was supposed to guard the entrance to the yard? Then the eye flickered and was gone. She jumped up and reached the spot just in time to see a German soldier leaving the yard. The terrible things about which she had been warned flashed through her mind. There could not be any mistake, she was in dire danger and all her friends with her. Although shaking with fear she kept a cool head. Mechanically she began to follow all the precautions in which she had been trained. She must first pack away all her equipment. Then she must obliterate any trace of her presence, her box and the table she used, and finally, with a personal stroke of genius she set about spreading a light layer of dust, rust and dirt where she had been, even adding a few artistic cobwebs. Then fear turned to shock and shaking like a leaf she returned to Vincent's house. Fortunately he saw her from the office where he was dealing with a customer, and realizing from her appearance that something was amiss he excused himself and came to her. 'You must go away immediately,' he decided, when he heard what had happened. 'I'll have to use my car whatever the risk. You must not be found here.' At that moment Philippe's car drew up outside. Some strange sort of sixth sense had communicated itself to him, making him feel something was wrong. Consequently he had turned back to investigate. It was a fortunate chance. Within minutes Muriel and her equipment were safely stowed in the back seat and the car was on its way.

The Germans did come later to follow up the soldier's story. They hadn't believed him, it sounded so incredible, but they were forced to do something. They screeched to a halt outside the garage but their investigations were half-hearted and apologetic, particularly when they were confronted by an obviously unused scrap dump, so thickly coated with the accumulated grime of many years that it patently had housed no-one, let alone a radio operator and all her equipment. Their informant was a fool and a dreamer. They were sorry to have disturbed the good Monsieur Vincent — such a helpful man — but of course he would understand. Duty was duty. They clicked their heels and shot out their arms in salute; 'Heil Hitler.' Then they departed in a cloud of dust. The unfortunate, bewildered soldier received 10 days detention.

Muriel moved to a new lodging, this time posing as a secretary on sick leave from Paris, who had to take medicines every few hours even at night. The family was not to be concerned if they heard her alarm go off at odd times. Philippe, having now become her uncle, dropped by regularly to watch her progress and was her most constant visitor, often taking her off for long walks in the good country air.

In fact there was a great deal in the air, for this was the time of a build-up in night drops of arms and equipment for the resistance which SOE was at last able to arrange with the RAF and USAAF. Operators like Muriel were now fully stretched, keeping up the flow of information needed by the planes — dropping zones, types of weapons, quantities, times.

There was more, too. For some time the resistance had considered how it might damage the arsenal that the Germans had created at Michenon, a former French army depot now enlarged by the Germans with the aid of forced labour to cover 50 acres. It stored shells, ammunition and bombs for use of the troops in north France and the Atlantic Wall, but the resistance could not attack it because it was so heavily guarded by troops, dogs and electrified fences. Then news was brought to Philippe that several goods trains were to collect supplies from the camp on 7 May. London was told and on that very afternoon passed a message through Muriel to say that Allied planes would bomb the camp from the air after dark. Already resistance saboteurs had blown up the lines to prevent the trains from leaving, and the local populace, with people working in the camp, were warned by word of mouth.

That night, just about midnight, the air raid sirens began to wail. First

came the pathfinder planes to mark the target with incendiaries, and when it was well alight and as bright as day they were followed by bombers of the RAF and USAAF. Soon all hell was let loose. The camp erupted with explosions shaking the ground up to nearly 20 miles away, while the air was filled with flying debris and flames. It became like a volcano. Those who escaped only

A Sologne landscape in Muriel's circuit.

ran into traps laid by the resistance. As a result of the raid, the wholesale destruction of the Arsenal undoubtedly seriously affected later German operations in Normandy. Afterwards, French escape lines were busy rescuing Allied airmen from the five bombers which had crashed during the raid.

Muriel had been kept busy sending and receiving signals during this activity, so it was not surprising that she looked rather tired and strained when things had quietened. The terrible explosions nearby too, had left her white and shaky. This would not do for a radio operator. Partly for this reason, and partly for her safety since Germans were reacting violently to the raid, Philippe arranged for her air traffic to be handled by other operators and sent her for a short break with another family with three daughters, some distance away. Later she was moved to the family home of a blacksmith at Vernou and given a little work to do, but still not too much.

One morning shortly after visiting her, Philippe had another premonition of something being wrong. He returned to find the family in an uproar. It appeared that they had breakfasted together as usual and

Muriel was very quiet. She had a headache and felt rather tired, so afterwards she said that she would go and lie down in her room for a while. Then even while she was turning to go, she had collapsed in a heap on the floor. 'Well, almost struck down you might say,' said Monsieur. Philippe went to look at her and found her lying on her bed, breathing but still unconscious. It seemed nothing could wake her. 'We must call a doctor,' said Philippe. They tried one, and then another, and then a third. The last one was at home and came around at once. After he had examined Muriel he shook his head and looked grave. He diagnosed meningitis. 'Only a hospital can save her.'

Now they were in a dilemma. The Germans kept a careful check on any persons admitted to hospital — a check meant to catch such people as Muriel or Philippe — and he knew that their papers would not stand up to such close scrutiny. Could he afford the risk? In the face of a question of life or death there seemed little choice. He telephoned for an ambulance. With the story that they were evacuees from Paris and that he was her uncle, Philippe accompanied Muriel in the ambulance to Romorantin and saw her admitted to the hospital. It was run by nuns who were both efficient and kind. Perhaps they suspected the truth but they never disclosed it.

A scene in Romorantin.

Another doctor came to examine Muriel as soon as she was settled. Anxious to know what was to happen, and fearful that she might speak English in delirium or give herself away, Philippe remained. The prognosis was bad. Only a very painful lumbar puncture would help and it must be done immediately. 'Would Monsieur give his consent?' 'Very well.'

The hospital provisions were very elementary. The operation was not for the squeamish, but Philippe bravely supported Muriel in his arms while it was done. Afterwards, despite the danger and the host of things that were waiting to be done with D-Day hardly two weeks away, he stayed in the darkened room by her bedside. Perhaps they could save her. Perhaps she would suddenly open her eyes and ask what had happened. Instead he saw her lying there white as marble, unlike the vital laughing girl he had known. She seemed to have left him and gone a long way away where none could follow. Soon after, still unconscious, she died.

It struck Philippe like a physical blow, but there was no time to grieve. Because they were in hospital there were many formalities to go through

Assisting the Resistance

An unusual photograph showing the path of bonfires laid out in the dark by the resistance,
for the approaching aircraft at the bottom left of the picture. (Weidenfeld & Nicolson)

Left *American aircraft drop food, guns and ammunition to the Resistance on Vercors.* (Imperial War Museum)

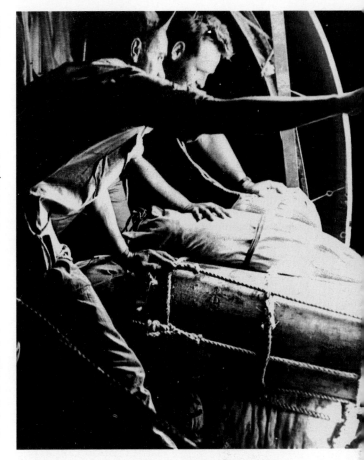

Right *What it was like in the aircraft dropping supplies. The crew chief dispatches the containers first, and the packages follow afterwards in successive passes.* (Weidenfeld & Nicolson)

Below *Gathering parachutes and supplies after an air drop. Yvonne Baseden* (**Chapter 12**) *worked her radio at the dropping zone from start to finish of a similar operation.* (Imperial War Museum)

Left *Parachuting into France from a midnight drop. For the agent this was only the beginning. What lay ahead?* (Weidenfeld & Nicolson)

Below left *Parachute landings were not always perfect, nor in the right place. Reception committees might be resistants, Germans or other unexpected things like an unconcerned herd of cows.* (Imperial War Museum)

Right *In their makeshift camp, an SOE man trains members of the French Resistance on the use of the new weapons that had been supplied to them by air drops. Pearl Witherington* **(Chapter 10)**, *Anne-Marie Walters* **(Chapter 11)** *and Sonya Butt* **(Chapter 17)** *took on regular training duties, as occasionally did some of the others.* (Weidenfeld & Nicolson)

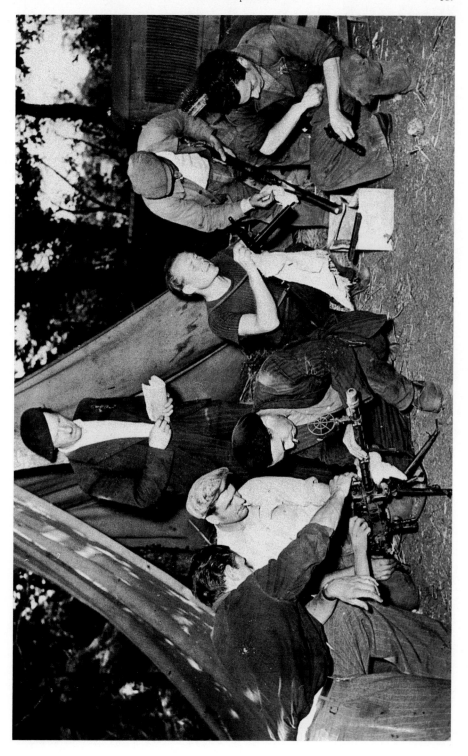

Above *The results of sabotage on the power house of a factory.* (Weidenfeld & Nicolson)

Below *Electric pylons brought down by the Resistance across the railway line to Paris on Hitler's 55th birthday, 20 May 1944.* (Weidenfeld & Nicolson)

Above *A derailed train beside a viaduct on the Limoges-Ucel line blown up the Maquis.* (Imperial War Museum)

Below *The Michenon works on the day after the air raid, set up by Muriel Byck* **(Chapter 14)** *on her radio.* (Weidenfeld & Nicolson)

Above *A Lysander has just landed to a special daylight reception in the mountains, among members of the Resistance.* (Group Captain F. Griffiths)

Below *Sibyl Sturrock, the WAAF who worked for SIS behind enemy lines with the Jugoslav partisans, greets the Red Army Russian Mission in Croatia in 1945.* (Lady Stewart)

and now he and his people were in greater danger. He was forced to break the news to friends coming to find out how Muriel fared, and for fear of discovery he had to forbid them to attend her funeral. He also had to answer many questions. Afterwards he had to arrange for the interment and walk alone behind the hearse to the cemetery. (She was buried under her assumed name and still wearing her gold cross.) Then fate dealt her last stroke. As the burial service proceeded, two cars came to a sharp halt outside the gates. It was the Germans. Fortunately, with unusual delicacy, they waited for the service to end, by which time Philippe had slipped through the graveyard, over the wall and out of their hands.

Later he was to learn that Muriel had suffered from meningitis once before as a child, a secret she had meticulously hidden from SOE knowing that, because of the faint risk of it recurring, they would never have allowed her to return to France. So great was her courage and her desire to see and serve her beloved country once again that she felt that the danger to her own life was a risk worth taking. And this she had done, playing her part in a small piece of history and endearing herself to all who knew her.

For many years her grave was tended by the townspeople of Romorantin, who regarded her as a heroine of the resistance and on every 23 May, the anniversary of her death in 1944, they brought flowers in her memory. She is also commemorated on their town memorial. Much later her grave was moved to the War Cemetery at Pornic to join the war dead from the British Services who are buried in this region.

15
Sweet Geneviève

Philippa Latour

'We both worked with my brother in Normandy where for security reasons we kept very much apart from one another, meeting only when necessary.'
Lise Villameur (de Baissac)

On 1 May 1944, Pippa Latour found herself dangling at the end of a parachute, rapidly sailing towards the reception party awaiting her in the shadows of the moonlit field. With her came one of the small transceivers developed by SOE, as she was to become another wireless operator at what was to become a frantically busy period in the life of the new Scientist circuit. There was also the ever-present danger of the Germans, as the area was thick with troops and Gestapo. Of particular danger to Pippa were the German Direction Finders, growing more skilled in locating wireless operators. The Germans also had several captive sets and false circuits from which they played misleading information to London pretending they were British. Sometimes London realized this and used them for its own purposes in a complicated radio game, but some it never spotted. A few were nearby, so consequently for her own safety Pippa had to start a wandering life, rarely able to stay in one place for more than a few days, and often for only one. Fortunately, the girl on her bicycle was a very familiar sight in most of France, where other forms of transport for the population were becoming daily more rare as the Germans commandeered most vehicles and trains. But there was always the snap check or the unexpected search on the road or in a house, which could trap anyone who was not both careful, cunning and courageous.

Naturally, Pippa had several wireless sets, which she located at various houses over the area where she transmitted, so that if a message was urgent she could use the set nearest to where she found herself. She had been given the code name Geneviève and by this she was known in the circuit. At the beginning she was rather lost and overwhelmed by her situation practically on the battle front, but shortly she developed more confidence and became almost too bold. Twice while she was in a house transmitting, there was a banging on the door, and the command, 'Open, Police.' While she hurriedly removed the evidence of her set and papers, she could hear the Germans talking to the lady of the house. Once it was only to ask questions. Here Pippa appeared shortly without undue concern, and in a charming manner satisfied the police without causing any suspicion of her clandestine activity. Another time the police searched a different house that she was at the time using, but the

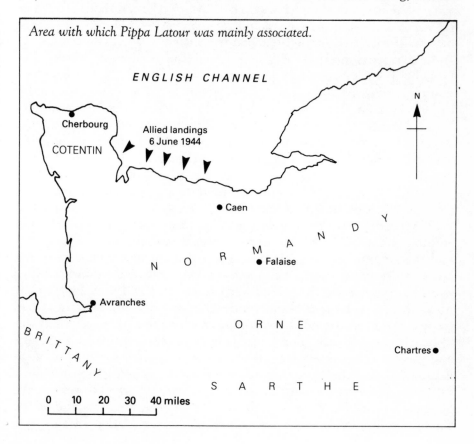

Area with which Pippa Latour was mainly associated.

ENGLISH CHANNEL

N

Cherbourg

COTENTIN

Allied landings
6 June 1944

Caen

N O R M A N D Y

Falaise

Avranches

ORNE

B R I T T A N Y

Chartres

S A R T H E

0 10 20 30 40 miles

set was well hidden and she spun such a convincing story for her presence that again her questioners were thrown off the scent. Both times she escaped by a mixture of coolness, presence of mind and good luck.

Like many SOE agents Philippa Latour was born outside Britain, in Durban in March 1921, where her father Philippe, a Frenchman, had married Louise, who was a British citizen living in South Africa. Pippa, as her friends called her, came to Britain and joined the WAAF in November 1941, when she was 20. She trained in the difficult trade of flight mechanic for airframes, but was later accepted into SOE in November 1943 and commissioned as an Honorary Section Officer.

She was intended to join the Scientist circuit, which under its organizer Claude de Baissac had

Orne — a typical farmhouse.

suffered a great deal of change since Mary Herbert had arrived at Bordeaux in the Gironde during the late part of 1942. During its greatest days in 1943, Scientist had reached from Paris to the Pyrénées. Its size and its interconnection with the crumbling edifice of Prosper had brought about the recall of Claude in August 1943. By November 1943, disasters in nearby circuits and the crippling activities of a double agent had dealt it an almost irrecoverable blow, despite the best efforts of Roger Landes, the wireless operator who had taken Claude's place. Roger attempted to leave some useful contacts still ready to function before he too had to flee, although he courageously returned to the area in early 1944 to form the new circuit, Actor, out of the ruins of what remained. Scientist had therefore been, in the parlance of the resistance, more or less scorched or burned out.

1944 was the year intended by the Allies to see the liberation of France and to this end SOE bent its efforts to prepare members of the resistance and the circuits that organized and supplied them. Its aims were that areas to the south should be able to prevent large-scale movements of German troops towards the northern battle area and that areas in the north should, as far as possible, hinder the Germans and help the Allied troops. However, the northern area near where the Allied invasion was to take place was weak. There was a big gap in the existing SOE circuits and there was no secret army in the wings ready to assist the Allies. In February 1944, therefore, Claude de Baissac, as one of SOE's most experienced agents was sent to the area around Chartres to reform the Scientist circuit. He brought with him his wireless operator, and at the beginning of April his sister Lise joined him as his courier. By this time his Scientist circuit was functioning well and had spread to cover a large part of Normandy, just short of the coast. Now London decided that he needed further help, particularly as he was very close to the area shortly to be used by Operation Overlord. This was when Pippa made her welcome appearance.

In the normal way, the members of the SOE team kept well away from one another, so as not to raise the Germans' suspicions or allow them to capture more than one member at a time, but it was nearly always necessary for the courier to see the organizer and sometimes the wireless operator to pass messages. In an emergency, when time was of the essence, however, the organizer himself had to be present to send and receive urgent information through the wireless operator. One such occasion was during the build-up of the days before the Normandy landings, only a month after Pippa arrived. At that time Claude, Lise and Pippa, worked in the same house. There on the first floor of a half-derelict farmhouse, with wooden benches for seating, straw for bedding and no water or food except what they foraged for themselves, they coded and decoded the many messages Pippa sent to and received from London. Then they passed them on to various members of the organization to follow the instructions they had been given. This was a short but hectic period, day

Part of the Normandy coast near the D Day landings.

and night, when the importance of their mission had to override the risk they were taking. In any case they hoped from the information they were recording that within days the Germans would have far more important things to take their attention than the capture of a few British SOE members.

Then arrived 6 June 1944, the great day for which all of France had been waiting, when they heard that the combined forces of the Allies had landed on the shores of Normandy. All the SOE circuits were already carrying out their allotted tasks of sabotage, but the landings obviously affected Pippa and her circuit greatly as they were so near. It also enhanced her danger, since the area was soon full of German troops hurring to the battle front. Although the landings were themselves very successful (the Germans being caught by surprise with low-grade troops defending the coast) the British, American and Canadian troops with a small party of Frenchmen taking part were soon brought to a standstill by stronger German resistance, which became tougher and fiercer the further they advanced

inland. The Allies had also believed that local resistance groups would
come to their aid and were severely disillusioned to find that the French
in the coastal towns and farms were none too eager to have their rich
orchards, fields and houses fought over by armies of *any* nationality.

The British and Canadians found themselves held up by an
inopportune panzer division for nearly a month just outside William the
Conqueror's favourite city of Caen, which had been expected to fall on
the first day; while to their west, the Americans mainly concentrated on
extending their bridgehead, making it over 60 miles long by 12 July. This
delay enabled the Germans to bring up their tanks and anti-armour
weapons, generally more powerful than those of the Allies, and also their
best troops, who fought with almost religious fanaticism. Moreover the
Allies had not fully realized the implications of fighting in the bocage
country of Normandy with its deep ditches topped by thick hedges, a gift
for defence and a bad stumbling block for attack.

Pippa's circuit therefore found itself playing a role not usually designed
for members of SOE. As virtually every foot of soil was being fought over,
information on German strength and troop positions could give a vital
advantage to the invading armies. In May, Pippa had set up a reception
for a two-man team, immediately sent by Claude to establish a sub-circuit
called Verger close to Caen. It was to prove very useful both in sabotage
and information until the two agents were captured and shot by the
Germans in early July. Their demise was shortly followed by another
reception arranged by Pippa, this time in a meadow near Avranches, for
Jack Hayes, who set up another sub-circuit called Helmsman in the
Cotentin peninsula. Using about 30 messengers, it successfully got
information through the enemy lines to the Americans. Meanwhile
Claude had moved the main base of his activities forward to the

A landscape in Normandy where Pippa travelled.

département of Orne, where his sabotage teams could do more damage to the arriving German forces and German forward troop dispositions could be relayed to the Allies.

July saw the turning point in the struggle for Normandy ending with the capture of Avranches, and August saw the gradual repulse of the German forces sent to oppose the Allies, speeded up by risings engineered by the French Forces of the Interior, the FFI. In that heady month Paris was taken back by its own citizens and the German troops were in full retreat.

During this period Pippa had many narrow escapes, flitting to and fro over Orne from one hidden radio set to another, or following after Lise who frequently carried her wirelesses ahead of Pippa. One day during the German retreat, she was on her way to a distant farmhouse from where her next transmission was expected to go out. As the area was filled with Germans, Claude, having no one else to spare and knowing that it was not safe to let her go alone, sent his sister Lise to accompany her. The Allied victories which Pippa constantly heard on the BBC had sometimes made her less careful of her safety and less conscious of the danger surrounding her. This worried Claude, as his pianists were too valuable to lose, and Pippa was both too young and bold for her own safety, only measuring the demoralization of the mass of soldiery by those units she saw in flight, rather than the individual soldier, who might be driven to revenge if he suspected her mission. They were both on their bicycles and Lise was carrying some spare parts for the set, hidden in the belt around the waist of her dress, believing that what was in full view was less likely to be searched.

As they came to a bend in the country road they had taken, believing it was clear of Germans, they saw a soldier at the side examining all those passing by. There was no way of avoiding him, so they rode casually up to him and getting down from their bicycles produced their papers for his inspection. But more followed. He wanted to search them for arms or sabotage materials. The resistance had been quite active over the past week in this area, and the Germans knew that they were being helped by many in the locality who, with the Germans in retreat, were becoming more open in their hostility. A thorough search might mean removing clothes and examining different parts of the body and was usually carried out at the police headquarters, but a wayside search usually meant passing the hands over the body, clothes and all, to detect any unusual lumps or bumps on the person. Pippa was all right, but would the German find the parts in Lise's belt? Quietly Pippa submitted to the search. Then it was Lise's turn. What would they do if he discovered the spares? A minute lasted like an hour, and then Pippa felt like laughing. The German did not bother with the belt, not even noticing that it was rather an odd shape. He merely grunted, and stood back motioning them to go.

The search was satisfactory. They mounted their bikes, overwhelmed with relief, when suddenly there was a clatter on the road at their feet. One of the spare parts had fallen out of Lise's belt. Surely this was the end? To Pippa's astonishment the German hardly seemed to notice, being already busy with another couple riding behind them. Quickly Lise bent to retrieve the part and then they were off cycling like the wind, in case the German had second thoughts. But he didn't and they got away without further mishap. Nevertheless they had both had a great fright.

Claude was the first to meet the advanced troops in July 1944, at the local Mayor's office of a recently liberated village. There he was standing with Lise, both immaculately turned out in uniform, when the first soldiers from a 'Geordie' regiment turned up. 'Where have they come from?' asked one. His companion shrugged. 'Oot o' the sky,' he replied, with more truth than he realized.

In August, Pippa stood at the side of the road as the American army drove into the village where she was staying. She waved, shouted and laughed with the best of them, as the motorcade drove up the main street with stars and stripes on cars and uniforms. Everyone was clapping and cheering, catching at the hands of the men and smothering those that could be reached with flowers and kisses. No one particularly noticed the girl from SOE, in her faded summer dress, and yet she as much as any of them had paved the way for their victory. She had sent over 135 messages to London and carried out her mission safely and successfully. Now for her at that moment her work was over, the war had ended and France was at last free.

16
Toll For The Brave

Lilian Verna Rolfe

'Jeune anglaise volontaire... elle parvint grace à ses solides connaissances techniques et à son beau sang-froid a transmettre... Après l'arrestation de son chef, elle n'en continua pas moins courageusement son travail au milieu du danger croissant... Rest un vivant symbole de l'amitié Franco-Britannique.'

Citation for Croix de Guerre, 1946

A dark-haired girl, with steady dark eyes and a mouth made for smiling — this was how Lilian Verna Rolfe appeared when she came from Rio de Janeiro, Brazil, to live in Woking at the outbreak of war. With her was her twin sister, Helen, her British father, George, and her Russian mother, Alexandra. Her parents had met and married in Paris where their twins were born in the V11 Arrondissement on 26 April 1914. So the girls passed from one world war into another.

Lilian became an airwoman in May 1943, starting like so many girls in so-called general duties. On the shoulder of her uniform, she proudly sported her Brazil flash showing the country from whence she had come. Shortly her patriotism, her steadiness, her maturity and her fluency in several languages made it only a small step to being offered a place in SOE, which she joined officially in November 1943, destined to be sent to work in the field in France.

Strangely, a number of normally reliable sources shroud many events in her career as an agent in mystery, even disagreeing on her type of work. However, her French honours citation made in 1946, a WAAF record and family papers at the Imperial War Museum, coincide on many details and follow the most likely course, which is the one given here.

Her organizer, George Wilkinson, codenamed Étienne, was sent to France in early April 1944 to set up a new circuit to be called Historian in the area containing the towns of Nangis, Montargis and Orléans, part of which had been covered by the now destroyed Prosper circuit. To his west, Headmaster was coming back into action after many difficulties; to his southern flank Ventriloquist was reviving, and Wrestler was soon to arise under the redoubtable leadership of Pearl Witherington out of the ashes of Stationer. The rise and fall of so many circuits in this area shows the high detection ratio so near to Paris, the hub of German counter-espionage and wireless monitoring services where the Gestapo was now dominant. It was therefore a highly dangerous assignment. On top of it all, the Germans were becoming understandably nervous knowing that an Allied invasion upon the north coast of France was likely to take place soon, and redoubled their efforts to arrest sympathizers and members of the resistance, as well as any agents who guided and supplied them. Nor were they too proper in the methods they used to produce information or to vent their rage on those who withheld it.

Lilian was set down as part of Operation Umpire by one of two Lysanders bringing agents to the Touraine area, arriving near Bléré from Tangmere airfield on 6 May 1944, some time after George had started on his travels around his region, making contacts and trying to build up his

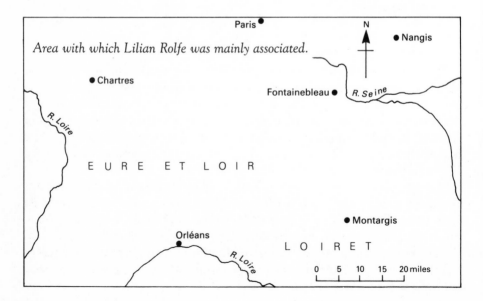

Area with which Lilian Rolfe was mainly associated.

new circuit. When she arrived she carried a tiny transmitter and receiver strapped to her body. It was more fragile than the sturdier B2, one reason why she did not parachute in. The A Mark III was one of the new breed

of radios produced by the skilful designers working for SOE in the war of the boffins, where men on both sides tried to outdo one another with their ingenious inventions in many fields, so that they could keep one step ahead of the other side. Lilian's radio measured in total $10 \times 7 \times 5$ in and weighed as little as 5½ lb (2.5 kg) without its case or accessories, which took it up to 9 lb (4 kg). It sacrificed range for

A scene in the Loire Valley.

size, its 5 watt output only technically capable of 400 miles but really able to transmit well over 500 miles extremely clearly, a range more than adequate for the area covered by Historian. She had little cause to use it, however, as she was separated from her organizer for several weeks, as he travelled around his circuit. She was able therefore to settle in the area, establish her cover story, meet and get over the shock of her first Germans, get to know the routes she would have to use with her bike and make some useful contacts of her own, including the leaders of the local Maquis. Apart from a few messages she used her wireless very little until George, having got the circuit organized, came back to find her. Then she started work with him in earnest, under her code name of Nadine.

By now the messages she was receiving warned that D-Day was fast approaching and the volume of traffic through her set suddenly shot up astronomically. Daily she made contact with London, handling requests and instructions for the Maquis and resistance groups in the area. As a result a great quantity of armaments were sent and parachuted in successfully to the dropping zones which she had notified to London, supplies much needed by the men who impatiently awaited the orders for them to be used in mass attacks on the enemy once Operation Overlord was launched.

In an area infested with Gestapo and Milice, Lilian took every possible precaution not to let her set or herself fall into enemy hands. Although the sheer quantity of air traffic made her work at all hours of the day and night, she also remembered her training and endeavoured to be on the move from one place to another, both in the countryside and in safe houses, as she knew that the Germans had detection vans trying to track down her messages as fast as she sent them. Receiving them was not so dangerous, as the destination of a signal could not be traced. It needed no imagination to realize that the Germans had their most skilled Direction Finders hot on her trail, a compliment to her technique and effectiveness but a compliment she could well do without.

Then at last came the instructions everyone had been expecting. The Allies had set foot on French soil. In the previous and following nights there was an outburst of sabotage over the length and breadth, not only of Lilian's circuit, but also the whole extent of France. It was now not so much a question of encouraging sabotage but preventing it happening undirected, lest precious hoarded supplies be frittered away on unimportant targets.

Historian also played its part in hampering the German troops sent north and east to defend the Allied bridgeheads around Caen and the Cherbourg peninsula. Guerilla tactics were most effective, sniping at stragglers, cutting communications, derailing trains and generally disrupting the orderly arrival of tanks and troops at the battleground. These actions were stiffened and sometimes led by no more than three persons of uniformed Jedburgh or SAS teams of mixed nationalities. Historian itself received at least one SAS unit in June 1944.

Drawing of the A Mark III transceiver, the nearest set to miniaturization. The transmitter and receiver are in one container, while the headset, morse key, crystals and the small box containing a 6 volt vibrator, to enable a change-over from the mains electricity supply to a car battery, come separately. Complete in its suitcase it measures only 13 × 9 × 4 ins and weighs less than 9 lbs. (Drawing by Lt Col P. Lorain)

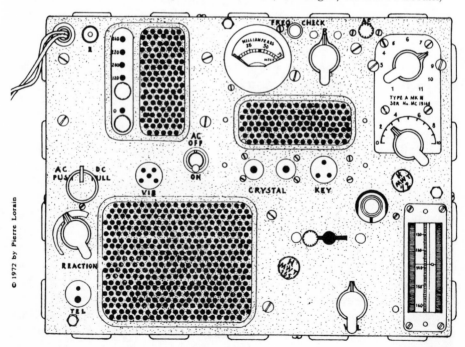

Guided over the last miles of its flight by the Eureka ground beacon operated by the kneeling figure, a Hudson aircraft touches down, disgorges its passengers and loads up on a field somewhere in France, closely guarded by armed members of the resistance. (Drawing by Lt Col P. Lorain)

At the end of this month of frantic activity and turmoil, George fell victim to the Gestapo and was captured near Orléans. By now he had been sent several more assistants, who with Lilian's help and the aid of the local leader of the Maquis, carried on with his work, ensuring continuity of all the plans that had been carefully laid in the previous month. Resistance continued to grow and large numbers joined with the local Maquis. At the beginning of July, Lilian took part in an engagement against a force of enemy troops, while the Allied forces were still struggling to break through the Germans fighting fiercely along the strip of Normandy they were containing.

During the month of July, the Gestapo, preparing to evacuate Montargis, made a final purge of all known or suspected members of the resistance. Consequently there were many arrests, among whom were some of George's assistants. Others disappeared or lay low until the danger period had passed. But worse was to come. In pursuit of one of the resistance leaders the Germans raided a house at Nangis. The man they were looking for was not there, but they found a girl who was lodging there at the time whose papers did not satisfy their inspection. She was roughly arrested, handcuffed and taken to their headquarters at Orléans, where they shortly discovered, much to their surprise, that they had netted a far more important member of the resistance group. She was none other than the wireless operator of the SOE circuit — Lilian Rolfe.

For Lilian this meant her transfer to Paris to the rough, intensive interrogation of the fearsome Gestapo, of which she had been warned during training. Neither then nor at any time in the future did she give the Germans any information that would have been of the slightest use to them, and they must have realized this, because she was quickly sent to Fresnes prison. But time was running out for the Germans, as the Allies started to advance, aided by many of the local French forces who often took over towns and districts themselves ahead of the liberating armies. In mid-August the Gestapo staff left Paris, the city being freed by its own people a week later. One of the Paris Gestapo's final gestures on 8 August 1944 was to put its remaining 37 SOE men and women prisoners — most by now languishing in Fresnes prison — on a transport to deport them all to Germany.

Thus Lilian found herself with two other SOE women sent to Ravensbrück women's concentration camp. Here packed like sardines, living in filth and squalor, with constant Appells, starvation rations, degradation and endless labour, she spent her first three weeks in the main camp. The Red Cross parcels which might have somewhat alleviated her lot were forbidden to all French and Russian prisoners.

Torgau was a dependent camp, not far from Ravensbrück, and housed those who were considered fit enough to do forced labour, such as work in local factories, farms or roads. Because such heavy work was expected of them, food was slightly better, guards more relaxed and conditions did not seem as bad as those on the main camp. Lilian was sent there with her two companions on a working party. Having rather more strength and enough leisure, the three SOE girls therefore started to consider the possibilities of an escape from the camp and talked over various options when they were in their huts for the night. They felt that having an objective helped them through difficult days and in any case all prisoners of war knew it was their duty to attempt escape.

The only trouble was that although they should have been classed as prisoners of war, the Germans had ignored this fact and were treating them as civil malcontents or political prisoners, and apart from not sending them to a prisoner of war camp — often a death sentence although they did not know it — they had never been brought to trial. In fact none of the SOE girls was tried, so their imprisonment was breaking all the rules of war drawn up in the Geneva Convention to which Germany had subscribed. But this was a small matter in comparison with the terrible crimes of which the Germans were later found guilty.

Unfortunately for Lilian, before their plans to escape had materialized she was sent back to the main camp with her two companions, their stint at Torgau completed. Then because they had fared so well on their first labour camp the three girls were sent on a second draft of forced labour, this time to Königsberg where they were to work on clearing and construction work for a new airfield. It was now winter, freezing cold, with ice and snow. They were thinly clothed for the conditions, the food was bad and there was very little of it. They had to lift and carry heavy weights, to dig in deep frozen water for hours on end, to fill swamps with sand, to cut and lay slabs of turf, to hew and haul down trees and tree stumps, to drag boulders and equipment, all in the open, without covering or shelter. There was no medical treatment and many died from pneumonia, dysentery, cholera and tuberculosis, if they did not break down from sheer exhaustion, malnutrition or cruel treatment by the guards, who thought nothing of beating women staggering with heavy loads or almost dying on their feet. The women were completely expendable, and the guards vented their fears, frustrations and often warped natures on the poor starving wretches who worked there. Indeed when the German Air Force came to occupy the camp, so painstakingly created, even they were horrified by what they saw. Under these conditions, Lilian no longer spoke of escape. It was all she could do to survive. She was already sick with a spot on her lung and her breathing becoming hard and laboured. All her former cheerfulness failed her and she found it hard not to sink into the torpor which usually preceded a loss of the will to live, and then death.

It was therefore with relief that she heard that the three of them had been recalled to the main camp in January of 1945, by an order of the German Secret Police countersigned by the Camp Commandant. She may have guessed that the Allies were already encircling Germany, but she was now so weak that it seemed of little moment. On her return she was not sent to her former hut but to the punishment block, where she occupied a dark, cold, windowless cell, scarcely big enough to lie down. After some time she was removed from there and put into a block of isolation cells, near where a large crematorium had been built to take the many corpses that the camp conditions produced. Possibly the Germans hoped to hide the evidence of their actions from the rapidly advancing Russian and Anglo-American forces.

From here on about the 5 February 1945 in the evening, she was summoned to the crematorium yard with her two companions. Lilian's strength had so failed that she was carried out on a stretcher. She must have known then what would happen. Smart in his high boots and peaked cap, his buttons gleaming, the Camp Commandant read out a short order from Berlin saying that the prisoners were condemned to death. Also present were the camp doctor and dentist with three SS guards. Then the Camp Commandant gave the order and the girls were brought forward one by one. Each was then shot from behind with a small calibre pistol through the back of the neck, those waiting guarded by two soldiers and watching the death of the others. What agony of mind did they suffer at what they beheld, knowing there was no escape. Lilian met her death without flinching and her bravery together with those of her friends deeply impressed all those taking part. Afterwards their bodies were taken to the crematorium and burned. By then Lilian probably had the satisfaction of knowing that the country for which she was giving her life had been freed.

There is, however, as in several important points in Lilian's life, a slightly different and unpleasant ending, recorded by Mary Lindell, who survived her imprisonment at Ravensbrück, as did Yvonne Baseden. She thinks that when the girls returned from their work Kommando near Königsberg, they had been told that they would then be sent to the prisoner of war camp near Lake Constance, but as is now known no women SOE agents were ever sent there. It was a fiction used to hide a death sentence. Consequently, Mary felt that their deaths were as a direct result of this. Moreover she knew that the normal method of execution at Ravensbrück was hanging and she was reliably informed that the clothes of the three girls had been handed back to the store unsoiled. Therefore she believed that this was how they died. Such second-hand evidence balanced against the sworn evidence of the Camp Commandant is difficult to reconcile — except that they did die, but whether swiftly or slowly only Lilian in her last hours knew. It was a sad end to a brave venture, saddest since it was so close to the war ending.

17
Wink As You Jump

Sonya Esmée Florence Butt

'What little I was able to do was motivated by my love for France and because I could not imagine not doing my utmost when my country was at war.'

Sonya Butt

While she was still in training, on her first jump from an aircraft over Tatton Park, she looked over her shoulder and winked at her neighbour, a French Canadian officer called Captain d'Artois. He was preparing for a similar mission and was filled with admiration at such light-hearted daring and beauty. There and then he determined to marry such a courageous girl, if they both survived their descent into occupied France.

Coming from an RAF family living in Woking, Sonya Butt joined the WAAF at the earliest possible moment at the end of 1941, when she was just 17½ years of age. Her trade was administration which she detested, and was only too pleased to transfer into SOE in 1943. When she joined SOE she was among the ex-airwomen of whom Cécile Lefort, who died at Ravensbrück aged 44, was the oldest, and she, Sonya, was the youngest.

Sonya was to be assigned as a courier to Christopher Hudson, codenamed Albin, organizer of the Headmaster circuit. Originally covering the area west of Lyon around Clermont Ferrand, Christopher had the misfortune of being arrested almost as soon as he landed in 1942, and then the incredible luck of escaping from prison. He was now head of a more-or-less new circuit, still called Headmaster, but in the Sarthe area, centring around the cathedral town of Le Mans to the south of Normandy, and backing up Claude de Baissac's Scientist. These circuits were therefore well in place for the areas ahead of the forthcoming invasion, and played their part skilfully in damaging and delaying the German forces being rushed up to the front.

Sonya was one of the latest WAAF landed in France before the invasion, arriving on the 28 May 1944, only nine days before D-Day. Supplies to the Maquis had been greatly increased in 1944, but many of the weapons were new to the raw recruits who needed instruction on how to handle them so that they would not be as much of a danger to themselves as to others. Anne-Marie Walters and Pearl Witherington had been most successful in this role, and Sonya, codenamed Blanche, was given the special training necessary to help in the same work. Shortly after her arrival, one of the agents dropped with her was shot during one of the many guerrilla engagements fought by the Maquis against the Germans. Sonya therefore took over his post as weapons training officer, fitting this in with her other work during the confused days that followed. In her own words, 'I filled in wherever the need arose.'

As Christopher's courier, she also had to carry money and messages and maintain liaison between the different, very dispersed, resistance groups, Maquis and their organizers, over an area infested with German troops, the Gestapo, the French police and the Milice. Frenchmen and agents feared the latter almost more than the others, since they were chosen from local men, collaborating with the Germans, very sharp-witted and suspicious, who knew their area well and often enjoyed their

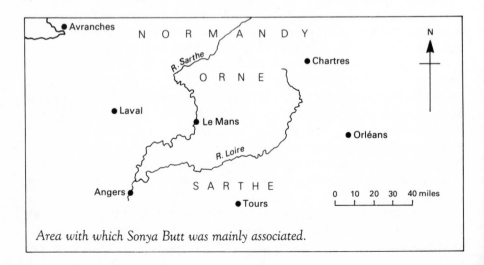

Area with which Sonya Butt was mainly associated.

feeling of power, turning into petty tyrants and sadists towards their
fellows on the slightest excuse. Many were little better than thugs. These
were the kind of people against whom Sonya had to pit her wits as she
cycled from one place to another, inviting danger, running many risks
and having many narrow escapes, saved by a convincing cover story, a
clear, cool head and a daily fund of great courage and determination.

Once she was stopped by two Germans as she walked along the road.
Flashing her most charming smile, she produced the papers for which
they asked and, used to the procedure by now, waited for the questions
and for her documents to be
returned. They were looking at
her rather strangely and her heart
skipped a beat. Did they know
something about her? Had
someone informed and collected a
ransom, or were they searching
for someone else? One of them
beckoned imperiously. 'We need
to examine your papers more
closely. Come with us.'

*Pickers at work in the vineyards — a
familiar scene to Sonya as she cycled
around the circuit.*

As she was escorted along,
Sonya racked her brains to work
out what might be wrong. Did she
have the wrong stamp on her
papers? Was there a wrong date? Would they realize that the papers were
forgeries, albeit very clever ones? Outwardly the injured innocent but
inwardly in a turmoil, she wondered if this was to be the end of her brief
mission. She was taken to a small room, where a man at a large desk
once more examined her papers and started asking questions. Her knees
were shaking, but she knew that innocent or guilty, every Frenchwoman
would be afraid. She protested volubly at such treatment, wondering
what more was to come. Her interrogator tapped her papers
thoughtfully, looking hard in her face. Then she was sent to a dark,
cheerless cell. This is it, she thought, but she determined to keep to her
present cover story as a young girl visiting friends. No one came and
morning slipped into afternoon. She suspected that the Germans were
checking her story.

At length there was the sound of a key turning in the lock, and the
heavy door swung open. The German guard outside beckoned. 'Come,'
he barked. Sonya's heart dropped. Were there to be more questions?
Down some long corridors, she was at length taken into a large office,
busy with many desks and many Germans. She was taken to one behind
which sat a man who asked her name and nodded. 'Your papers,' he
said, handing them over to her. 'You may go now.' She felt weak. It was

all over. She was free. There was no time to dally, however. She must get out as quickly as possible. Thanking everyone in sight, she hurried out of the room and to freedom. It had taken four hours, and had been the narrowest of escapes so far.

Sonya had dark hair and eyes with a gentle mouth but a determined nose and chin. Her youth and good looks might have misled her enemies but not her friends, and she quickly earned the liking and respect — not easily won — of those with whom she worked. Young as she was, her cool head and knowledge gave her an air of authority, so that she

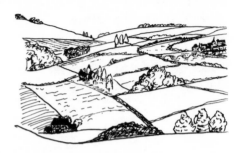

The rolling countryside of Sarthe where Sonya travelled on her missions.

eventually became, in function if not in name, the second in command of the circuit. She took care, however, to sink well into the background and avoid drawing any attention to herself, particularly from the Germans working in her area. Indeed, the house where she frequently stayed was not far from the requisitioned home of the Gestapo chief, whom she often saw in his comings and goings. These became so regular that he would nod acknowledgement as she passed, never dreaming of her true rôle. Or had he decided to have her watched? Had this perhaps been the reason for her arrest? At least he must have been satisfied and soon had far more important matters to claim his full attention.

The Normandy landings brought great activity, both in the field of sabotage and, later, guerilla attacks as enemy troops passed through Headmaster's Sarthe and then tangled with Scientist in the Orne *département* where Pippa Latour worked. Most SOE organizations functioned well.

Nevertheless, there were and had been problems for SOE circuits, not so much concerning the enemy, which were relatively clear-cut, but among the French themselves. In early days it had been the belligerence of the communists and the supporters of Vichy, including much of the Roman Catholic church, but this had been settled after the invasion of Russia and the unoccupied zone of France by the Germans. Later, differences surfaced among the French of various political persuasions, and a great gulf opened between the supporters of General de Gaulle and the resistance inspired and supplied by F Section. In the field, agents working for various factions usually found a satisfactory compromise, but battles were fought above their heads very bitterly in the safety of council chambers in England and America, often resulting in confusion where there should have been co-ordination.

This was aside from the difficulties that SOE met in getting authorizations, planes and supplies from the UK for its agents. There were also a lot of mistakes in its own organization, and in this minefield of divided loyalties and delicate consciences, organizers and couriers had to tread carefully.

Many Frenchmen could not believe that British SOE agents did not have an ulterior motive in helping France and that their ideals could be and were altruistic and even romantic. Pippa Latour and Pearl Witherington were both most successful in handling these problems and so was Sonya. It needed much tact and skill.

Sonya remained acting as Christopher's courier in the Headmaster circuit. Some of the fiercest battles were fought between the Allies and the Germans around Avranches and Falaise, but in August the Americans, after securing Brittany, swept down towards Le Mans. Then

the wonderful day eventually arrived when the pounding guns, the rattle of firing and the crump of falling bombs told her that the battle was nearing her refuge. Finally the streets filled with retreating Germans followed close after by the advancing Americans. That was a day she would never forget, and it must have seemed that for her the war was at last over. She could relax without looking over her shoulder and fearing the knock on the door foretelling her arrest.

Sarthe — a typical farmhouse.

But this was not the end. Of course there was the tidying up of SOE operations and staff, and a happy round of celebrating with resistance members amid rivers of wine and back-slapping, but there was more. Reporting to the headquarters of the advancing army with her organizer she found that she could still help greatly, because her knowledge of people and terrain in her many journeys to the south was of great use to the Generals. Suddenly she found herself cast in a new role, after they had milked all the information out of her that they needed. Would she act as a courier bringing more intelligence on enemy dispositions and stores from behind enemy lines? It was highly dangerous work that only a person familiar with the region and able to contact friends in enemy-occupied areas could do. True to her character she hardly paused before agreeing. She knew the risks, but she also knew that she was one of those best suited to do it successfully.

Thus began a new phase in her mission, where she consciously travelled into the areas still occupied by the Germans, through the battleground where the opposed armies fought it out, with the whistle of stray shells over her head and sometimes cratering the ground around her while she hunted for her contacts who had often gone to underground cellars or to the hiding places of the Maquis. As she drove her bicycle along the dry dusty lanes, a young girl in a summer dress and headscarf, she was shot at several times, whether by the Maquis or by the Germans she was not always sure.

Once, two Germans jumped out at her, suspecting that anyone of the local population was helping their enemies. They were only the dregs of the once proud German army and glad to find someone weaker than they to vent their rage and humiliation upon. They knocked her off her bike, threw her to the ground and at gun-point demanded to know what she was doing. If they had really known they would have killed her. They slapped her face until her nose and lips bled and forced their attentions on her, despite her struggles and screams. She was unarmed. There was no one to help her and no one came to her aid. Her quick wits enabled her to convince them at length that she was no more than what she seemed, a peasant girl from the country, so they left her by the roadside, shaken and bleeding but alive. Gathering her torn dress around her, she finally managed to reach the house of a friendly family and take shelter for the night.

Next day, more determined than ever, and not allowing the incident to shake either her nerves or courage she continued on her way, collecting and passing on the information with which she had been entrusted. Then she turned around and made her way back to where she had started, noting that the Americans had advanced quite a long way since she had left them. How glad and relieved she was to see their smiling faces again!

These dangerous missions she undertook not once but several times, selflessly running great risks in her willingness to help in the cause of liberating France. At length she saw the Germans driven out of the major part of France. One further task remained. Wearing her full airforce blue WAAF uniform and cap, she eventually returned to identify some of her earlier friends and enemies. When the door of one cell in the local prison was opened, she came face to face with the Gestapo chief with whom she had casually and fleetingly had a nodding acquaintance. When recognition dawned, he stared at her in amazement. He could hardly believe that such a young girl had been an important agent in the downfall of himself and his army; nor, in view of the determined opposition from such unusual and courageous people, should he have been so surprised at his defeat. With a shrug at their reversed situations, he courteously saluted a brave opponent.

In early October, Sonya returned safely to Britain, her mission completed. She was still only 20. Later on, she again met Guy d'Artois, also back successfully from his mission, and redeeming his promise they were married.

18
The Polish Pimpernel

Christine Granville
(Krystina Gizycka)

'To use the word brave or courage about her would be a wrong use of words.'

Francis Cammaerts

'Her incredible exploits...only came to light after her death, but for courage and audacity they have no equal.'

'FANY Invicta' Dame Irene Ward (Hutchinson)

How can anyone pin down this most volatile and venturesome of women who darts across the pages of history like a brilliant bird of passage, refusing to be categorized? Christine Granville's French organizer, Francis Cammaerts, found her 'independent, humorous and fiercely anti-pompous', and the custodian of SOE archives agrees that she was no respecter of bureaucratic distinctions. Even at the outbreak of war there were queries as to whom she really belonged and for whom she worked, for already she was valued. Her chief motivation, for ever nearest her heart, was to help by all in her power, to free her dismembered and conquered homeland — Poland. All other activities were merely means to that end.

Briefly and tenuously she worked with one of the precursors of SOE, Section D, before passing to the SOE Polish Section, followed by belonging jointly to the Polish and Middle Eastern Section. In France she was accredited, in the words of Colonel Buckmaster, 'fleetingly to F Section', although not officially part of it, as she appears to have been sent to assist in the DF Section on escapes. She received her honorary WAAF commission in time for her expected task in Italy. Nevertheless much of her time she appears to have acted on her own inspiration, as a free agent. However, on the basis of her brief connection with the WAAF, in whose uniform she had her official photograph, I include her in my account, since in part the WAAF can claim a small share in her honours with SOE.

Born the daughter of a Polish count and his Jewish wife, she was outstandingly beautiful, intelligent and unconventional. A Polish Countess by her second marriage, her life altered dramatically when she and her husband left their travels abroad to come to London when Poland was overrun by Germany. From that time forward she was ready to oppose the Germans by every means in her power, and those means were not inconsiderable, as she had a gift for languages, and enormous range of contacts in high places and unquenchable courage. She would admit nothing as being impossible.

Consequently, at the greatest risk to herself, from late 1939 onwards she could be found helping the resistance, arranging escapes, and collecting information for those fighting Germany. These activities took her to France, Poland, Hungary, and even Germany. She was issued with her British passport and name, to help her escape arrest on her car journey through Yugoslavia and Bulgaria to Turkey where, with another task accomplished, she continued through Syria down to Egypt, with a slight later diversion to Lebanon. It was ironic that with her multifarious activities, most sides, at one time or other, suspected her of being a German spy!

In 1943, while she waited to be rehabilitated yet again by the British authorities, she learned to be a wireless operator and to parachute, the intention at that time being to use her efforts to mobilize her Polish compatriots serving as prisoners and recruits of the Germans in France. She also tried to learn to shoot and ride a bike, neither with notable success despite the fact that she was a fine athlete and that her skiing skills had often saved her own and other lives. Then she was sent to Algiers in 1944 to become the first woman agent dropped by the Massingham organization into France.

Meanwhile in France, her future SOE organizer Francis Cammaerts, codenamed Roger, was looking after his vast circuit in the south-east known as Jockey, which stretched from Isère to the Côte d'Azur, the Maritime Alps to the Ardèche. With the Allied invasion of the south coast expected almost hourly in the summer of 1944, his work had so multiplied that he needed another assistant, preferably a courier — Cécile

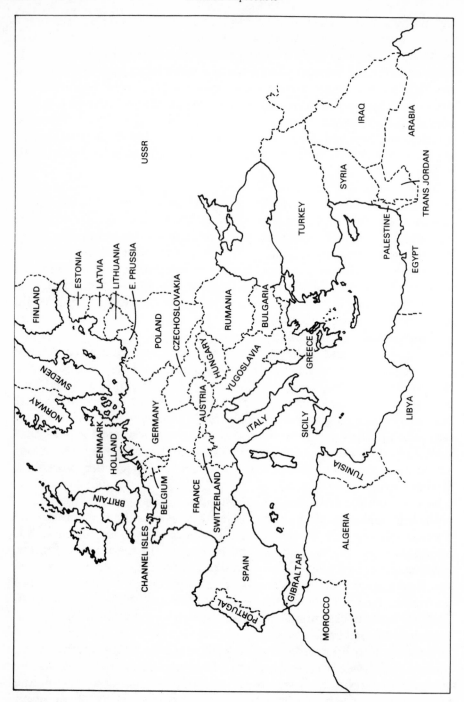

The countries of pre-war Europe (about 1935). Christine Granville travelled widely over some of these areas.

Lefort, one of his earlier couriers, had been lost to him by an unforeseen accident in September 1943, and although he had several wireless operators, one had recently been captured. This time he appealed to SOE Algiers, his area being so wide that he could employ someone in Crest to the north contacting London, while another at Mont-Dauphin in the south maintained contact with Algiers — much nearer for him. He suggested that they send him a woman as she would be less conspicuous.

Christine's arrival in France was as tempestuous as her life. Francis had arranged a dropping zone near the Vercors, but the plane arrived from Algiers on 7 July 1944 after a very rough ride in a raging gale, so that although those with her landed safely in the right place, she was blown four miles off course near Vassieu, and landed so heavily that the butt of the revolver she was carrying was shattered and she was badly bruised. It was pitch dark and she had no idea where she was. Therefore, very wisely she hid her parachute and sat quietly waiting for daylight. She was dressed like a peasant girl and her French was so perfect that when at length a search party of Maquisards discovered her, they thought she was one of themselves. It took a little time before her field name Pauline and her code words told them that she was the one they were seeking. In her identity documents she masqueraded as Madame Jacqueline Armand.

When she finally met Francis, she found that they were kindred souls, he a tall, modest, seemingly easy-going young man, she dark-haired, slender and vivacious, with a hurried, breathy voice, and ready to travel at the drop of a hat with only a knapsack and tote bag, showing little pride about her clothes or hair. To Francis she was a perfect assistant needing little direction, full of initiative, and becoming cooler and more convincing the tighter the situation. One instance was when she was caught by a German patrol carrying an SOE escape map printed on silk. Without hesitation she whipped it out and tied it around her head, like a headscarf, her actions so natural that the Germans never noticed.

She arrived just over a month after the Normandy invasions in the north, and five-and-a-half weeks before the Allied invasions in the south. Some of her earliest tasks were to arrange drops of arms for the increasingly active Maquis, many arms coming from Algiers, where the containers seem to have been worse packed than those from Britain, destroying or badly damaging a large proportion of their contents. Another difficult rôle, while treading gently among the sensitivities of the various political allegiances and groupings of the time, was to reinforce Francis's words of caution not to begin any uprising until it was bound to succeed. He preferred that his men should act like insects, stinging the enemy but slipping away before they could be caught, and avoiding a pitched battle where they could be destroyed by superior forces. Nevertheless, around Lyon Christine organized numerous damaging sabotage attacks. By now most of the roads and main railway lines along

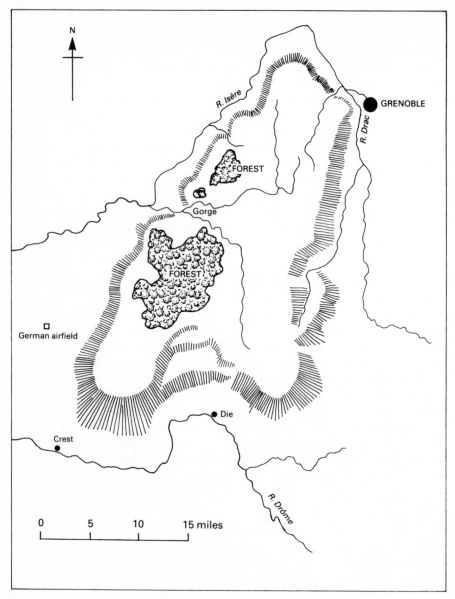

Sketch map of the Vercors plateau with its forests, steep cliffs and ravines.

which the Germans were sending reinforcements north were badly disrupted, including the Route Hannibal and the Route Napoléon.

Despite words of caution, the French were impatient of restraint, and especially in the area around Vercors. This was an immense, blue-grey limestone plateau in the shape of an arrowhead, about 40 miles (64 km) long and 18 miles (29 km) at its widest end. At its tip, its cliffs towered high above the road and mountain tracks. It was cut by a huge river gorge and several mountain passes, as well as man-made tunnels, bridges and roads, and managed to hold rich orchards and farmland, numerous little villages, rocky outcrops honeycombed with caves and dark, impenetrable forests. Thus it was almost a self-contained, independent world and had already received uniformed operational and interallied groups to help train young men into a liberation army in an area which was a magnet for all those fleeing forced labour or impatient for action. The troops were, however, short of heavy artillery, anti-aircraft guns and anti-tank weapons which, though constantly requested, never came. At the same time there was a series of misunderstandings — prime of which may have been the message brought back from Algiers by Chavant, the communist leader of the resistance in that area, which was soon to number over 3,000 Maquis. It called on the people to rise on D Day — 'Bouclez le Vercors le Jour J' — and was unfortunately read to mean the day of the landings in the north rather than those in the south, causing the towns on and around the plateau to rise too soon, on 7 June 1944. Thus for six heady weeks the tricolour flew over the plateau.

Faced by an event he could not stop, Francis had to make the best of it. Based in a safe house on Vercors, he sent Christine crossing and recrossing the area, with advice and requests for arms, food and uniforms, which were demanded from both Algiers and Baker Street. Both knew that such outright defiance by the area could not be ignored by the Germans, no matter how embattled they were on other fronts, and that the final blow would come soon. A daylight drop of 600 containers by 36 British-based United States Army Air Force Liberators on 25 June brought some supplies and light weapons. Later the red and white parachutes dropped by 72 United States Army Air Force Flying Fortresses, on the morning of 14 July, bringing a thousand containers of Sten guns, ammunition and clothes, still brought no heavy weapons, but drew much German shelling moments after the drop. On 18 July, up to three German divisions of 10,000 men with air support began their first full attack. Christine watched it from the top of the plateau, where Francis now had his headquarters, with tears in her throat for the bravery of the doomed patriots. Vainly Francis appealed to SOE for the right weapons for the men, warning that such help withheld could only turn the French against the British after all his efforts to gain their trust. Nothing came.

On 21 July, the Germans sent in gliders with 200 crack SS troops. They mowed down the lightly armed Maquis who still desperately tried to hold on, but it was useless, and on 23 July the French Commander gave the order to disperse. There followed terrible acts of German barbarity on those captured, the wounded were shot and the civilians suffered terrible reprisals by an enraged enemy. One woman resister was left to die with her entrails around her neck. The martyrdom of Vercors left only one useful result. It deterred other resisters from making the same mistake.

During the battle, realizing all too soon that everything was lost and there was nothing to stop it, Francis, Christine and a leader of the FFI with a few companions escaped to a southern pass connecting with the town of Die below, and then at dead of night climbed and scrambled down. On their way through the precipitous beech woods they heard the tunnel they had used being blown up behind them. Eventually they arrived 70 miles away in less than 24 hours, scratched and burned but alive. Here, in his second base at Seynes-les-Alpes, Francis continued the struggle and here although physically and mentally drained from the tragedy and their escape, Christine went back to work.

Her next mission was to make contact with a group of Italian partisans. After the surrender of Italy to the Allies in 1943, the Germans had found to their fury that the Italian soldiers considered that they too had finished with the war. Some were forcibly kept in their place by heavy German troops, but they made only token resistance and many hundreds deserted to reinforce their own Italian partisans who had always disliked the war policies of Mussolini. Their behaviour was most marked on the Italian border with France, and

Bonneval. Christine revelled in this mountainous area.

SOE wanted to win over their active co-operation with the Allies. Fired with enthusiasm for such a challenging role, Christine's eyes began to sparkle and she set off gaily with a light, dancing step. To find the partisans meant a long, gruelling journey into the Italian Alps, where she had to pass through German lines, manned by trigger-happy, nervous soldiery and Italian groups equally trigger-happy and more likely to shoot first and ask questions afterwards. It was hot and the mountains shimmered in the sunshine. In this heat she travelled partly by motor cycle and partly by foot, lapping up the sunshine like a lizard.

On the way she had many adventures. Usually she posed as an ignorant young peasant girl, and this guise worked when she was twice stopped by German guards. On another occasion she was guiding a young Italian to the nearest Maquis, when she was stopped by a German patrol. She knew that these soldiers would not believe her and the Italian with her had no papers, so thinking all was lost, she whipped out two live grenades from her haversack and held them in her hands as she put them up in answer to their challenge. Then, in German, she told the guards that if they approached any nearer she would blow them all up. They stopped in horror, saw that she meant her threat and in a minute they could hardly be seen for dust. The Italian with her, not quite understanding, had also been tempted to run away but thought she was bluffing. He was therefore much relieved when she returned the grenades to her satchel and they continued their amicable way to their destination. She finally located the group to which she had been sent, where her coming was greeted with much shooting into the air and hugging. The 200-strong group was most willing to accept the help that Christine was able to offer on behalf of SOE.

When she had made the dangerous journey back, she was sent off once again on a similar mission, this time to try to influence the Russians serving in the Oriental Legion of the German 19th Army. This legion was made up of a mixture of nationalities, drawn from the countries cowed or occupied by the conquering German armies, who had often joined their enemies to gain better treatment for their families or to earn money in an otherwise unemployed situation in their shattered country. As the supply of German manpower dwindled, the Germans were forced to the expedient of incorporating more of these foreign mercenaries into the army, and there were even some reluctant Poles among them. Nevertheless the Germans were never too certain of these men's loyalties. Many could speak neither German nor French, but this was considered an asset as they could not easily be subverted by the arguments of the French. Some coming from very deprived areas could be exceedingly brutal and lawless in carrying out what they were told were their duties, and these men were increasingly employed on patrols and searches. As there were many people of Mongol appearance in their ranks, the French dubbed them all Mongols, and there is no doubt that the French feared them almost more than the German troops.

It was to this restless and malevolent force that Christine was now dispatched to gain recruits for the Maquis or at worst encourage deserters from the legion. Her gift for languages made her welcome and her arguments were so effective that hundreds swarmed out to join the local resistance forces, where they may have been nearly as much of a headache as they had been to the Germans.

On this journey, while she was trying to avoid one of the nightly German patrols, one of the men's guard dogs, a large Alsatian, scented her as she lay under some bushes by the wayside. It streaked off, far ahead of its handler and finally pounced on her. It seemed the end of her mission. Then a strange thing happened. Christine had always possessed the gift of charm to a high degree. Few men could resist her — and she had many lovers, most of whom bored her once acquired — but she loved everyone and everything. This unusual gift also extended to the animal kingdom. Thus when the dog's handler whistled and called to his charge, the Alsatian only whined softly, licked Christine's hand and lay down quietly beside her, having in that moment instantly transferred its loyalties. Its handler disappeared still calling vainly, the dog never moved. It remained with her for the rest of the journey, guarding her jealously and cavorting like a puppy around her. Indeed it stayed with her until given to a friend when she left France.

Another useful errand on which she embarked was to try to persuade the foreign soldiers in the German-held fort at Col de Larche to desert. Finding that they were Polish and therefore her compatriots, she decided to climb the mountain where the fort stood, to try to speak to them in their own tongue. She found a guide willing to take her, and then embarked on the cruel walk up the nearly 2,000 ft high mountain. They followed narrow winding mountain tracks often more suitable for goats than humans, and she often fell or slithered down, scratching herself

A mountain village perched high in the Alps, such as Christine would have visited on her missions.

on pine needles and sharp rocks as she sought to stop, leaving her face, legs and hands bleeding, and her clothing torn. They stopped overnight on the mountainside and carried on again next day. Reaching the fort at last, her task of subverting the garrison seemed easy beside that of the ascent and later the descent, but she achieved her goal and the Poles were eager to join the resistance.

With so much success and the Allies beginning to advance into France from the north, it appeared that nothing could go wrong. The invasion of the Côte d'Azur seemed almost superfluous, but the plans for this forged ahead. Naturally enough the French patriots of the south awaited it with increasing impatience. It was to be their liberation. Francis and Christine had been making ready for it since their arrival in France.

Then suddenly, three days before it was due, the impossible happened. Christine was away on yet another mission to the Italian border to subvert some more Poles serving with the *Wehrmacht* and Francis was returning with a newly arrived agent and a French major from a visit to see some local resistance leaders. They were driving in a Red-Cross marked vehicle. As they reached the town of Digne, an air raid siren wailed. To avert suspicion they took cover, arranging to meet the car on the other side of the town after the raid had finished. All went as planned and they climbed into the car and had started back for Seyne, when they ran into a new barricade manned by Mongols, where the bridge spanned the river. They were about to be let pass, however, when they were stopped by a member of the Milice who was in the car behind them. He discovered that the bank notes they carried had consecutive numbers. Immediately suspicious, they were bundled into his car and taken off to the central prison for questioning and the next day moved to the Gestapo headquarters in the Villa Rose, where they were again roughly questioned and later returned to their former prison in the death cell.

While this went on, the Allies had landed on the Riviera with remarkably few casualties and little opposition from the Germans, who were retreating almost as fast as the Allies advanced, assisted by the French resistance who were at last able to show their true colours after so many years of waiting. It was only a matter of time before the town of Digne where Francis and his friends were imprisoned would be overrun. But would the troops be soon enough to save them?

They weren't. Instead it was left to Christine, who receiving news of their capture and knowing that if the Germans knew Francis's real identity he would be shot out of hand and that time was against him, rushed back to her headquarters to pick up all the gold she could borrow. Then riding the bike which she so hated and feared, she pedalled the 25 miles to Digne, where she slipped through the prison gates and circled the building, busy with people, singing a song Francis would recognize. As luck would have it, Francis in his cell heard her and joined in, so that she was able to locate him and know he was still there. Then with a headscarf hiding her dark hair, she approached a few local gendarmes, posing as Francis's wife and begging their help to let her take him some necessities like soap and shaving cream. One older than the rest, pitying her distress, advised her to see a liaison officer between the French police and the Gestapo. The name once known, she was off to demand an interview with the man. Then she took probably the greatest risk of her life. She told him that the Gestapo had captured three important British agents, and that she, a niece of the much-feared General Montgomery, was the wife of one of them. If they died, the advancing troops and the Maquis would take a terrible revenge on the perpetrators. Shaken, the man explained that he could do nothing but he would help her gain access to a Belgian, who was the official interpreter of the Gestapo. He craftily added that bribing such a man would cost over two million francs, an impossible sum to anyone less than who she said she was. The same afternoon she was taken by the liaison officer to the interpreter, who turned out to be the man who had arrested her friends. For three hours she promised Allied protection, cajoled, bargained and threatened. She even admitted to being a British wireless operator, showing her listeners some useless wireless crystals, to show her identity and contacts. All the while she could not help noticing the interpreter's shining revolver case and the death's head on his Gestapo cap. They drank real coffee and the two men seemed impressed by her arguments and air of authority. They promised to help if she

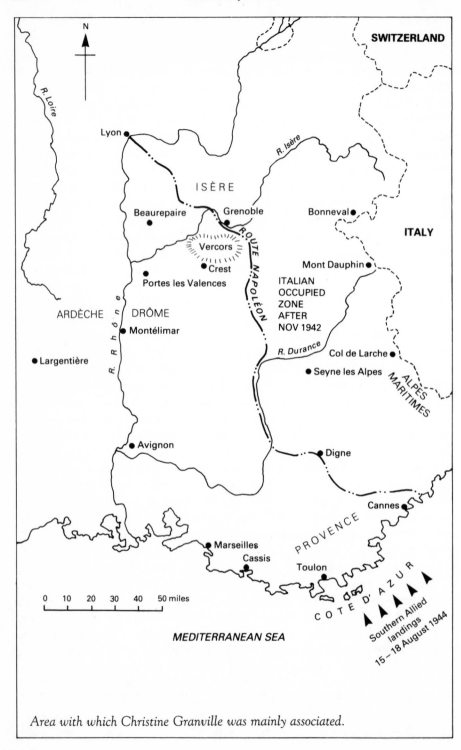

Area with which Christine Granville was mainly associated.

could get the money and that they too could get away.

Again she leapt on to her hated bike and pedalled like mad back to Seyne-les-Alpes, where she found the wireless operator and had an urgent message sent to Algiers demanding the money immediately. Then she was off again to organize the dropping zone. Fortunately all went according to plan, and a rubber pouch of money was dropped to the waiting girl. Meanwhile the Maquis were talking of a rescue by attacking the prison in force, but knowing that they had little chance of success and that her way was the only possible, one she held them off, and then went to sleep during the hours of darkness when no one could travel, with the heavy pouch containing the two million francs under her bed. At daylight she commandeered a car and set off again for Digne. On her way she stopped to return another officer to Seyne, expecting that if Francis escaped, the town would be a dangerous place for agents. Then she went back to Digne, handed over the money and waited. Miraculously, after a delay the interpreter appeared outside the gates leading his three captives, who had imagined that they had been summoned to be shot in the prison yard. They all jumped into his car when told, and he drove out of the town. The sentries seeing the uniformed driver, waved him on. No one dared speak, until he picked up a solitary figure waiting at the side of the road. It was Christine! A short time afterwards the driver jumped out and buried his Gestapo uniform before driving on. Then Christine leaned from her front seat and said, 'It worked.'

When at last they arrived safely at Seyne, they heard that Digne had been captured by the Americans a few hours previously. Leaving their captive rescuers in safety, after a night's sleep Christine and Francis set off to find the American headquarters to see if there were any other things they could do to help. One General rudely brushed aside their offers but an American Captain asked Christine's help to turn the allegiance of a detachment of German-uniformed Poles held as prisoners in a nearby valley. As the Americans expected a heavy German counter attack very soon, they could do without these prisoners but with these extra numbers. Undeterred by this odd request Christine grasped a megaphone and spoke to the men. In response they stripped the hated uniform off to the waist and joined the Americans. The General was not pleased, however, at her 'messing about' with his prisoners. That evening the story was picked up by a war correspondent and the General shortly found himself removed.

Later they drove to another American General's headquarters. Their welcome was very different and again they were given a task, this time to instruct the members of the resistance throughout the three *départements* up to Lyon to protect the American army as it advanced. This done, Christine and Francis went their separate ways, but with continuing affection on both sides. Christine finally reported her mission complete at the regional headquarters in Avignon, from where she hitched a lift to London.

However, this was not to end her connection with SOE. She was now asked if she would go to help the Polish cause in Italy. Kitted in WAAF uniform, she was flown to join the Polish Mission at Bari in November 1944, at much the same time as her honorary WAAF commission was confirmed. During the whole autumn she had agonized over the unwillingness or inability of the Allies to assist the uprising in Warsaw, and now she saw it crushed. Her arrival in Italy was therefore too late and except for assisting the transfer of some more German-employed Polish troops to the Allies, she could do nothing more except return to report to London that the mission had failed. In its place she was offered employment by the movement section of the General Headquarters, Middle East at Cairo, which she accepted and there she remained until demobilized as a Flight Officer in May 1945.

There she would have dropped out of sight, as did most of the other agents of SOE, but for a macabre accident. In 1952, her name reappeared sadly but briefly after her murder in London by a rejected lover, the victim of that gift of attraction which had now proved fatal.

19
Fear No More

'Keep your fears to yourself, but share your courage with others.'
Robert Louis Stephenson

'My overall impression of those girls was how young and normal they were.'

Peggy Heard

Britain has always had the closest of ties with France whether in time of war or peace. Her language was our courtly tongue for many centuries, and from Alcuin to Mary Queen of Scots and the *entente cordiale* of Edward VII, our country has frequently exchanged scholars, brides, and even rulers over the years.

It was therefore natural that our two nations should be drawn together in the war against Germany, and particularly so after the fall of France, when only Britain remained free. This was the reason for the creation of the French Section of SOE. To the French, SOE was the tangible evidence that it was not wrong to cherish the wish for liberation and that there was an outsider who still cared enough for their ideals and for them as a people to be prepared to sacrifice its agents' lives on their behalf. Greater love hath no man! There was comfort too in the thought that their race was not forgotten, relegated to the dusty annals of conquest. They could hope for a successful end to their struggle, even though it was a long way out of sight. Indeed SOE's epitaph might well be, that it kept alive the flickering flame of hope in a conquered country, for hope is indestructible, the strongest weapon in any armoury.

Nevertheless, SOE's work would not have been possible without the co-operation and sacrifice of the many brave members of the resistance. For every agent who advised, directed and supplied the underground, there were hundreds of ordinary French men and women who daily risked their own and their families' lives to support them. At best, an agent could return to London if he suspected discovery, but for the French, there was nowhere to go in an occupied country. Their toll was grievous.

Guy Moquet was a French hostage shot by the Germans at Chateaubriant in 1942. In this moving testimonial of courage the young boy, before his execution, scribbles a short note to his mother: 'Of course I would like to have lived, but what I want most of all is that my death shall be of some use. I say goodbye for the last time to all my friends and my brother whom I love so much. May he learn to be a man. At 17½ my life has been so short but I have no regrets.'

The figures for those who suffered and died are so large that accuracy is practically impossible. Perhaps 24,000 men and women were executed by the Germans in France and over 115,000 deported to concentration camps, of whom no more than 40,000 returned alive. The Maquis lost well over 30,000 killed in action. Beside these totals, SOE losses seem infinitesimal. Such was the price that the children of France paid for their freedom, their enemy being all around them.

It was sad after this co-operative effort that when liberation came, one of the first reactions of a returning triumphant de Gaulle was to order all SOE agents out of the country at 48 hours notice. 'Your place is not here.' He had long mistrusted the motives and political alignments of Churchill and Roosevelt, and fearing a communist takeover or state confusion he activated his own plans to ensure control of the French government by his supporters. It was left to other councils to redress the injustice, give awards and citations and organize the reunions of the many friends individual agents had made in their circuits.

At the beginning of SOE's existence, it was not impossible but at least highly improbable that women would be sent as clandestine agents overseas. Then, when the question began to be considered, it was felt that

"WHY DON'T THEY LIKE US, HEINRICH?"

IN OCCUPIED TERRITORY

Cartoon by Low showing Hitler and Himmler discussing the problem of occupied Europe. (London Evening Standard)

it was not impossible but improbable that they would make good agents. Against the odds they proved a success and thus *Mission Improbable* was born. As it turned out, it was France which received most of these women agents and it is the stories of those connected with the Women's Auxiliary Air Force which have filled these pages. To set the record straight, however, mention must be made of one or two other women, who do not fit into the former categories.

Such was Marguerite (Peggy) Knight, the daughter of a British army officer, born in Paris and speaking fluent French. She joined the WAAF at the beginning of the war in September 1939, but was invalided out in the following May, and returned to her civilian job as a shorthand typist with an engineering firm. Then one day she was present at a party given in the lounge of a London hotel. While the social chatter went on around, her attention was caught by a man, whose book seemed to have slipped from under his arm without his noticing it. When she retrieved it he had moved away, giving her time to glance at the cover, the title of which appeared to be in French. Probably its owner could also speak it. Unobtrusively she found her quarry and almost apologetically handed his book back, adding a few courteous and appropriate words in French. The man raised his eyebrows and complimented her on her good accent. Then switching the conversation to French he soon found out how fluent she was. Before the party broke up she found herself the possessor of a name and telephone number, which she was to ring up if she wanted to change her job. This was her entry into SOE and in April 1944 she joined the FANY. On 6 May 1944, after less than a fortnight's training, she was parachuted into France to act as a courier, code named Nicole, with the Donkeyman circuit working in the Yonne under Roger Bardet. Here she bravely carried out liaison missions, reconnaissances into enemy lines and sabotage operations, until her circuit was overrun by the Allies. In December 1944 she resigned from the FANY on her marriage, when her surname became the ubiquitous Smith.

It is also worth notice that Nancy Grace Augusta Fiocca, née Wake, whose SOE exploits have become almost legendary, and who was a member of the FANY during the war, ultimately joined the WAAF as a Pilot Officer in 1952.

All these were exceptional people! How would a young girl of today react to a similar challenge? Would she have enough idealism to be willing to risk her life for her country? Could she show the same high courage and wisdom in the field? Would she be able to face the cold reality of torture and death for her work? Hard questions, but in judging these women of the past, judge also how well you would respond if you were one of them. A comparison between now and then must make us more understanding.

It is always interesting to speculate on the characteristics of unusual people such as these women of SOE whose lives have been recorded in this book. Their attitudes to war differed radically from those of men. They were neither so bloodthirsty nor so cruel. They hated the enemy in the mass and injustice when they saw it, but they often felt contempt or pity for individuals. They did not relish killing, whether it be Germans, other people or themselves. Few used the guns and none the lethal tablets with which they were supplied. Their ideas were more romantic and unselfish, idealistic and yet practical. They enjoyed the battle of wits, outsmarting the enemy, the sense of adventure, protecting the innocent and highly valued the love of their friends and country. France and Britain were one country to them, many being in any case of dual nationality. The adrenalin of danger was not normally to their taste, but it brought out the best in them whenever necessary.

Their loyalty was never faulted, despite capture and torture. Threats or opposition usually made them more determined. They were hard workers, sensitive and quick-witted innovators and it goes without saying that they were endowed with intelligence and a good memory. They were usually high-spirited, healthy and charming, even if they lacked beauty — and many were remarkably beautiful. Indeed to be ordinary looking and inconspicuous was a distinct advantage. Their cheerfulness too, was remarked by those around them, where a sense of humour was a valuable asset.

It is also clear that many of them were individualists for whom release from the unimportant or petty rules at home gave them unexpected freedom to discover new qualities hitherto unsuspected in themselves. Their earlier reports might have said 'impatient of discipline' or 'unconventional'. In the field these qualities became assets, aided with a quick mind and the charisma of youth, which turned many into leaders that men respected and willingly followed. The loner also came into her own, as she had acquired over her lifetime inner resources to keep her going, not needing the bolstering of company in what had to be secretive work, done alone, and very much on her own initiative.

All the girls would have found it difficult to carry out their missions unless they had been consummate actresses, studying each new person that they were to become and slipping into it like a character on the stage. The sheer bravery and bravado for which this called mirrored the tremendous amount of self-assurance needed to carry it off successfully, though sometimes this did lead to unexpected carelessness. Generally, being careful kept the girl free, and it was bad luck or the merest accident, rather than any fault of their own, that brought about their capture. Obviously those who arrived in the earlier years or were in the field longest ran the greater risk, but even those who arrived shortly before liberation were more or less vulnerable according to their area of country and the efficiency of German counter-intelligence.

That they were courageous, their actions speak for themselves, but this must not give the impression that most were also fearless. Indeed many felt and came face to face with gut-twisting, terrible fear. It was just that having coolly balanced the dangers with their objective of helping to free France, they felt the risk worth taking, and if the worst came to the worst they accepted it as part of the price. They were frequently afraid, lonely and prey to doubts and depression but they were too proud to show their fear. Their chief faults often lay in their innocence and their sometimes misplaced trustfulness. Their British nationality sometimes showed in their looks for which they could hardly be responsible, a slight variation in their tone rather than a lack of fluency in French, and despite all efforts, in their choice of clothes.

All of them were volunteers. Age made no difference, though many were exceptionally young. The war was not of their making and their main wish was to finish it as shortly as possible. Exceptional times called for exceptional actions; afterwards they only wanted to return to normality.

In the overall picture is it perhaps optimistic to believe that a small body of 500 men and women, hastily trained and widely scattered over a territory about two-and-a-quarter times the size of Britain can be anything more than a minor irritant to a huge army of occupation? On the face of it, this would seem to be the situation confronting the members of SOE in France.

In their small groups of three or so, were their operations properly run? The organizers were usually men of discretion, flair and ability, who brought the resistance much-needed leadership and co-ordination. There are always some exceptions to any rule, but it is surprising that there were so few. Many of their deeds are long remembered and their courage has passed into local legend. The same applies to their couriers, men and women, native and British, who took incredible risks to keep the circuits functional. Little of this effort would have been possible, however, without the painstaking work of the wireless operators — many of them women — who by keeping up the contact with London, or later Algiers, exchanged information and arranged safe supply drops and targets, running perhaps the greatest risks of all because their transmissions made them more easily traced.

SOE's members have often been criticized because, at the start at least, some of their sabotage work with the resistance failed or was not very effective, and the same went for a number of the aircraft bombing raids they arranged. Sometimes these killed innocent civilians and lost many valuable patriots. On the other hand, these people were the source of most of the sabotage materials and arms which came into the hands of the resistance, and indeed made resistance possible. Colonel Buckmaster states that by denying the Germans many of the products of the French factories commandeered for war work, industrial sabotage often saved the population from aerial attacks thus preserving many civilian lives.

Guerrilla action is unfortunately usually muddled and messy, and consequently it is more disliked by established forces than regular action. An enemy that fights and then melts away may be thought to be more cowardly, but it survives to fight another day. It also provokes more savage reaction. The German practice of taking hostages may have banked down opposition for a time but it also increased hatred for the oppressor, ready to erupt with greater violence when the enemy hold weakened.

The cost in lives, of the ordinary French population, the resisters and the agents was undeniably great as has been seen, and it may have been greater because of the rashness of some of its members despite wiser councils, because by its nature resistance attracts those most impatient and active in opposition. Nevertheless, those losses signalled to the Germans the fundamental depth of French patriotism for which SOE only served as focus and harness.

Was the cost in time, money and lives wasteful, or worth all the effort put into it by Britain and SOE? Incredibly it seems that its impact was far greater than such an undertaking would appear to deserve. Against the odds, the resisters working with the circuits are estimated to have been worth perhaps 10-15 extra divisions of regular troops. They kept the Germans jumpy, always looking over their shoulders, diverting their manpower and tying down numerous forces of transport, weapons and soldiers much needed after D-Day at the front, and making their retreat, particularly in the south, into a rout. In general, SOE occupied the Germans' best counter-intelligence personnel, including some of their most skilled interrogators, and kept them always distrustful and distrusted by their conquests. General Eisenhower, impressed by the support of the resistance in France, considered that their efforts had eased the route of his forces and shortened the war in Europe by nine months, surely the best result of all.

Of the men and women who had been behind so much of this assistance, and who had lost nearly one quarter of their number in the process, he said, 'Finally I must express my great admiration for the brave and often spectacular exploits of the agents and special groups under the control of the Special Forces Headquarters.'

Afterwards in the distribution of ranks and awards to those in the field and those at home, there was, as there always has been, an obvious gulf. Rewards were haphazard, to say the least, for those who had risked their lives living dangerously in the field and for those who died unseen, silent and alone in a foreign land. But among the brave such returns are insignificant. They know their own worth!

Perhaps their best reward and memorial is that we have all lived through half a century of peace.

Postscript

Sibyl Anne Sturrock

Although this book deals with the missions of WAAF to France, as part of SOE, it would be unfair to exclude mention of one other British WAAF dropped behind German lines to assist the resistance in a different enemy-occupied country. She, however, belonged not to SOE but SIS, the Special Intelligence Service working for the Foreign Office. Nevertheless her role was so unusual that it deserves special mention here.

Sibyl Anne Sturrock, or Chibi as she was known by her friends, had a cosmopolitan upbringing and was fluent in several languages. She was born in Berlin in 1921, thus making German her first language learned from her German nurse. Since her father worked in our Foreign Office he was subject to constant moves, the next being Hungary and then Yugoslavia, where Sibyl attended the local French school in Belgrade, learning French simultaneously with Serbo-Croat. Later she was sent to a boarding school in Vienna, but always returning to her much-loved home in Belgrade.

In 1941 her father was killed, heroically rescuing Yugoslav children from a bombed Red Cross ship in Suez, but by this time Sibyl had come to England and was in the WAAF, which she joined in July 1940. Eventually she became a Sergeant wireless operator employed on Direction Finding (DF), and a convinced anti-fascist. She quickly found the rules and petty discipline of her life restrictive, being of an independent, outspoken nature, and felt her abilities wasted until SIS, recognizing her peculiar talents, had her seconded to its service. At its insistence she was sent for officer training before working at the Yugoslav desk in London and Bari.

In wartime Yugoslavia the political picture was at least as complicated as that in France. The King was in exile and the country occupied by both Germans and Italians. There were also two rival bodies in the resistance — the pro-royalist Serb Mihailović, with his četnics, and the pro-communist Tito, with his partisans. There was already civil war in the country between nationalities while the rivalry between the two resistance parties often damaged the other more than the common enemy. Neither SOE nor SIS was too finicky about long-term political results, siding with whichever resistance party seemed most likely to drive out the Germans (and sometimes helping both sides at once). But gradually Britain began to side more strongly with the more active Tito.

Into this problem area, Sibyl was parachuted in September 1944, to work on operations, intelligence gathering and building up good relations with the Yugoslavs, under the leadership of her organizer Major John Ennals and their wireless operator Eli Zohar. They were attached to the 10th Corps of the partisan forces of General Tito in the partly liberated territory of Moslavina, about 45 km south-east of the Croatian capital of Zagreb, and surrounded by enemy-held lines of communications.

In the winter snow, at the end of the year, she travelled with the partisans on foot and on horseback as they retreated painfully, step by step into Slavonia. 'Life was very serious and danger a constant companion.' Her willingness to share their hardships and champion their cause made her very popular and helped to establish confidence between the Allied and partisan authorities.

By about March 1945, they had gone back as far as they would go and the Yugoslav army prepared to take the offensive, eventually advancing into Podravina and joining with the advancing Red Army of Russia, Sibyl still accompanying them. In May 1945 Zagreb was finally liberated and she took part in the great Victory march through the city. Now her part in the war was over and shortly afterwards she left.

Appendix A
Alphabetical Table of Names and Main Details

Surname	Forename	Place and date of birth	Joined WAAF/ Number	Trade	Date joined SOE, and WAAF number	Method and date of arrival in France	Code name	Circuit
BASEDEN	Yvonne	Paris 20.1.22	4.9.40 4189	Clerk General Duties Intelligence	24.5.43 4189	Parachute 19.3.44	Odette	Scholar
BEEKMAN	Yolande Elsa Maria	Paris 28.10.11	1941 2004266	Clerk General Duties Wireless Operator	15.2.43 9902	Landed 17.9.43	Mariette	Musician
BUTT	Sonya Esmée Florence	Kent 14.5.24	14.11.41 454240	Admini-stration	11.12.43 9910	Parachute 28.5.44	Blanche	Headmaster
BYCK	Muriel Tamara	London 4.6.18	1942 2071428	Clerk General Duties	31.1.44 9911	Parachute 9.4.44	Michèle	Ventriloquist
CORMEAU	Beatrice Yvonne	Shanghai 18.12.09	11.41 2027172	Admini-stration	15.2.43 9903	Parachute 23.8.43	Annette	Wheelwright
GRAN-VILLE	Christine (Krystina)	Poland 1.5.15	—	—	31.11.44 9914	Parachute 7.7.44	Pauline	Jockey
HERBERT	Mary Katherine	Ireland 1.10.03	19.9.41 452631 1541	Clerk General Duties Intelligence	05.42 1541	Felucca 30.10.42	Claudine	Scientist
INAYAT-KHAN	Noor-un-nisa (Nora)	Moscow 1.1.14	11.40 424598	Wireless Operator	8.2.43 9901	Landed 17.6.43	Madeleine	Phono
LATOUR	Phyllis	Durban 8.4.21	11.41 718483	Flight Mech (Aircraft)	1.11.43 8108/9909	Parachute 1.5.44	Geneviève	Scientist
LEFORT	Cécile Margot	London 30.4.00	6.41 452845	WAAF Police	1943 9900	Landed 17.6.43	Alice	Jockey
O'SULLI-VAN	Patricia Maureen	Dublin 3.1.18	6.41 450686	Aircraft Hand General Duties	8.12.43 8109 9908	Parachute 23.3.44	Simonet	Fireman
ROLFE	Lilian Verna	Paris 26.4.14	16.5.43 2149745	Aircraft Hand General Duties	24.11.43 9907	Landed 6.5.44	Nadine	Historian
ROWDEN	Diana Hope	London 31.1.15	5.9.41 4193	Intelligence	18.3.43 4193	Landed 17.6.43	Paulette	Acrobat/ Stockbroker
WALTERS	Anne-Marie	Geneva 16.3.23	1941 2001920	Clerk General Duties	6.7.43 9905	Parachute 4.1.44	Colette	Wheelwright
WITHER—INGTON	Cécile Pearl	Paris 24.6.14	3.9.43 —	Intelligence	8.6.43 9904	Parachute 23.9.43	Marie	Stationer/ Wrestler

Area	Organizer	Last rank	Work	Arrests	Results	Awards	Surname changes
Jura	Baron Gonzagues St Geniès (Lucien)	Flight Officer	Wireless Operator	Dôle 16.6.44 Dijon Prison Ravensbrück 1944	28.4.45 Released from Ravensbrück	C de G[1] MBE[2]	m. Bailey Burney
St Quentin	Gustave Bieler (Guy)	Section Officer (Hon)	Wireless Operator	St Quentin 13.1.44 Ave Foch/ Fresnes Karlsrühe 13.5.44	12.9.44 Shot in Dachau	C de G MID[3]	née Unternährer
Sarthe	Christopher. S. Hudson (Albin)	Assistant Section Officer (Hon)	Courier	6.44	Survived	MBE MID	m. d'Artois
Sologne	Philippe de Vomécourt (Antoine Major St Paul)	Assistant Section Officer (Hon)	Wireless Operator	–	23.5.44 Died from meningitis at Romorantin	MID	–
Gascony	George Starr (Hilaire)	Flight Officer (Hon)	Wireless Operator	–	Survived	C de G L d'H[4] MBE	née Biesterfeld m. Farrow
South-east France	Francis Cammaerts (Roger)	Flight Officer (Hon)	Courier	–	Survived Murdered in London 1952	C de G MBE GM[5]	née Skarbek m. Gerlich Gizycki
Gironde	Claude de Baissac (David) Roger Landes (Aristide)	Section Officer	Courier	Poitiers 18.2.44	Survived Died 23.1.83		m. de Baissac
Paris	Emile Henri Garry (Cinema/ Phono)	Assistant Section Officer (Hon)	Wireless Operator	Ave Foch 13.10.43 Pforzheim 27.11.43	12.9.44 Shot in Dachau	GC MBE C de G MID	–
Normandy Orne	Claude de Baissac (David)	Section Officer (Hon)	Wireless Operator	–	Survived	C de G MBE	m. Boyle
South-east France	Francis Cammaerts (Roger)	Assistant Section Officer (Hon)	Courier	Lyon 16.9.43 Ave Foch Ravensbrück 1943	2.45 Died in Ravensbrück	C de G MID	née MacKenzie
Limoges	Edmund R & Percy E Mayer (Maurice & Barthelemy)	Section Officer (Hon)	Wireless Operator	–	Survived	C de G MBE	m. Alvey
Orléans	George Wilkinson (Etienne)	Assistant Section Officer (Hon)	Wireless Operator	Orléans 3.7.44 Ave Foche/Fresnes Ravensbrück 8.8.44	5.2.45 Shot in Ravensbrück	C de G MBE MID	–
Jura	John Starr (Bob)	Section Officer	Courier	07.43, Lons 17.11.43 Ave Foch 18.11.43 Fresnes 5.12.43 Karlsrühe 13.5.44	6.7.44 Lethal injection in Natzweiler	C de G MBE MID	–
Gascony	George Starr (Hilaire)	Assistant Section Officer (Hon)	Courier	–	8.44 Escaped over Pyrénées	MBE	m. Comert
Auvergne	Maurice Southgate (Hector)	Flight Officer (Hon)	Courier Organizer	–	Survived	C de G L d'H MBE	m. Cornioley

[1] Croix de Guerre   [2] Member of the British Empire   [3] Mentioned in Dispatches   [4] Legion d'Honore   [5] George Medal

Appendix B
Diary Of Main
Events

DATES	SOE	FRANCE	WAR IN THE WEST
1931-8		June 1936 Rearmament begins	1931 Stock market crash 1933 Hitler, German Chancellor 1935 German conscription Germany annexes Saar Italy invades Ethiopia US neutrality 1936 Rhineland occupied Spanish Civil War March 1938 Austria annexed Sept 1938 Munich Agreement 27 Sept 1938 UK ATS formed (with RAF) Sept 1938-March 1939 Czechoslovakia dismembered
1939		31 March France and UK guarantee Polish independence 1 Sept France and UK order total mobilization 3 Sept France and UK ultimatum to Germany - war declared	13 April Italy annexes Albania April UK male conscription 28 June WAAF formed Aug USSR-German Pact 1 Sept Germany invades Poland 30 Nov USSR invades Finland

DATES	SOE	FRANCE	WAR IN THE WEST
1940 April		Phoney War	9 Germany attacks Norway and Denmark
May		10 Germany attacks France	10 Germany invades Belgium, Holland and Luxembourg Chamberlain resigns in UK Churchill becomes PM 22 Germany and Italy Pact
		24–4 June Dunkirk evacuation	
June			10 Italy joins in war
		14 Paris falls	15 USSR occupies Baltic States
		16 Reynaud resigns Pétain new PM 17 France sues for peace 18 De Gaulle (in UK) urges France to resist 22 French-German Armistice	18 USSR congratulates Germany on French conquest 25 UK agrees French Armistice if French fleet excluded 28 UK recognizes de Gaulle 30 Germany invades Channel Islands
July		1 Pétain's government moves to Vichy — unoccupied France 3 UK navy seizes or sinks French fleet at Oran and Mers-el-Kebir 10 French parliament votes itself out 11 Pétain Chief of State	
Sept	22 SOE set up under Dalton		July-Sept Battle of Britain 7 Sept—May 1941 London blitz 16 US military conscription

DATES	SOE	FRANCE	WAR IN THE WEST

1940
Oct
Nov
 	
Dec
			28 Italians attack Greece
			14 Coventry. Mass
			  bombing begins on
			  provincial cities
			9 UK begins offensive
			  in North Africa
			  against Italians

1941
Jan
 	
Feb
 	
April
 	
May
 	
June
 	
July
 	
Aug
 	
Sept
 	
Nov
 	
Dec
	
	First SOE agents to
	  France
	First W/T messages
	First para equipment
	  drop
	
	Special Duties Squadron
	  formed
	
	Buckmaster head of
	  F Section
		3 Bread ration 10 oz
		  daily
		
		Coal strike in Nord and
		  Pas de Calais
		  départements
		
		24 Cardinals and
		  archbishops pledge
		  loyalty to Vichy
		
		10 Germans shoot 10
		  hostages for 1 German
		  soldier killed
		
		220 sabotage acts in
		  Paris
			
			10 US begins Lease-lend
			  to UK
			12 Germans land in
			  Tripoli
			6 Germany invades
			  Yugoslavia and Greece
			25 Women's Services
			  UK part of armed
			  forces of Crown
			20 Germany invades
			  Crete
			22 Germany attacks
			  USSR
			
			Sept 1941–Jan 1943
			  Seige of Leningrad
			
			5 Battle of Moscow
			7 Japan attacks US
			  fleet
			Japan declares war on
			  US and UK
			9 China declares war
			  on Japan
			11 Germany and Italy
			  declare war on US
			  Conscription for UK
			  women

1942
Jan
	Free French Intelligence
	  Service becomes
	  BCRA
		1 Moulin arrives from
		  UK to unite resistance
		  under de Gaulle	

DATES	SOE	FRANCE	WAR IN THE WEST
1942 Feb	Selborne replaces Dalton as head of MEW		
Mar	138 and 161 Squadrons at Tempsford	27 Raid on St Nazaire	
April	Cabinet allows women for field in SOE		
May	Plan to invade France, spring 1943 Directive on minor SOE actions SIS supplies have priority over SOE	29 Vichy Jews — yellow star	
June	OSS formed in US Dutch networks disaster eventually implicates Prosper		
July		16 'Foreign' Jews arrested in Paris 19 'Family Hostage' law	
Aug		British and French raid on Dieppe fails	
Sept			Sept 1942–Feb 1943 Germans attack Stalingrad
Oct	31 Mary Herbert lands (Scientist)	Strike against STP in Lyon	
Nov		Vichy breaks relations with US	4 Battle of El Alamein Axis retreat in North Africa 8 Allies land in Algeria and Morocco (Operation Torch)
	10 Massingham set up near Algiers	11 Germans over-run Vichy 27 French fleet at Toulon scuttles itself to prevent German control 29 French armistice army disbanded	
Dec		24 Darlan assassinated in Algiers	
1943 Jan		11 Subways closed to save electricity	

DATES	SOE	FRANCE	WAR IN THE WEST
1943			12 Casablanca Conference (US and UK) demands unconditional German surrender
Feb		30 Vichy creates Milice 15 Travaille Obligatoire (STO) registration by Vichy	
Mar		Savoy and Vercors Maquis formed Mar–May Various resistance movements begin to unite	
May			12 Axis surrenders in North Africa
		27 Moulin President of 1st CNR (resistance) meeting in Paris	
June	Psychological selection introduced for new agents More aircraft for SOE Lighter wirelesses issued 17 Noor Inayat Khan lands (Cinema) Cécile Lefort lands (Jockey) Diana Rowden lands (Acrobat)		
July		21 Moulin arrested Prosper arrests begin	10 Sicily invaded by Allies 25 Mussolini deposed
Aug		31 Germans take over Italian occupied zone	14 Rome an Open City
Sept	23 Yvonne Cormeau para (Wheelwright) SOE section in Bari Gubbins Head of SOE (CD) 17 Yolande Beekman lands (Musician) 23 Pearl Witherington para (Stationer)	Maquis battles in Corrèze	3 Allies land on Italy 8 Italian surrender made public 9 Allies land at Salerno 10 Germans occupy Rome Italian fleet joins Allies

DATES	SOE	FRANCE	WAR IN THE WEST
1943 Oct		5 Corsica liberated by Free French	13 Italy declares war on Germany
Nov		5 Peugeot works damaged	28 Teheran Conference (UK, US, USSR)
Dec	'F' Test Sabotage Instructions		
1944 Jan	4 Anne-Marie Walters para (Wheelwright) F answerable to Combined Chiefs of Staff as well as War Cabinet US aircraft join in drops	20 Milice Courts Martial set up by Vichy	3 USSR enters Poland
Feb		1 STO extended to men 16–60 Resistance combined into FFI Eysses Prison breakout SS takes over Abwehr, Paris	
Mar	19 Yvonne Baseden para (Scholar) 23 Patricia O'Sullivan para (Fireman)	De Gaulle appoints Koenig to represent FFI with Allies in UK and Cochet in Algiers	19 Germans occupy Hungary
Apr	9 Muriel Byck para (Ventriloquist)	4 De Gaulle Commander of FF forces	
May	1 Philippa Latour para (Scientist) 6 Lilian Rolfe lands (Historian) 13 Convoy of women SOE from Paris to Karlsrühe	7 Michenon arsenal bombed	French-Italian resisters declare friendship on Alps

DATES	SOE	FRANCE	WAR IN THE WEST

1944
 	
June
	28 Sonya Butt para
	  (Headmaster)
	Jedburgh & SAS parties
	  begin landings
	Koenig in SHAEF to
	  command SOE, OSS
	  & BCRA
		
		6 Normandy landings
		  by Allies
		8 Bayeux liberated
		10 Oradour massacre
		30 Cotentin Peninsula
		  cleared
			4 Rome taken by Allies
			
			13 VI attacks on UK
			  start

July	7 Christine Granville
	  para (Jockey)
		Caen taken
		Cochet of Algiers to
		  command FFI of south
		23 Vercors rising
		  crushed
			20 Assassination of
			  Hitler fails

Aug			1 Aug–2 Oct Warsaw rising

	8 Convoy of SOE
	women from Paris to
	Ravensbrück
	
	17 Av Foch staff leave
	Paris
		15 Allies land in south
		  France
		Allies take Orléans and
		  Châtres
			
			23 Rumania surrenders
			  to USSR

Sept		25 Paris liberated
		26 De Gaulle arrives in
		  Paris
		28 Toulon and
		  Marseilles freed
		FFI absorbed into
		  French army
		3 Lyon freed
			
			3 Brussels freed
			8 V2 rockets on UK

	SOE Ops in France end	11 Allied armies from north and south meet 12 Dijon freed 20 Bologne freed	 17 Arnhem disaster
Oct			4 Greek landings 6 USSR enters Czechoslovakiá
	Judex missions		22 Yugoslav partisans enter Belgrade

DATES	SOE	FRANCE	WAR IN THE WEST

1944
 	
Dec
		28 De Gaulle orders
		  resistance to disarm
		German offensive in
		  Ardennes fails	

1945
 	
Feb
 	
Apr
		
		26 Pétain arrested
			12 Budapest taken by
			  USSR
			17 USSR takes Warsaw
			4 Yalta Conference (UK,
			  US, USSR)
			Germans leave Hungary
			  and retreat into
			  Yugoslavia
			
			28 Mussolini killed
			30 Hitler's suicide
			29 Apr–8 May
			  Emergency food flights
			  to Netherlands

May
 	
Aug
Sept
			5 Germans in
			  Netherlands,
			  Denmark
			  and Bavaria surrender
			8 Zagreb freed
			9 Germans sign uncon-
			  ditional surrender
			Atom bombs on Japan
			2 Japan signs surrender

1946 Jan	SOE closed down		

Appendix C
Acknowledgements

I wish to thank the following individuals for so kindly spending their time and patience in helping me in lengthy correspondence and telephone calls resolving weighty problems or providing little details that pieced together the jigsaw of information that came to form this book, and for giving permission to use their published works.

Sonya d'Artois (Canada); Irene Bramley; John Brown; Ray Brandish; Maurice Buckmaster; Dr Bullen and Joanne Buggins of the Imperial War Museum; Yvonne Burney (Portugal); Francis Cammaerts (France); Eva Chew; Nancy Chilver; Simon Cobley of Weidenfeld and Nicolson Archives; Jean-Claude Comert (France); Pearl Cornioley (France); Gervase Cowell of the Foreign and Commonwealth Office; Margaret Davidson of the FANY; M. Deschamps (France); Yvonne Farrow; Michael Foot; Yvonne George; June Gozzard; Frank Griffiths; Peggy Heard; Ken Hemmings; Paula Irwin; Roger Landes; Bob Large; Peter Lee of the Special Forces Club; Pierre Lorain (France); Moira McCairns; Ole Malm (Norway); Keith Melton (USA); Mrs Midgley of the Commonwealth War Graves Commission; Lord Montague of Beaulieu; Nora Mortimer; Pearl Panton; Claudine Pappe (USA); Valerie Pearman-Smith; Gwyneth Pritchard; Mrs Raftree of RAF Personnel Management Centre, Gloucester; Audrey Ririe; Dee Scandrett; Diana Scruton; Winifred Smith (New Zealand); Mr & Mrs J. Smithers; Faith Spencer-Chapman; Lady Sibyl Stewart; Dorothy Stott; M. Tabarant (France); Maddie Turner; Hugh Verity; Lise Villameur (France); Irene Warner.

Also the following bodies/publishers for permission to use some of their material.

Aerofilms Ltd; Air Historical Branch (RAF); Century Hutchinson Publishing Group Ltd; East-West Publications Ltd; Evening Standard Co Ltd; George Mann Books and Allan Wingate; George Weidenfeld & Nicolson Ltd; Hamish Hamilton; Her Majesty's Stationery Office; Ian Allan Ltd; Imperial War Museum; Macmillan Publishers Ltd; Oxford Public Library; RAF Escaping Society; United Nations (London, Paris, Geneva, New York); WRAF Directorate.

Appendix D
Bibliography

Beevor, J.G. *SOE Recollections & Reflections 1940-45* (Bodley Head, 1981)
Bell, L. *Sabotage* (Laurie, 1957)
Buckmaster, M. *They Fought Alone* (Odhams, 1958)
Buckmaster, M. *Specially Employed* (Batchworth, 1952)
Burney, C. *Solitary Confinement* (Macmillan, 1961)
Butler, E. *Amateur Agent* (Harrap, 1963)
Colvin, I. Ed, *Colonel Henri's Story — Bleicher* (Kimber, 1954)
Cookridge, E.H. *Inside SOE* (Arthur Barker, 1966)
Cookridge, E.H. *They Came From The Sky* (Heinemann, 1965)
Cookridge, E.H. *Sisters of Delilah* (Oldbourne, 1959)
Dalton, H. *The Fateful Years* (Muller, 1957)
Dank, M. *The French Against The French* (Cassell, 1974)
Foot, M.R.D. *SOE In France* (HMSO, 1966)
Foot, M.R.D. *Resistance* (Eyre & Methuen Ltd, 1976)
Foot, M.R.D. *SOE 1940-46* (BBC, 1984)
Foot, M.R.D. *Six Faces of Courage* (Eyre & Methuen Ltd, 1978)
Gavin, C. *None Dare Call It Treason* (Hodder & Stoughton, 1978)
Griffiths, F. *Winged Hours* (Kimber, 1981)
Griffiths, F. *Angel Visits* (Harmsworth, 1986)
Hastings, M. *Das Reich* (Michael Joseph, 1981)
Hinsley, F.H. *British Intelligence In The 2nd World War* (3 vols) (HMSO 1981)
Howarth, P. Ed, *Special Operations* (Routledge & Kegan Paul, 1955)
Hawes, S. & R. White, Ed, *Resistance in Europe 1939-45* (Allen Lane, 1975)
Jones, L. *A Quiet Courage* (Bantam Press, 1990)
King, S. *Jacqueline* (Arms & Armour, 1989)
Ladd, J. & Melton, K. *Clandestine Warfare* (Blandford, 1988)
Long, H. *Safe Houses Are Dangerous* (Kimber, 1985)
Lorain, P. (translated D. Khan) *Secret Warfare* (Orbis, 1984)
Marshall, B. *The White Rabbit* (Evans, 1952)
Marshall, R. *All The King's Men* (Collins, 1988)
Masson, M. *Christine (A search for Christine Granville)* (Hamish Hamilton, 1975)

Michel, H. *The Shadow War* (Andre Deutsch, 1972)

Nicholas, E. *Death Be Not Proud* (Cresset, 1958; White Lion, 1973)

Overton-Fuller, J. *Noor-Un-Nisa Inayat Khan (Madeleine)* (Gollancz, 1952; East-West Publications, Rotterdam, 1971, 1989)

Overton-Fuller, J. *The German Penetration of SOE* (Kimber & Co, 1975)

Overton-Fuller, J. *The Starr Affair* (Gollancz, 1954)

Paine, L. *The Abwehr* (Robert Hale, 1984)

Popham, H. *FANY 1907-84* (Secker & Warburg, 1984)

Rossiter, M. *Women In The Resistance* (Praeger Publishers, USA, 1986)

Ruby, M. *F Section SOE* (Leo Cooper, 1985)

Russell, Lord of Liverpool. *Scourge Of The Swastika* (Cassell, 1954)

Stafford, D. *Britain & European Resistance 1940-45* (Macmillan, 1980)

Sweet-Escott, B. *Baker Street Irregular* (Methuen, 1965)

Sweets, J.F. *Choices In Vichy France* (OUP, 1986)

Taylor, E. *Women Who Went To War* (Grafton, 1989)

Tickell, J. *Moon Squadron* (Allan Wingate, 1956)

Verity, H. *We Landed By Moonlight* (Ian Allan Ltd, 1978)

Vomécourt, P. de *Who Lived To See The Day* (Hutchinson, 1961)

Walters, A.M. *Moondrop To Gascony* (Macmillan, 1946)

Ward, Dame I. *FANY Invicta* (Hutchinson, 1955)

Webb, A.M. Ed, *The Natzweiler Trial* (William Hodge, 1949)

Wynne, B. *Count Five and Die* (George Mann, 1958)

Wynne, B. *No Drums... No Trumpets* (A Barker Ltd, 1961)

General

Bowyer, C. *Royal Air Force Handbook 1939-45* (Allan, 1984)

Boyd, A. *Atlas of World Affairs* (Methuen)

Baudot, M. *Historical Encyclopaedia of WW2* (Macmillan, 1982)

Campbell, C. *World War II Fact Book* (Black Cat, 1985)

Gander, T. *Encyclopaedia Of The Modern RAF* (Patrick Stephens, 1984 and 1987)

Gorlaski, R. *World War II Almanac '31-45* (Hamish Hamilton, 1981)

Mercer, D.K. Ed, *Chronicle of the 20th Century* (Longmans, 1988)

Messenger, C. *WW2 Chronological Atlas* (Bloomsbury, 1989)

Terraine, J. *Right Of The Line* (Hodder & Stoughton, 1985)

Times Concise Atlas of the World

Waller & Vaughan Rees *Women In Wartime* (Optima, 1987)

Index